Impact

Impact

A whole year's worth of teaching materials for 5–12s

- Useful Insights Into Reaching a Totally New Generation
- Over 100 games • 52 Unique Stories, Bible Texts and Bible Lessons
- Step-by-step Curriculum Guide • Illustrations
- Major Format Ideas • Contemporary Magazine-style Programme
- The Curriculum That Really Works

Mark Griffiths

MONARCH
BOOKS

Mill Hill, London and Grand Rapids, Michigan

First published in 2003 in the UK by Monarch Books, Concorde House,
Grenville Place, Mill Hill, London NW7 3SA.

Distributed by:
UK: STL, PO Box 300, Kingstown Broadway, Carlisle, Cumbria CA3 0QS;
USA: Kregel Publications, PO Box 2607, Grand Rapids, Michigan 49501.

ISBN 1 85424 593 7 (UK)

British Library Cataloguing Data
A catalogue record for this book is available
from the British Library.

Designed and produced for the publishers by
Gazelle Creative Productions Ltd,
Concorde House, Grenville Place, Mill Hill, London NW7 3SA.

For my own children Nia, Owen and Elliot,
and for Ethan... When we don't understand, we trust.

Impact (im'paekt),
v. to affect or influence

Whoever learns to communicate
to a generation ultimately
has the power to influence
that generation

FOREWORD

Mark Griffiths opens *Impact* with the stark question: *Can these bones live?* Can a book become an instrument of bringing children to faith? The answer is: *Absolutely!*

Following his first manual, *Fusion*, Mark provides 52 more programmes for Christian-based sessions for children of all ages and situations. He includes practical information on those aspects that underpin successful children's work: publicity, good planning, use of leaders, pastoral care, and the logistics of running a programme. His enthusiasm for enabling children to hear the Good News jumps off the pages and will encourage and equip the most jaded children's leader, even on a cold Friday night, when the hall heating has been accidentally turned off!

I am delighted to commend *Impact* with its scriptural basis and down-to-earth approach to meeting children where they are – in every sense. Both it and its companion, *Fusion*, provide excellent resources where they are desperately needed, helping children to hear the gospel and encounter the living God.

Margaret Withers
Archbishop's Officer for Evangelism among Children

A FEW WORDS FROM THE AUTHOR

This book can be an instrument for producing an army of warriors or it can be a pile of dry bones. The difference is the same as in Ezekiel 37. If God comes and breathes life into it, it will live and change lives and impact communities. If God doesn't breathe life into it, then you have in your hands nothing more than a book of ideas.

Can these bones live? Absolutely.

God wants them to live. He longs to use you to change the lives of countless boys and girls. He stands on the edge of heaven, waiting to abundantly bless everything you put your hands to. What is he waiting for? You! He is patiently waiting for you to ask. God wants to breathe life into your children's programme.

There is an increasing understanding amongst church leaders of both the need for and the profound impact of quality children's ministry. UK government research completed in 2001 concluded that every community needs a children's centre.* This research identified the benefits of such endeavours as being:

- **Economic** – the activities of the children's centre would allow parents to work longer hours and allow more parents to return to the workplace.
- **Social** – the centres would become focal points for social interaction between parents and children.
- **Moral** – sex and drugs education and other health issues could be addressed from such centres.

However, if we can understand the opportunity that this research presents and if we move quickly, then the church can own many of these children's centres and add a fourth dimension:

- **Spiritual** – a children's club within the centre that exists to promote God's agenda.

If righteousness can exalt a nation then I am very confident that our communities can be positively affected by such works. I dare to believe that our nation will see children's outreach clubs attended by hundreds and even thousands – and even some thriving churches growing from children's clubs.

The curriculum returns to the gospel message again and again. As your club grows, children will join who have never heard the gospel before – give them the opportunity to hear it, even if you think the time is not quite ready for them to respond. It is also no accident that the curriculum starts and ends with a missionary series. I believe that some of those boys and girls who will come to listen and learn from you over the coming weeks and years will themselves become a vital and active part of the kingdom of God – impacting their world for Jesus.

Sometimes the material touches on sensitive areas such as death and divorce. It is important that we don't avoid these subjects (they are an inevitable part of life), but at the same time we mustn't open the proverbial can of worms and then walk away. Let us continue to involve ourselves in the lives of boys and girls, and allow the kingdom's influence to extend into homes that have never before experienced the love of the Creator God.

Mark Griffiths
January 2003

---

* Government research undertaken by Kids Club Network UK.

CONTENTS

THE STEP-BY-STEP GUIDE TO ESTABLISHING A THRIVING CHILDREN'S OUTREACH PROGRAMME

There are many issues that need to be weighed before you start an outreach children's club, because once something is up and running it is very hard to change its form or shape. It has always been my preference to start from scratch; taking over from someone else is always going to be difficult. It is my intention in the very near future to write a book that covers the unique elements of starting from scratch and the continuing development and running of children's ministry. Here I have simply attempted to overview the process of starting, and more importantly maintaining, a thriving children's work.

Before you start

In children's ministry, there is the temptation to wait until all the conditions are right before you start. You might feel you should wait until you have the right staff, wait until you are all experts at the programme, wait until you have all the equipment you need. Forget it! Start.

It will never be the perfect time. God blesses people on the journey, not while they're waiting for the perfect conditions.

Promotion

If nobody knows your club exists it is unlikely that anyone will attend. Praying for a good attendance is good, but praying without doing throws us into the "faith without works" category. Do something. Produce a leaflet (I've enclosed an example in Appendix 1). Ask your local schools to distribute it; pop into the morning assembly and mention it to the children; mailshot your whole district. Stand outside your local school dressed as Mickey Mouse and hand out the leaflet (get permission from the head teacher first); put an advert in the local paper; offer an incentive to come – free Mars bar this week! Promote it.

Arrival

Arrival and departure is important. Have a good register that keeps track of children's names, addresses and any ailments that you should be aware of. Have a contact number for parents. Talk to parents; allow them to see your face. It's hard for a parent to trust an anonymous name on the bottom of a sheet of paper. It's much easier to trust someone they've seen and met.

Charge a small admission fee. The more self-sufficient the club can be, the better. Remember: I am suggesting that these clubs can be the seeds for new churches. Some will need to be completely self-sufficient.

What's important

It is enough for now to stress that the things that are important to us must be incorporated into the way we run. Here are some principles that I hold as important:

- Children will only listen to you if you listen to them.
- Children will only listen to you if you will have fun with them.
- Children will only listen to you if they like you.
- Children are individuals and like different things.

I believe in these principles, therefore I would not consider starting an outreach club without incorporating these things into it. Run each session for a couple of hours, but make the first part free play, e.g., face-painting, computer games (some children like computers), pool/snooker. Provide a coffee bar area (if children will only listen to you if you listen to them, then create a place where they can talk to you – a coffee bar) and a craft area (some children like crafts). Don't be so naive as to think that all the children will like everything.

For the first hour, let them choose what they do. For the next hour or so, run the programme. It is important not to fall into the trap of teaching that all children are unique, different and special and then insisting that they all play the set game on arrival.

Hall set-up and structure

Registration and Tuck Shop		
Blue Team	**Red Team**	**Yellow Team**
A		B
OHP and Video	Stage Area	Score Board

WHY THREE TEAMS?

If two teams are used, then usually there is a winning team and a losing team. Having three teams allows one team to win and the others to come joint second. It allows an element of healthy competitiveness without there needing to be a loser. Other children's groups (some very large groups) work with two teams, one of boys and the other of girls. There are two main disadvantages to this system: there is very rarely an equal mix of boys and girls; it leads to unnecessary tension between the teams and also with social services, who will frown on the practice. (Wherever possible it will pay you to keep government organisations positively inclined towards your work – Jesus had favour with God *and men*.)

Staffing

REGISTRATION

Three team members should be responsible for registration. This is where you meet the parents. This is the initial contact point. First impressions do last, so put some of your best people here. The registration people will also need to be armed with information regarding trips, etc. This is your public relations department.

TEAM LEADERS

There should be a sprinkling of leaders in each team. Problems should not be dealt with from the front but sorted quickly from within the team. It will be a process of education for the staff as well as for the children.

SCOREKEEPER

A competent and upbeat member of the team is needed who will periodically announce the scores.

TECHNICAL SUPPORT

A person who can operate PA systems, videos, OHPs, etc. is invaluable. If done well, this will help you greatly. If done badly, this can destroy your programme.

FRONT PEOPLE

Two front people will be responsible for illustrations. If you work with two front people who know what they are doing and have obvious communication gifts, then introduce a third person who can develop and learn. As they come to maturity in this gift, release more responsibility to them. This is a continuous process which allows you to move or sow out into other children's works. The choice of the third person is very important. He or she may not be particularly gifted, but must be humble, teachable and have the heart of a servant. Don't choose anyone without these qualifications.

OTHERS

If you run crafts as part of your programme, then you will need artistic people. A qualified first-aider should not be overlooked. Members of the team will also need to be involved in the weekly visitation programme.

The programme from beginning to end

WELCOME (3 minutes)

This is a chance to welcome the children, but also an opportunity to have fun with them. Remember, if you will not have fun with them, they will not listen to you. I prefer to lead the programme with two people at the front. This allows comical banter between them. Think differently! Have the two leaders dressed as Barney Rubble™ and Fred Flintstone™ to walk on and welcome the children. Be creative!

RULES (2 minutes)

If there are no clear rules, then the children have no discipline guidelines – they cannot be reprimanded for not obeying rules that they have never heard. Only two simple rules are necessary:

- Nobody leaves their seat. If a child needs to go to the toilet, he or she must put a hand up and ask permission from a leader.
- When the whistle blows, everyone stops speaking, sits down, focuses on the front and makes no sound. If you are uncomfortable with the use of a whistle, you can use a horn, or a special word.

These two simple rules will keep everything controlled. Children feel safer and more secure in a disciplined atmosphere.

There must be a method of enforcing the rules. We use the following twofold system:

Positive enforcement:

If a team is particularly good (e.g. they sit well, listen well, cheer the loudest, or win a game), they get to roll dice. The score from the dice is added to their overall score. The team with the most points at the end of the term gets the biggest prizes; the other teams receive smaller prizes (e.g. at the end of the Easter term the members of the winning team receive Easter Eggs; the others receive cream eggs).

Negative enforcement:

If a child talks after the whistle has gone or is not sitting and facing the front, their team instantly loses six points.

PRAYER (5 minutes)

This can be divided into two sections:

Giving thanks: Children who have prayed for something the week before (or several weeks before) and whose prayers have been answered should be asked to come and tell the others how God answered their prayer.

Bringing needs: Some of the children will want to pray for certain things. Allow them to come and mention what they are praying for, and ask God together to answer their prayer.

Remember, when children have prayers answered they need to be invited to the front so that everyone can give God thanks.

PRAISE (7 minutes)

This involves singing some lively songs. There are two slots for praise. Make sure you use the first slot for songs they know which contain lots of actions. New songs can be introduced in the second section. Some of the children may not enjoy singing – award six points for the best team singing; suddenly you'll find they enjoy it a lot more!

GAME 1 (5 minutes)

Games differ from week to week. But the following points are important:

- In order to play a game they must answer a question on the previous week's lesson.
- Choose one person from each team and then allow that person to choose the rest of the team.
- For games which mention point A and point B, see the hall plan.
- Give points for the teams that cheer people the loudest.
- Play fast music while the game runs – live music, if possible.
- The first team to complete the game must sit down.

PRAISE (10 minutes)

This second praise slot is longer, with several songs being used together. Encourage banners, streamers, dancing, etc. Allow some of the children to form a praise group that stands with a microphone to lead the others. I have included a list of good CDs for children in Appendix 5.

FUN ITEM 1 (5 minutes)

We use several fun items to enhance the programme. You can be creative with your ideas, but we recommend the following:

Guess The Leader: We reveal an interesting fact regarding one of the leaders, e.g. "This leader used to live in Spain." Then four leaders are chosen who all try and convince the children that they used to live in Spain. The children then have to guess the leader who was telling the truth. A variation on this theme is to show a picture of the leader as a baby; the leaders all have to try and convince the children that they are the person in the picture.

Strip Search: Here is an idea from Saturday morning television that will help with getting to know the children or leaders. Play some background music. Invite a leader (or a child) to sit in a seat at the front. Then for one minute ask the leader questions such as: "Awake or asleep?" The leader will then answer by telling you whether they prefer to be awake or asleep. These are some samples, but there are many more that can be used:

- "Awake or asleep?"
- "Music or reading?"

- "Chocolate or fruit?"
- "Will or Gareth (from the TV show *Pop Idol*)?"

Buy It or Bin It: This is a chance for music and video reviews. Ask the children to bring in the videos they watch and the music they listen to. This may not seem overtly Christian, but it is incredibly educational! Form a panel of three (one leader and two children) and allow them to view three videos/CDs for 30 seconds each. Then ask them whether they would buy them or bin them, and why. Periodically introduce Christian music. This teaches the children critical thought, which is very important for their development.

Who Wants To Be A Chocoholic?: This is based on the television game show *Who Wants To Be A Millionaire?* A child is chosen from the audience. They are asked questions in increasing degrees of difficulty. They are given four answers to the questions and have to choose the right one. For a right answer they gain more chocolate; for a wrong answer they lose it all. The trick is to know when to quit and take the chocolate. The children have two lifelines: they can ask the audience or a leader the answer to a question.

Aerobics Workout: A piece of music is played and the children copy the leader at the front performing their aerobic workout.

This slot can also be used for all sorts of fun items such as puppet skits, etc. Use the time to have fun with the children.

GAME 2 (5 minutes)

Make sure that the people who take part in Game 2 are different from those who were involved in Game 1.

FUN ITEM 2 (5 minutes)

Other items may be added to the first section, such as video clips of an outing, interviews with community members, etc. Use your imagination.

Special Note:	All the items within the programme need to be joined together quite rapidly. The usual length of a session is just under two hours. Younger children may not cope with the full length of the programme. Condense the programme and introduce a simple craft time if you are working with children under seven years old.

BIBLE TEXT (3 minutes)

We display the memory verse on the OHP from the start of preaching time and refer to it frequently, but you may prefer to encourage the children to memorise the text. There are many ways to teach a Bible text. A few ideas are given below, but there are literally hundreds of possibilities. Be creative.

- Write the words of the Bible text on balloons and burst a balloon as each word of the verse is read.
- Make the verse into a jigsaw puzzle.
- Write the verse on an object which communicates its message, e.g. "You are a light to my path" can be written on a lamp or a drawing of a bulb.
- "The Lord is my shepherd" can be written on five cut-out sheep.

Remember that memorisation of the verse is not as important as understanding. Children may win a prize if they can quote "The Lord is my shepherd", but their lives will be changed if they understand it.

- Unless stated otherwise, all Scripture quotations are from the *Contemporary English Version*. New Testament © American Bible Society 1991, 1992, 1995. Used by permission. Anglicisation © British & Foreign Bible Society 1996.

Copies of each of the Bible texts are included in Appendix 3 for you to photocopy onto acetate.

ANNOUNCEMENTS (2 minutes)

Summer camps, play schemes, colouring competitions, birthdays, special events, etc. all need mentioning here. If you are going to celebrate birthdays, you must be consistent – don't mention birthdays one week and then give them a miss for two weeks, as some children will miss out and feel hurt.

INTERVIEW (5 minutes)

Invite one of the leaders (or one of the children) to come and tell the group what Jesus has done for them; how he has helped them in work or school; how he cares for them; how they first made their decision to become a Christian. If the person is very nervous, interview them. If they are more confident, allow them to speak freely, taking notice of the timing allowed for this section.

WORSHIP (10 minutes)

This is a quieter time of worship where songs such as Ishmael's "Father God" can be introduced. Encourage the children who know the words to close their eyes and begin to think about King Jesus. Take your time here; it is important to introduce them to worship.

We instruct the children that praise is generally loud and lively, a time when we have fun singing to God. Worship is when we come closer to God, and think about God more. Worship comes from our hearts and our minds. It involves all our emotions. The definitions of praise and worship may be much broader and more theological than this, but a bite-sized theological portion is more easily swallowed by an eight-year-old.

PREACHING TIME

The rest of the programme falls under the heading "preaching time". This will include all Bible lessons, illustrations and the story. Take three minutes to explain the rules.

Time for a very special announcement

Inform the children that they are now moving into preaching time, which is the most important thing that happens. Inform them that this section can change their lives. There are special rules; when the whistle blows next, preaching time has begun. In preaching time:

- Nobody leaves to go to the toilet. In fact, nobody moves.
- Anyone talking loses six points straightaway, without discussion.

However, a leader will be walking around with tuck shop tokens or sweets and will place them in the hands of anyone who really deserves one:

- You must be excellent to receive one. Being good is not enough; anyone can be good.
- You must keep facing the front. If you look at the leader (whom we refer to as a "quiet seat" watcher) he or she will not give you a token/sweet.
- If you get a sweet/token and play with it (or try and open it), it will be taken from you.

Blow the whistle (the whistle can be put away now; it will no longer be needed).

BIBLE LESSON (5 minutes)

There are various ideas to help with the presentation of the Bible lesson:

- Dress some of the children up as characters in the story.
- Use videos. The list of recommended resources in Appendix 5 will give you some ideas.
- If you are presenting the story in narrative form, then tell the story as Hollywood would – don't just read the account.

ILLUSTRATIONS 1–3 (5 minutes each)

Illustrations can take many forms – object lessons, short drama sketches, video clips, testimonies, etc. – basically anything which can be used to present the overall lesson.

STORY (10 minutes)

The story is a modern parable, which rolls all the themes presented so far into one neat narrative package. Again, various methods can be used to enhance the presentation:

* Use some of the children as characters in the story.
* Draw some of the characters on flash cards or acetates.
* Keep it dramatic. Use your body and voice to maximise the presentation.

PRAYER/RESPONSE (5 minutes)

Always ask for a response. Make an appeal. Ask any children who felt the lesson had applied to them to stand. If the lesson required forgiveness, pray a prayer of forgiveness together. Let the children respond by repeating the prayer after you. There must be a response.

NEXT WEEK (3 minutes)

Highlight next week's programme. Keep it exciting: "Next week everyone who comes will get a cream egg", "Next week we'll hear the concluding part of this exciting story", etc.

THE FINISHING TOUCH (2 minutes)

Give the children a picture which reinforces the day's lesson to take home. Ask them to colour and return it. The best pictures will win prizes. Ask a leader to dismiss the children a row at a time. Head for the door and say goodbye to the children, then talk to some parents. Mix!

And the most important part

What happens next is the reason why many clubs start with 80 children, have 60 the following week, and eventually drop down to five children, which they accept as their average running level. They will run at this level until the following year when they restart. Because of good promotion, they will start again with 80.

The way to break the cycle is as follows:

All the things you did to get 80 children coming during week 1 need to be repeated for week 2. Hand out more leaflets; put flyers through more doors; visit more schools. Add to this a visit to the home of every child that attended in the first week. Don't worry about this – it simply involves knocking on a door and handing the mum/dad a colouring competition for the child to complete and return during the following week's club (there's an example in Appendix 1). Offer a prize for the best entry.

If some of the children live too far away, use the postal service. The effect of this will be that week 2 will have a higher attendance than week 1. At the end of week 2, repeat all this again. And again after week 3, and again…

All hard work brings profit!

I've deliberately included three single lessons at the start of the book before the series begin, so that time can be given to attracting new children. In this way, no child needs to feel that they have missed the start of the series.

Make the link

Make sure you regularly try to include the children and their parents in your wider church activities. Invite them to church barbecues, fun days, etc. as well as to your Christmas and Easter services – this is paramount if you plan to use this method to plant new churches.

PROGRAMME ENHANCEMENTS

The role of music within the programme

For the first section until preaching time, music is present almost all the time.
Play quiet, ambient music when explaining rules; use loud music for games.
The contrast of total silence in preaching time seems to
help the children listen and focus on the discussion.

Preaching

The material you have in front of you is designed to be preached. Preach it with fire and passion, and with gentleness and compassion. Such a proclamation will sometimes bypass the head and speak directly into the heart. The need of the day is children's workers who are full of the Holy Ghost, who will proclaim, in a relevant and contemporary manner, the message of the cross and the principles of God's word.

Don't just tell cute stories – change lives!

This is the part that can't be taught. The message either burns within you or it doesn't. If it burns inside, then lives will be changed. If it doesn't, pray until it does.

Crafts

It is always useful to have a good craft activity that relates to the overall theme for the week. Assign a creative person to come up with an idea each week, based on the theme. When the children take things home it helps reinforce the message and at the same time allows a Christian activity into a potentially non-Christian home.

Pictures

Many of the illustrations need pictures. The Internet is a great place to find any piece of artwork you may need. Either use Microsoft Word – go to Insert and then ClipArt and then choose the Internet option; or go to www.ask.com and type in a description of the picture. Another useful source is the computer programme Microsoft Encarta. It is relatively cheap and is a gold mine of pictures on a huge range of topics. In all honesty, the process of getting pictures is more difficult if you don't have access to a computer, but your local library should be a useful place to look. A conversation with the librarian on copyright might be advisable before you start photocopying pictures from books.

Personal references

From time to time the illustrations are from my own personal experiences. In this context I usually use first person narrative. There are two options: probably the best route would be to replace the illustration with one from your own experience. Failing that, tell the story and use the third person: "The person who wrote this book once went to…" or "I know a person who once went to…"

THINKING OF GIUING UP?
READ THIS FIRST

(Feel free to photocopy and distribute this article to your children's team.)

Seventy per cent of the leaders who headed up the biggest Assemblies of God children's congregations in the United States in 1990 were not in any form of ministry by the turn of the millennium. The greatest negative factor in children's ministry in the United States and the United Kingdom is the massive turnover of leaders. Some leave because God has called them to another ministry; some use this as an excuse to get out; most simply drop out. It's easier to stay at home and watch your favourite TV programme on a cold winter evening than to drag yourself away from the fire and into a hall of screaming children – particularly when the club isn't going as well as you would like. The children are restless; the toilets are blocked again; the deacons are writing you nasty letters; there are discipline problems.

We all face challenges. They are there to prove and improve us. Before you give up I invite you to keep reading.

1 Samuel 30 contains a very interesting account. David and his men had been journeying long and hard. He had led his men valiantly. He had lived with incredible standards of integrity and righteousness. He had always done the right thing. He was now returning to camp, hoping to come back to his wife and children and enjoy a time of rest and relaxation before continuing. Then suddenly, as he rode into camp, he saw smoke billowing high into the air. Ziklag was on fire. His possessions were in flames. As he came closer, the enormity of the situation hit him. Not only were all his possessions on fire, but his wife and children and everything he and his men owned were gone.

And, as if the situation couldn't get any worse, his friends, those he had helped, those he had encouraged when they were downcast and depressed, those he had carried when they couldn't support themselves – those selfsame men now wanted to kill him; they wanted to stone their leader to death.

David was facing one of his bleakest moments. He had entered a dark time – a time that no one is immune from – a defining moment in his life. Several weeks after this episode, David would ride triumphantly into Jerusalem to be crowned king. He would prove to be the greatest king that Israel would ever have (apart from King Jesus himself). But before he got to Jerusalem, he had to get through Ziklag.

Ziklag represents that defining moment in our lives when we face a choice: to move on to a level that is way above average, or else to decide that mediocrity is where we will live out our lives. It is the central base around which all else hinges. Ziklag is David's final test before kingship. If he passes this test, he will walk on into triumph and glory; if he fails, the shepherd boy will at best return to his sheep; at worst he will die.

David's past was incredibly exciting. He had been anointed king by Samuel the prophet. He had defeated Goliath. He had gathered to himself men and women who were depressed, discouraged, in debt and desperate – and he had made them great. But at Ziklag he faced the defining moment.

We all come there. We must. Anyone worth anything in God's kingdom must pass the Ziklag test. They must prove faithful under intense pressure; they must be of sufficient mettle that they don't shrink away at the first sign of opposition. Allow me to make some general observations on David's predicament that may help us also:

1. The decision was David's. God willed for him to get up and deal with the situation, but God would never override his special gift to humankind, the gift of free will. The decision here was David's, and David's alone.

2. He was on his own. Nobody was going to help him up.

   i) He had no physical support – his men were not going to support or help him; on the contrary, they wanted to kill him.

ii)   He had no material support – all his material possessions had been taken.
iii) He had no emotional support – his wife and children had been taken away; his emotional shelter was gone.

It so happens that there isn't always someone there to help you up – sometimes God designs it that way. Devoid of everything, what would David do? God allowed a similar experience to befall Job in order that God could prove and improve him.

3.   Those David had worked with, those he had strengthened and encouraged, now wanted to stone him. Anyone who has ever held a position of responsibility will understand the emotions that this brings up.

I genuinely believe that we must all face that place of Ziklag, that place where two different futures open up before us. And for every person who comes through to be a king, I wonder how many people return to being shepherds. Having a destiny is not enough; being prophesied over is not enough. Many people have a destiny but may never see it fulfilled.

It would perhaps be true to say that 90% of our life is governed by our decisions and only 10% by unforeseen circumstances. However, I think it is our response and our decision process within that 10% that defines us. It is that decision we make in the unforeseen circumstance, that decision when we feel devoid of everything, that decision in the Ziklag time, which makes the difference.

Ziklag means the time when nobody wants to support our vision to reach boys and girls for Jesus, that time when nobody wants to work with us, that time when we are physically and emotionally drained. It is when we drag ourselves out week after week, through those cold autumnal evenings and those depressing winter nights, to do what we are convinced God has called us to do. In those times, it does not help to learn that it is God himself who destines us to be devoid of support and encouragement. But it is so important that God allows us to go through these times, for ultimately it is the builder that defines the shape of the building. If God can get his builders right, then there is no real problem with what they build. Paul, for example, was like a master builder. The early church was bound to be good and strong and full of God, because that was what Paul was like. The builder defines the shape.

And David was always going to prove himself at Ziklag. Sun Tze, a ninth-century Chinese general, commented in his book *The Art of War* that victories are won before the battles even begin. Likewise, David had been through many tests that prepared him for Ziklag. At the time, the other tests must have seemed difficult, but they all prepared the man of God for the next rung of the ladder. So let's see what we can learn from David:

1.   He had an open and honest relationship with God.
     David wasn't praying liturgical prayers that he had memorised; David had cultivated an open and honest relationship with the Creator of the universe. He told God how he felt.

2.   He knew about the power of praise.
     Psychologists are only just beginning to realise the potential of music to change our moods and emotions. David knew more than this; he knew that God himself inhabited the praise of his people. Through praise David could lift his feelings, his emotions and his spirit, and thus be in a position to overcome in every situation.

3.   He knew how to draw power from a different place.
     New Age gurus talk of our need to draw power from within, to draw strength from something mystical inside us. (This idea is almost certainly a distortion of the assertion in Ecclesiastes that eternity has been hidden in our hearts.) But David knew that it wasn't mystical power from within that he needed, but supernatural power from without. He needed to draw strength from his God, as he had done so many times in the past.

If we can build these principles very firmly into our lives *before the battle* – then we will always be successful and live our lives on a level that is way above average. Let us remember the sobering thought that for every person who goes on to be a "king", there are many who return to being "shepherds". To change this generation of boys and girls, we desperately need some people who will operate on a level way above average. I believe that God is raising those people up right now. But they must pass through Ziklag.

Experts are hewn out of the bedrock of experience. Do you want to be great? Then get through Ziklag. There are boys and girls being abused right now who have a chance of healing because of who you are and what you do. There are children who now have a hope of eternal life because of what you do. There are boys and girls who would have grown up to be drug dealers and dangerous criminals, who would have shipwrecked their lives, but will not do so now – because of who you are and what you do.

For the sake of this generation – don't give up, not now, not ever.

THE CURRICULUM IN VARIOUS CONTEXTS

The evangelistic children's club

The material was written with this context in mind. The format should be used as it appears, but feel free to add your own games and illustrations as you see fit. The stories at the end of each lesson may not suit everyone. Some people will prefer to add visual aids to them; some people will prefer not to use them at all and instead add an extra illustration. If it works for you, then it is right for you. Go with what feels comfortable.

The holiday play scheme

It is always difficult to determine how much of the Christian message can be packaged into what is essentially a community project. I recommend that the format is followed as listed, but only one of the illustrations and the story is used.

The Bible week

Follow the guidelines for the evangelistic children's club but opt for series that have five parts or that can be shortened to five parts.

The school assembly

The stories may be used as they are, or a single illustration expanded to form the fifteen-minute school assembly block.

The church Sunday school

The first section will need condensing, but the preaching time could be used in this context without any major amendments. It is important to work out how you want to format your Sunday school. We prefer our Sunday school programme (by which we mean the children's programme that runs while the preaching takes place on Sundays) to follow the programme of praise, worship, Bible texts, illustrations and story.

Summer camp

Within this context, I would maintain the format as it stands, but expand the illustrations and Bible lessons. I would not normally use the stories, but instead bring about opportunities for response from the illustrations.

PRESENTING THE CURRICULUM ALONE

There are some new dynamics that come into play when you present alone; an opportunity to interweave the whole thing occurs. Let me explain:

Children like to track with you; as soon as they know the end of the story, they are no longer interested. As soon as they can see conclusions, they tend to switch off and wait patiently (sometimes not so patiently) for you to get to the application. In the light of this, the more things you can throw into the air without conclusion, the better. They will track with you until all the pieces have landed, so to speak, and if the application itself can go into the story then you will have done a great job of communicating.

I realise this may come across as slightly complicated, so let me illustrate with an example from "Elizabeth's Accident", the first of the "One-off Lessons":

- Display the Bible verse.
- Start the story of the prodigal son from the Bible lesson, but only take it to the point where the prodigal is in a desperate state and thinking about returning to his dad.
- Then start the story... "There was another girl thinking of returning to her dad. Her name was Elizabeth..."
- When you reach the part where Elizabeth is sick, you could move to Illustration 2 – "The Spoiled T-shirt".
- Then use Illustration 1.
- Then use Illustration 3.
- Then return to complete the Elizabeth story.
- Then complete the prodigal son story.
- Refer back to the Bible text.
- Finally, mention that there is a loving Father God who is looking for some people to come back to him tonight/today; no matter what they have done, he wants to take their sin away.

It's a complicated process which needs some work and much use before it becomes second nature. However, when it does, you will captivate your audience and communicate effectively to a generation.

One-Off Lessons

Three One-off Lessons

Introduction

Title	Themes covered
1 Elizabeth's Accident	God wants to forgive
2 It Doesn't Always Make Sense	It doesn't always make sense
3 Sin Is At Your Door	The nature of sin

 Series Overview

This section consists of three one-off lessons. They are not connected in any way other than that they all have a strong gospel emphasis. It is intended that they be used to start up your new children's clubs. This means that for the first three weeks you can begin to build up the numbers of children who attend, without being concerned that parts of the series will be missed.

The first lesson is aimed at communicating simply and effectively the heart of the gospel message: God wants a relationship with us, but we have no means of coming to him, so God has made the way possible through Christ.

The second lesson may be quite difficult to present, but it is a very important lesson. There are so many children out there who need to know that God is with them even when things go wrong.

The third lesson deals with the nature of sin and the way that sin operates to mess up our lives. The message from Genesis 4:7 is quite clear: "Sin wants to destroy you, but don't let it!"

① Elizabeth's Accident

	Programme	Item
Section 1	Welcome	
	Rules	
	Prayer	
	Praise	
	Game 1	Blockage
	Praise (x2)	
	Fun Item 1	
	Game 2	Bridge
	Fun Item 2	
	Bible Text	Isaiah 1:18
	Announcements	
	Interview	
	Worship (x2)	
Section 2 **Preaching** **Time**	Bible Lesson	The Prodigal Son
	Illustration 1	Blockage
	Illustration 2	The Spoiled T-shirt
	Illustration 3	The Bridge
	Story	Elizabeth's Accident
	Prayer	

 **verview** This lesson is aimed at communicating simply and effectively the heart of the gospel message: God wants a relationship with us, but we have no means of coming to him, so God has made the way possible through Christ.

Game 1

Blockage

PREPARATION	Five chairs per team placed between points A and B in a line so that the children are able to crawl through the legs. Five objects per team placed under each of the chairs.
PLAYERS	Five players per team.
SET-UP	Players stand at A in relay formation (i.e. one player goes first; the next player waits until that first person comes back before they go).
OBJECT	The first person runs to the chairs, goes underneath, unblocks the tunnel by collecting one of the objects and then returns. The next player then goes. This is repeated until all the objects are collected from under the chairs. The last player runs to the chairs, goes under, touches a point at B and returns.
WINNING	The first team to complete the game wins.

Game 2

Bridge

PREPARATION	Two pieces of masking tape stretched across the ground. There should be about three metres between each of the pieces, as shown below. Four chairs per team are placed at A.

A
B

PLAYERS	Five players from each team.
SET-UP	The teams line up at A in relay formation.
OBJECT	The first player goes and places a chair just over the masking tape line. The next player then does the same until the chairs stretch across the imaginary chasm. This is repeated until four chairs are placed. The fifth player runs across the top of the chairs to B.
WINNING	The first team to get their player across wins.

PreachingTime

 **BIBLE LESSON**

THE PRODIGAL SON (Luke 15)

"Your sins are scarlet red, but they will be whiter than snow or wool." (Isaiah 1:18)

The children could be invited to act this out.

Once a man had two sons. The younger son said to his father, "Give me my share of the property." So the father divided his property between his two sons.

Not long after that, the younger son packed up everything he owned and left for a foreign country, where he wasted all his money. He had spent everything and soon he had nothing to eat.

He went to work for a man in that country, and the man sent him out to take care of his pigs. The man was so desperate that he would have been glad to eat what the pigs were eating, but no one gave him a thing.

Finally, he came to his senses and said, "My father's workers have plenty to eat, and here I am, starving to death! I will go to my father and say to him, 'Father, I have sinned against God in heaven and against you. I am no longer good enough to be called your son. Treat me like one of your workers.' "

The younger son got up and started his

journey back home. But when he was still a long way off, his father saw him and felt sorry for him. He ran to his son and hugged and kissed him. The son said, "Father, I have sinned against God in heaven and against you. I am no longer good enough to be called your son."

But his father said to the servants, "Hurry and bring the best clothes and put them on him. Give him a ring for his finger, and sandals for his feet. This son of mine was dead, but has now come back to life. He was lost and has now been found." And they began to celebrate.

The father had longed for his son to come back. He knew he'd been foolish, but at least he was smart enough to come back home.

Blockage

Objects needed: *A tube and some bits of rolled-up newspaper.*

This is a tube. If I look through it I can see lots of beautiful faces – and a couple of leaders' faces! The tube is completely clear. If I was a lot smaller I could walk into it from this side and come out on the other side (if I was a lot, lot smaller!).

It was like this at the start of time. God was at this side, we were at the other side, and we could walk through and chat to each other any time we wanted. Imagine, being able to hang out with the Person who created the universe, the planet, me and you!

But then, because of the wrong things we did, the tube began to get blocked.

Begin to put pieces of paper in the tube.

Eventually, we couldn't talk to God any more. We had done so many wrong things that the tube was blocked.

Remember what we've been learning. The same thing is true – we couldn't do a thing about the blockage, so God himself came, disguised as Jesus, and began to clean out the tube. He just wants us to ask his forgiveness for messing up the tube in the first place.

Pull the pieces of paper out of the tube.

God really does want to spend time with us. We just have to ask him to forgive the wrong things we have done.

The Spoiled T-shirt

Objects needed: *A white T-shirt, paint and a paintbrush*

It's really easy to get your clothes dirty. You play a game of football – mud ends up on your shirt. You do some painting – paint ends up on your shirt. You slide down a mountain – grass stains.

But our lives can also get dirty with this thing called sin. Now sins are the bad things we do, the junk, rubbish, garbage in our lives. Let's pretend this white T-shirt is our life. Let's see what happens when we sin. Let's say I steal something from a shop. *Blot some paint onto the T-shirt.* The T-shirt gets messed up.

Let's say I swear at my parents. *Blot some paint onto the T-shirt.* The T-Shirt gets messed up.

Let's say I get into a fight. *Blot some paint onto the T-shirt.* The T-shirt gets messed up.

And all the time, our lives are getting more and more messed up. Just like this T-shirt, our lives get totally ruined. There's nothing we can do about it. But there is something God can do. If we ask him, he will come and clean up our lives and make our lives clean again. *Turn the T-shirt around the other way.*

We can be just like this T-shirt: as clean as the day it was bought.

The Bridge

Object needed: *Draw the illustration below, but omit the cross and do not cross out the word "death".**

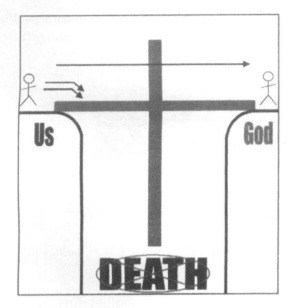

The Bible tells us that we have all done bad things. The Bible calls these things "sin". Sin separates us from God, just as you can see on this drawing. The Bible also tells us that, because we have done wrong things, one day we will die and not get to go to heaven.

So, how do we change this? How do we find a way of getting rid of sin and getting close to God again? The bad news is that we can't find a way. The good news is that God has already made a way for us.

Jesus died on the cross *(introduce the cross to the drawing)* so that all the wrong things we've done could be forgiven. And also, just to make it even better, if we ask Jesus to forgive the wrong things we have done and make him our leader, then when we die, we go straight to heaven. *(Put a line through death.)*

Remember, we can't do it ourselves, but God can help us if we ask him.

* Illustration based on "Becoming a Contagious Christian", produced by Willow Creek Community Church

● STORY – Elizabeth's Accident

Elizabeth was really quite a strange girl to look at. She was seven years of age. She always wore big lacy dresses which, even though she was a little bit fat, looked absolutely enormous on her. Her hair was plaited. But instead of hanging down nicely in two plaits, she insisted that the ends were pinned back up into her hair so that she looked like she had two elephants' ears.

She was quite unpleasant to know. She never said "please" or "thank you" and she always did what she wanted. In fact she was spoilt. Her dad

was a millionaire and anything she wanted she got, not by asking, but by demanding.

For the past six months Elizabeth had been at a boarding school [you may need to explain what a boarding school is] in England. Today she was leaving school to go and see her mum and dad for the summer holidays. She was American, her mum and dad were American, and the boarding school was in England. So it would be quite a journey home.

She had demanded that the housemistress buy her a new white dress, which she was now wearing. And so down the stairs she walked, wearing the dress. She stopped at the bottom while her chauffeur opened the car door, and in she got. No "please" or "thank you" – she simply got in and waited for him to close the door. And off they set for the airport.

At the airport the chauffeur opened the door; Elizabeth got out of the car and, escorted by a stewardess, walked to her aeroplane. The stewardess showed Elizabeth to her seat and told her that a food trolley and a drinks trolley would come past at regular intervals; she could have whatever she wanted from them. And so the plane took off.

After only a couple of minutes the drinks trolley went past: "Would you like anything?" the stewardess asked.

"Coke. I want Coke," demanded Elizabeth. "Glug, glug, glug!" – and it was gone.

Several minutes later the food trolley arrived. "Would you like anything?" the stewardess asked.

"Peanuts. I want KP peanuts," demanded Elizabeth. "Crunch, crunch, crunch" – and they were gone.

After another couple of minutes the drinks trolley was back. "Would you like anything?" the stewardess asked.

"Coke. I want Coke," demanded Elizabeth again. "Glug, glug, glug!" – and it was gone.

Then several minutes later the food trolley arrived. "Would you like anything?" the stewardess asked.

"More peanuts. I want peanuts. Crunch, crunch, crunch" – and they were gone too.

This went on for several hours. Every couple of minutes: "Glug, glug, glug, crunch, crunch, crunch, glug, glug, crunch, crunch, glug, crunch, glug, crunch." Loads and loads of peanuts, and bottles and bottles of Coke, all in Elizabeth's tummy.

Now this would have been OK normally, because she had quite a big tummy and it could hold a lot of Coke and peanuts. But the aeroplane went into a storm and the plane started going up and down, up and down, up and down…

Now *this* would have been OK, except all the people in the plane started going up and down, up and down, up and down…

Now *this* would have been OK, except Elizabeth started going up and down, up and down, up and down…

Now *this* would have been OK, except Elizabeth's tummy started going up and down, up and down, up and down…

Now even *this* would have been OK, except all the peanuts and Coke inside Elizabeth started going up and down, up and down, up and then… OUT!

All over the cabin shot this radioactive, supersonic, turbo-propelled, projectile sick. It left Elizabeth's mouth, it broke the sound barrier, it flew down the aeroplane, it knocked a lady's hat off, and hit the end of the cabin so hard the pilot thought he was going to crash.

Elizabeth's white dress was no longer white. It looked more like Joseph's Technicolour Dreamcoat than a white dress. It had greens and yellows and oranges and purples and blues. It was horrible.

This story was told to me by a man who was sitting opposite Elizabeth on the plane, and he said that not only did it look horrible, it smelt horrible; it was disgusting. Sometimes when God looks down on us he sees stuff on us, actually inside us. It looks like sick. It's all the junk, garbage and rubbish in our lives, the stuff the Bible calls sin.

Elizabeth had to sit there for another three hours. The man opposite her said it was horrible just to be near her. He couldn't wait for the aeroplane to stop and for Elizabeth to get off, and he was pretty convinced that when her father saw the state she was in, she was going to get smacked very hard indeed.

Eventually the plane landed. The man got off quickly and rushed through the airport so that he could see what would happen. He saw a man wearing a white shirt and smart tie and thought that must be Elizabeth's dad. And so he waited. He was absolutely convinced that she was in for trouble.

Elizabeth got off the plane and started walking towards her father. When she saw him, she opened her arms and started running towards him. The father saw his little girl and opened his arms and started running towards her. "That's a colourful dress," he thought to himself.

They ran until they were quite close. What was going to happen? "That really is a strange dress," Dad thought. They came closer and closer and closer, then…

"Aaaghhh!" The father saw what was really on the dress and stopped dead in his tracks. Elizabeth, however, didn't stop at all, but kept running and then jumped up towards her dad, her arms held wide. Dad was so shocked he just stood there. Closer and closer she flew through the air. What was her father going to do?

Some people wonder the same things about God, because he sees this stuff all down us which looks like sin, and we think he would at least push us away in disgust.

What was Elizabeth's father going to do? Elizabeth came closer and closer… until eventually she landed right in her dad's arms – and it went squelch! Her father didn't turn her away or move aside. He hugged his little girl close and didn't worry about the dress. He loved his little girl and had missed her so much.

And God is exactly the same; he knows what we are like and wants to accept us just as we are. After we come to him, we can then get rid of that sickly sin stuff. Elizabeth's father's shirt was ruined, but he was glad to have her back and didn't worry too much. After all, he was a millionaire.

It's amazing really, how God accepts us as we are. Sometimes we find it so hard to accept ourselves.

(Story adapted from a sermon illustration by Tony Campolo.)

2 It Doesn't Always Make Sense

	Programme	Item
Section 1	Welcome	
	Rules	
	Prayer	
	Praise	
	Game 1	It Doesn't Always Make Sense 1
	Praise (x2)	
	Fun Item 1	
	Game 2	It Doesn't Always Make Sense 2
	Fun Item 2	
	Bible Text	Romans 8:38
	Announcements	
	Interview	
	Worship (x2)	
Section 2	Bible Lesson	The Cross
Preaching	Illustration 1	Good Things
Time	Illustration 2	Bad Things
	Illustration 3	Time To Be Real
	Story	Victoria
	Prayer	

Overview This is quite a difficult lesson to present, but it is a very important lesson. There are so many children out there who need to know that God is with them even when things go wrong.

games

Game 1

It Doesn't Always Make Sense 1

PREPARATION   Five sheets of paper as follows per team:

a	b	c	d	e
1	2	3	4	5

f	g	h	i	j
6	7	8	9	10

k	l	m	n	o
11	12	13	14	15

p	q	r	s	t
16	17	18	19	20

u	v	w	x	y	z
21	22	23	24	25	26

And also the following coded message displayed on an acetate:

7.15.4.	8.5.12.16.19.	21.19.	9.14.
20.8.5.	7.15.15.4.	20.9.13.5.19.	

PLAYERS	Five players per team.
SET-UP	Players stand at A in relay formation. The above sheet is displayed on the acetate. The five sheets of paper are placed at B.
OBJECT	The first person runs from A to B. At B the person collects the sheet and returns to A. This is repeated until all the people have collected all the necessary sheets. The five people then use the decoding sheets they have collected to work out together what the coded message is.
WINNING	The first team to work out the message wins.

Game 2

It Doesn't Always Make Sense 2

PREPARATION   As above but with five different people, and the coded message has changed to:

7.15.4.	8.5.12.16.19.	21.19.	9.14.
20.8.5.	2.1.4.	20.9.13.5.19.	

PreachingTime

BIBLE LESSON   ## THE CROSS

"I am sure that nothing can separate us from God's love – not life or death, not angels or spirits, not the present or the future." (Romans 8:38)

This can be spoken, or you could use a video clip from Miracle Maker.

Jesus was arrested and taken away. The Roman soldiers made him carry his own wooden cross up a mountain to a place called Golgotha. Then the soldiers nailed him to the cross. They nailed his hands and his feet.

The Son of God was left there dying, hanging on a wooden cross. Blood was coming from his hands, from his feet and from the thorns that had been driven into his head. He could have commanded all the angels of heaven to come and rescue him, but he stayed there. He hung on the cross so that the wrong things we had done could be forgiven.

He hung there and at that moment all the wrong things done by every person who had ever lived and all the wrong things done by everyone who was yet to live, were piled on him. He was going to be punished for the whole human race. But he just hung there.

Jesus hung there dying. Eventually he asked for a drink, and a sponge containing cheap wine was placed on a stick and stretched up to him. He took a drink and then, realising that his work was now finished, he said: "Everything is done."

And with that, he hung his head, and the Son of God, who had never done one thing wrong, died.

Good Things

Object needed: *A sign saying "Good Times".*

In the old part of the Bible there is a psalm written by a man called David. David was a very special man; the Bible says that David was a man after God's own heart. He wrote these words: "If I were to climb up to the highest heavens, you would be there."

David here is saying to God: When things are right, when things are going well, when everything happens the way I wanted it to happen, I know that you will be with me.

Now David knew what he was talking about. God was with him when he was protecting his father's sheep as a young shepherd boy, God was with him when he was fighting a giant called Goliath, and God was with him when he was crowned one of the youngest kings in his country.

God wants to be with us in the good times.

Bad Things

Object needed: *A sign saying "Bad Times".*

There was another part to the psalm that David wrote. He wrote: "If I were to dig down to the world of the dead, you would also be there."

This time he meant something completely different. He wanted us to know that when everything wasn't going so well, when the things he had dreamed of lay in ruins at his feet, when people he thought were his friends turned against him, in fact in the very worst of times,  God was there.

Again David knew what he was talking about. God was with him when the king wanted to kill him and he had to run away and hide; God was with him when a man called Absolom tried to take the kingdom away from him; God was with him when his wife and children were taken away by another army called the Amalekites; and God was with him when his son died.

God also wants to be with us in the bad times.

Time To Be Real

The truth is this. Even though every day there are some great things that happen, if you picked up a newspaper you would also find a lot of bad things. Lots of people ask the question: "Why does God let bad things happen?"

The answer is: "I don't know; nobody does."

What we need to learn is that we don't know the answer to that particular question, but we do know something special: God loves people; he loves you, he loves me, he loves us. And when things go wrong and things make you sad, God loves you very, very much. He loves you just as much as he loved his own son Jesus.

● STORY – Victoria

Victoria was just like lots of other six-year-old girls. She liked to be with her friends; she liked to play with her Barbie dolls; she liked to watch lots of cartoons. But there was something that was different about Victoria. Victoria had leukaemia and because of it she was usually very weak, very ill and had to spend lots of time in hospital.

She had been in hospital for the last couple of months. It was now only two days before her seventh birthday and her dad came in to visit her. He talked to his little girl for a while and then he disappeared to speak to the doctor. When he came back he had a smile on his face. He announced, "It's settled. The doctor says that I can come and collect you tomorrow night and take you to the cinema. I've already invited your friends from school. Do you want to go?"

Victoria could hardly contain her excitement. She had been stuck in the hospital for what seemed like forever and even though she felt very weak she really wanted to see her friends again.

"The only sad part is that the doctor says I must bring you straight back here after the cinema visit," continued Dad.

Victoria didn't mind, as long as she could go to the cinema with her friends.

The following evening, Dad arrived in Victoria's room. She was already dressed and ready to go. They walked out of the room, down the stairs and out of the main door. Outside, there was a minibus full of laughing and giggling six- and seven-year-old girls, who went wild when they saw Victoria coming. They talked and laughed and giggled all the way to the cinema. Then they all piled off the bus and headed through the main doors, leaving Dad to pay for fourteen children. Then he went back to the bus. There was no way he was going to sit in the cinema with all those noisy girls!

He waited patiently. Eventually the cinema doors swung open and fourteen little girls tumbled out. They were all shouting and chattering and laughing. They climbed into the bus and Victoria jumped into the seat next to her dad. She was laughing so much she could hardly speak. Tears were running down her face.

"So what was it about?" Dad asked. But Victoria was laughing too much to explain. It took her ten minutes before she could bring herself to explain the movie, and even then she could only do it with the odd giggle sneaking out.

"Oh Dad, it was so funny!" she began. "It has got to be the funniest movie I have ever seen. Dad, there was this bit in the film, the funniest bit, when all the good guys and all the bad guys ended up facing each other in this big cake warehouse. They were looking for this diamond ring that had fallen into the cake mix and they were all searching. Then, Dad, they all started throwing cakes at each other. But that wasn't the best bit. Suddenly the baker came in and saw all his cakes flying everywhere. He looked so serious, Dad." At this point, Victoria had to stop again until she had finished laughing and then she continued, "Then, Dad, the good guys looked at the bad guys and the bad guys looked at the good guys and they winked. Then they started to throw cake at the baker. It was all over him. On his hat, down his trousers, up his nose. And, Dad, the funniest part of all: the baker just stood there and took it. He just took it. He just took it. He never did anything."

By now the minibus had arrived at the hospital and because Victoria was so tired her dad picked her up and carried her back up the stairs; he helped her into her pyjamas and put her to bed. Then he kissed her goodnight and went to take the rest of the children home.

The following day Dad was up early. He had arranged for the most amazing birthday cake for Victoria and he was on his way to pick it up. It was being made by the local baker and it had a big picture of Barbie on the top. It took him a while to collect it; then he made his way to the hospital.

He climbed up the stairs and began walking down the corridor towards Victoria's room. There he stopped in front of the doctor.

"Look, Doctor! What do you think of Victoria's cake? Isn't it amazing?"

The doctor looked at the cake and nodded his head slowly. Then he looked at Dad and began: "I've been trying to phone you all morning. Where were you?"

Dad looked down at the cake and explained, "I was at the baker's. Is there a problem?"

The doctor's voice was almost a whisper: "Sir, your daughter... she died this morning."

The father said nothing at all. He turned and walked back down the corridor, not saying a word. He walked down the stairs and out the door. He walked out on to the road. Cars swerved to avoid him; drivers shouted from their cars. He ignored them and kept walking.

Across the road there was an old Catholic church, and attached to the church was a statue of Jesus on the cross. The father looked up at the statue of Jesus and shouted, "Why? Why did you let my daughter die?"

And then with all his might he threw the cake at the statue. The cake began to run down the face of Jesus. The father stood there, staring.

Then as he looked up at Jesus on the cross, into the face of Jesus, he began to hear a voice in his head. It was the voice of his daughter from the night before: "He just took it, Dad. He didn't do anything. He just took it."

And Dad looked up at Jesus and began to realise the truth. Victoria might have died, but because Jesus had hung on the cross for the wrong things we've done, because he just took it – took all our sins – she had gone straight to heaven. Victoria was with God now and she wasn't weak any more. She wasn't in pain any more.

Dad didn't feel great; he didn't understand why God had let it happen, but he knew that God would be with him in the bad times, and he would see his little girl again one day, in heaven.

(Many of the lessons contained in this book could be used to invite the children to make a response. At times I have directed you to do so, but for the most part, listen to what God is saying.)

③ Sin Is At Your Door

	Programme	Item
Section 1	Welcome	
	Rules	
	Prayer	
	Praise	
	Game 1	Pendulum Run
	Praise (x2)	
	Fun Item 1	
	Game 2	Gingerbread Maker
	Fun Item 2	
	Bible Text	Genesis 4:7
	Announcements	
	Interview	
	Worship (x2)	
Section 2 Preaching Time	Bible Lesson	Cain And Abel
	Illustration 1	The Carriage
	Illustration 2	Pendulum Of Sin
	Story	The Gingerbread Man
	Prayer	

 **Overview** This lesson deals with the nature of sin and the way that sin operates to mess up our lives. The message from Genesis 4:7 is quite clear: "Sin wants to destroy you, but don't let it!"

Games

Game 1

Pendulum Run

PREPARATION	A chair per team placed halfway between A and B. A rope with a weight attached to it.
PLAYERS	Five players per team.
SET-UP	Players stand at A in relay formation. A leader per team stands on the chair and swings the pendulum back and forth at a leisurely pace.
OBJECT	The first person runs to the chair and scrambles underneath without being hit by the pendulum. If the pendulum does make contact, the person is out and the next player in their team starts their run. If they go through successfully, they return to the back of the line and the next person goes. The game continues until only one team has players left.
WINNING	The team left at the end wins.

Game 2

Gingerbread Maker

PREPARATION	A ball of play-dough per team and an assortment of small confectionery.
PLAYERS	Two players per team.
SET-UP	The two players per team stand in front of a small table with all the material listed above.
OBJECT	To put together the best-looking gingerbread man ever seen in 90 seconds.
WINNING	The best-looking gingerbread man wins.

Preaching Time

BIBLE LESSON **CAIN AND ABEL**

"Sin wants to destroy you, but don't let it!" (Genesis 4:7)

You could invite the children to act this out.

Adam and Eve had two sons. The first was called Cain; the second was called Abel. Abel became a sheep farmer, and his brother Cain became a vegetable farmer. One day Abel brought his best sheep to God to show God how much he loved him. Cain simply brought some of his vegetables.

God was very pleased with what Abel had brought, because he had brought the best he could. God was not so pleased with Cain. This made Cain very angry. But God saw his anger and said to him:

"Cain, be careful. Sin wants to destroy you, but don't let it! If you had brought a good gift, you would be happy now."

You see, Cain had a choice to make. He could stay away from the thing that was wrong or he could do what was wrong, but it was to be his choice and his choice only. It would have been just as easy for Cain to realise that he had done wrong and next time make sure he brought a good gift to God. But he was going to have to choose what to do.

Cain made his decision. He chose to let sin get the better of him and he went so far as to murder his brother Abel.

He had a choice to make but he chose incorrectly.

Illustration 1

The Carriage

Object needed: *A picture of a coach and horses.*

There was once a very wealthy man who lived in the United States of America at a time when the best method of transportation was by carriage and horses. He had a large cargo of gold that he needed to get from one end of America to the

other, and in order to do this he decided to hire the most suitable carriage driver he could find. He placed an advert in the paper and began to interview the three men who replied.

The rich man only had one question for the men who applied for the job: "Imagine you are driving my carriage and there is a very dangerous cliff with a fall of 200 metres to the rocks below – how would you get around this cliff?"

The first man came forward and thought for a while. Then he answered: "I could take the carriage within one metre of that cliff edge and continue on the journey."

The second answered: "I could take that carriage within 10cm of the edge of the cliff."

The third man thought long and hard before he answered. When he did speak, his reply was really quite surprising: "Sir, I would not take the carriage anywhere near the cliff edge."

The rich man didn't have to think for long. He gave the job to the third man. He wasn't interested in having the bravest or the cleverest man; he wanted the safest.

And likewise for us, it is not about getting as close as we can to doing wrong things without actually doing wrong things. It is about staying away from whatever is wrong.

Pendulum Of Sin

Object needed: *A large rope with a weight at the bottom – the whole illustration is much more effective if the item attached to the bottom of the rope could be set on fire. However, safety must never be sacrificed for effect, so don't attempt this if you can't guarantee safety.*

Ask someone to swing the rope back and forth.

This swinging pendulum represents sin. Sin means all the junk, the garbage, the rubbish that we can get ourselves caught up in. For example, we tell lies; we take things that don't belong to us; we are unkind to each other and don't treat each other with respect. All these things are sin, and we must stay away from them.

But we think that we can get a little closer to sin and still be OK.

Move closer to the swinging pendulum.

Now here we haven't actually got involved in sin. We have just got quite close to it. Maybe we hang out with people who steal things. But *we* don't steal things; we don't attempt it. But still, we are quite close and getting closer still.

We think we'll be OK, that nothing can happen to us. But we get too close.

Move so close as to be hit by the pendulum.

We must learn to keep away. If we get close we will end up messing up our lives. Keep away from sin.

● STORY – The Gingerbread Man

Has anybody heard the story of the gingerbread man? I'll tell you some of it.

One day, a woman makes a gingerbread man. She forms the head and the arms and the legs and the body. She puts some currant eyes on it and she places it in the oven. When she is quite sure that the gingerbread man will be ready, she opens the oven door... and out pops this rather rude and very loud gingerbread man! He announces that nobody is going to eat him and off he runs, shouting:

Run, run, as fast as you can,
You can't catch me, I'm the gingerbread man.

He passes a whole range of people, every time shouting to them as he passes:

Run, run, as fast as you can,
You can't catch me, I'm the gingerbread man.

He thinks he is the coolest! He thinks he is unstoppable; he thinks that nothing could ever harm him.

These are all dangerous thoughts, of course, but some of us think like this as well.

We think that nothing can ever hurt us or harm us. We are unstoppable. But that is not true. All the time, sin is trying to trip us up. It is trying to pull us down. It is, as the Bible says, trying to destroy us.

Do you remember the end of the story? A fox offers to take the gingerbread man across a river. The gingerbread man starts out riding on the fox's tail, but the fox says: "Come closer or you'll get wet there."

The gingerbread man, thinking that nothing could harm him, comes closer. He crawls onto the fox's back.

You see, the same thing happens again: we think that we can't be harmed and so we come closer to sin. But sin is just waiting to harm us.

The gingerbread man begins to get wet on the fox's back, so he is invited to sit on the fox's head. Then later he is asked to move up onto the fox's nose.

We think we can play with sin, but we can't. The junk, the garbage, the rubbish in our lives will stop us going to heaven and stop us being able to live our lives for King Jesus. We need to get rid of it and not go near it.

The gingerbread man didn't understand this. When he arrived on the fox's nose, the fox threw back his head and swallowed the gingerbread man.

Let's make sure our lives don't end so sadly. Keep away from sin.

Designer Living
A Model From Luke 9

A Series in Six Parts

Introduction

Bible Text	Title	Themes covered
1 Luke 9:1–6	Not What's In Your Bag, But What's In Your Life	Designed to fulfil a purpose
2 Luke 9:10–17	You Meet The Need	Designed to help others
3 Luke 9:18–21	Who Is Jesus?	Designed to be spectacular
4 Luke 9:22–27	It's Rarely Easy	Designed to be victorious
5 Luke 9:28–36	The Power Of God	Designed to do great things
6 Luke 9:57–62	Don't Look Back	Designed to finish the job

Series Overview

So much seems to happen in Luke 9 that it would be a shame not to devote a whole series to it. It is a pinnacle point in Jesus' dealing with his disciples. He begins to give them a much clearer idea of who he is and of the power of the God who sent him. He gives them instructions on how to live and ultimately he warns them of the need to keep on following him.

The third lesson makes the statement: "Lives touched by Jesus can't be anything other than spectacular." And the life story that ends each lesson is the story of Gladys Aylward. If there was ever a life touched by Jesus that became spectacular, this is it. The woman who was thrown out of Bible college rocked a nation.

Encourage the children to read through Luke 9 as the series develops and also draw up a table of the themes covered:

1	Designed to fulfil a purpose
2	Designed to help others
3	Designed to ?
4	Designed to ?
5	Designed to ?
6	Designed to ?

Fill in the theme on the table as you start each lesson. This timeline is included for your information:

Gladys Aylward's Timeline

1902–1928 Born and raised in London, little formal education, works as chambermaid
1928–1931 Makes a commitment to Christ, called to mission field, but rejected by China Inland Mission
1931–1932 Works for passage to China, leaves via the trans-Siberian railway
1932–1933 Arrives in China to work with Mrs Lawson, who later dies
1933–1936 Appointed by Mandarin as foot inspector, becomes Chinese citizen
1937–1938 When the Japanese invade her area, she leads 100 children to safety
1938–1970 Works with orphans, prisoners, Buddhists, until her death in 1970

Not What's In Your Bag, But What's In Your Life

	Programme	Item
Section 1	**Welcome**	
	Rules	
	Prayer	
	Praise	
	Game 1	In The Bag 1
	Praise (x2)	
	Fun Item 1	
	Game 2	In The Bag 2
	Fun Item 2	
	Bible Text	Luke 9:3
	Announcements	
	Interview	
	Worship (x2)	
Section 2	**Bible Lesson**	Luke 9:1–6
Preaching	**Illustration 1**	What's In The Bag?
Time	**Illustration 2**	The Carpenter's Pencil
	Illustration 3	Last One Picked
	Illustration 4	The Toolbox
	Story	Gladys Aylward (1)
	Prayer	

Overview Jesus sent the disciples out and forbade them to take anything with them. Why? Maybe Jesus wanted them to know that who they were was more important than what they could carry with them.

games

Game 1

In The Bag 1

PREPARATION Cut-outs of the human body and body parts: lungs, heart, kidneys, brain, liver, etc. An empty bag. All these items are per team.

PLAYERS Three per team.

SET-UP The players are lined up at A. The body parts are all positioned on the body at A. The bags are placed at B.

OBJECT The first player collects a part of the body, runs from A to B, places the part in the bag and returns to A. The next player does the same with another body part.

WINNING The first team to put all the parts in the bag and return wins.

Game 2

In The Bag 2

PREPARATION Cut-outs of the human body and body parts: lungs, heart, kidneys, brain, liver, etc. A bag. All these items are per team.

PLAYERS Three per team.

SET-UP The players are lined up at A. The body parts are placed in the bag at B.

OBJECT The first player runs from A to B, collects a body part from the bag and returns to A. The part is then placed on the body. The next player does the same with another body part.

WINNING The first team to put all the parts on the body wins.

Preaching Time

BIBLE LESSON LUKE 9:1–6

"He told them, 'Don't take anything with you! Don't take a walking stick or a travelling bag or food or money or even a change of clothes.'" (Luke 9:3)

Jesus called together his twelve apostles and gave them complete power over all demons and diseases. Then he sent them to tell about God's kingdom and to heal the sick.

He told them, "Don't take anything with you! Don't take a walking stick or a travelling bag or food or money or even a change of clothes. When you are welcomed into a home, stay there until you leave that town. If people won't welcome you, leave the town and shake the dust from your feet as a warning to them."

The apostles left and went from village to village, telling the good news and healing people everywhere.

Jesus didn't tell them to take along a suitcase full of stuff. In fact, he told them plainly that they didn't need lots of things; they didn't need lots of money or even a video projector or a CD player. Jesus wanted them to know that the only thing they needed was themselves.

And 2,000 years later, Jesus hasn't changed his mind. Jesus isn't looking for people who own a lot of stuff, people who can do clever tricks and play amazing instruments, people who have lots of things. Jesus just wants *us*. He wants us just as we are.

Illustration 1

What's In The Bag?

Objects needed: *A bag containing some coins, a designer T-shirt, some certificates.*

PERSON 1: God is going to be impressed by me. I've got a bag full of great things that will impress God.

PERSON 2: I don't think God is going to be impressed.

PERSON 1: Oh yes, he's going to be impressed. Here we go. *(Takes coins out of bag.)* I'm rich. I have so much money it's unbelievable. I have wonga everywhere. God is going to be impressed by this.

PERSON 2: Mate, God isn't impressed by your money.

PERSON 1: Are you sure? Well, it doesn't matter. I've got something else that will impress God. How about this? This is my designer T-shirt. If this doesn't impress God I'll be very surprised.

PERSON 2: Well, you'd better be very surprised because God isn't impressed by your clothes.

PERSON 1: I'm sure he is really; he's just pretending not to be.

PERSON 2: No, he's not pretending, mate. God is not impressed.

PERSON 1: Then I have one last shot. How about these certificates? I've passed so many exams; I have so many qualifications. God will be impressed now.

PERSON 2: He's not impressed!

PERSON 1: Of course he is!

PERSON 2: God's not impressed. He isn't impressed by the things we *have*. He's impressed by our lives. He's impressed by what's on the inside.

PERSON 1: What? He's impressed by my blood and bones and stuff?

PERSON 2: No! He's impressed by what you're like on the inside. Are you a good person? Are you a kind person? Stuff like that.

PERSON 1: Fair enough! Better take my bag away then.

The Carpenter's Pencil

Object needed: *A carpenter's pencil.*

Isn't this a strange-looking pencil? It's not round like normal pencils. It's flat. It's made like that for a very special reason. Anybody want to guess why?

The answer is that it's a carpenter's pencil.

And why is it flat? Well, it's designed on purpose. It's designed so that it won't roll. If the carpenter is working on a roof, for example, the pencil will not roll off.

The interesting thing is that *you* were also designed on purpose. God has something very special that he wants you to do for him. That's why he isn't impressed by what you may have, and he's also not particularly worried by the things that you don't have. God is interested in *you*. He created you for a purpose. You exist for a purpose. Life isn't about the things you can give. It's about you giving God *you*.

Last One Picked

Object needed: *None.*

Ask a couple of children to come and stand in a line.

When I was in school and we were going to play a game, we would all come and stand against the wall in a line like this. Then two people would choose teams. The first person would pick. If it was football, then I knew I was in trouble. I just wasn't very good at football. The first person would pick and he'd pick the best player and that wasn't me. He got picked because he was so skilful. Then the other person would pick and he would pick his best mate. And that wasn't me. And then the next would pick the strongest, and that wasn't me, and then the next would pick the cleverest and that wasn't me, either. And then the next would pick and so it would go on until there was only one person left...

And that was me. I was always the last to be picked because I just wasn't very good at football.

But God doesn't work like that. You see, he has designed each of us for a specific purpose. So when it's time for us to play our part God points straight at us. He created us for a purpose that only we can perform. We don't have to be worried about being picked last. God knows what he has designed us for and we will be his first choice.

The Toolbox

Object needed: *A toolbox.*

Here's a hammer. It's designed for a specific purpose: to hammer things, to bash nails! Here's a screwdriver. It's designed for screwing screws in. Everything in this box has a specific purpose. When the time is right, the builder takes out the perfect tool and uses it to do a job.

Each of us is like God's tools. He has created us for a specific purpose and he has placed us ready for him to use. You were created by an amazing God who wants to use you to do amazing things.

● STORY – Gladys Aylward (1)

Gladys was sitting in class with the rest of the students. It was 1928. She had waited a long time to come to college and now at last she was there. The college belonged to the China Inland Mission. Gladys was sure that God had told her to go to China as a missionary, and apparently this was the best place to learn.

She had been there for three months, but she wasn't doing particularly well. She wasn't very good at reading and writing and didn't enjoy all the studying.

However, she was sure that God had told her to go to China, so everything would be just fine. But Gladys was in for a shock. Before the end of the lesson, she was called out of the room and asked to go and see the headmaster. Gladys Aylward sat uneasily in the headmaster's office.

"Gladys," the principal said gently, "your grades for the first quarter are very poor. It would be a waste of time and money for you to continue."

"But," Gladys protested, "all my life I have felt that God wants me to be a missionary in China."

"Besides," the principal went on, "by the time you graduate, you will be almost 30. That's too old to learn a hard language like Chinese."

Shoulders sagging, she got up and began to get ready to leave the college. She was sure God wanted her to go to China, but she just wasn't clever enough. She had been kicked out of the only college that could get her into China.

But Gladys was making a mistake. God did want her to go to China. He wanted Gladys – not the certificate that the college would give her. She thought that she had to get things before she could go to China, but God just wanted her.

God was looking for someone who was willing, not someone who was clever or someone who could speak Chinese. God wanted her.

(To be continued…)

② You Meet The Need

	Programme	Item
Section 1	**Welcome**	
	Rules	
	Prayer	
	Praise	
	Game 1	Meet The Need (boys)
	Praise (x2)	
	Fun Item 1	
	Game 2	Meet The Need (girls)
	Fun Item 2	
	Bible Text	Luke 9:13
	Announcements	
	Interview	
	Worship (x2)	
Section 2	**Bible Lesson**	Luke 9:10–17
Preaching	**Illustration 1**	Weeds
Time	**Illustration 2**	The News
	Illustration 3	A Need To Meet
	Story	Gladys Aylward (2)
	Prayer	

 **verview** We tend to see the need; we are very happy to pray for the need; very often we tell others how we feel about the need. But somebody has to meet the need – maybe you!

Games

Game 1

Meet The Need (boys)

PREPARATION	Cut-outs of a homeless person, a drowning man, a thief, an unconscious lady; and a house, a life preserver, an ambulance, a policeman.
PLAYERS	Four boys per team.
SET-UP	The players are lined up at A. The first four pictures are placed at A. The second four pictures are placed at B.
OBJECT	The first player runs from A to B, collects a cut-out and returns. At A he must match the item to meet the need. The next players do the same.
WINNING	The first team to match all the items with their respective needs wins.

Game 2

Meet The Need (girls)

PREPARATION	Cut-outs of a homeless person, a drowning man, a thief, an unconscious lady; and a house, a life preserver, an ambulance, a policeman.
PLAYERS	Four girls per team.
SET-UP	The players are lined up at A. The first four pictures are placed at A. The second four pictures are placed at B.
OBJECT	The first player runs from A to B, collects a cut-out and returns. At A she must match the item to meet the need. The next players do the same.
WINNING	The first team to match all the items with their respective needs wins.

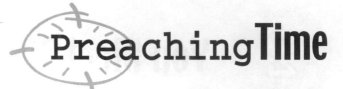

PreachingTime

BIBLE LESSON — LUKE 9:10–17

"Jesus answered, 'You give them something to eat.'" (Luke 9:13)

Act out the Bible lesson using some bread.

The apostles came back and told Jesus everything they had done. He then took them with him to the village of Bethsaida, where they could be alone. But a lot of people found out about this and followed him. Jesus welcomed them. He spoke to them about God's kingdom and healed everyone who was sick.

Late in the afternoon the twelve apostles came to Jesus and said, "Send the crowd to the villages and farms around here. They need to find a place to stay and something to eat. There is nothing in this place. It is like a desert!"

Jesus answered, "You give them something to eat."

But they replied, "We have only five small loaves of bread and two fish. If we are going to feed all these people, we will have to go and buy food." There were about five thousand men in the crowd.

Jesus said to his disciples, "Tell the people to sit in groups of fifty." They did this, and all the people sat down. Jesus took the five loaves and the two fish. He looked up toward heaven and blessed the food. Then he broke the bread and fish and handed them to his disciples to give to the people.

Everyone ate all they wanted. What was left over filled twelve baskets.

Illustration 1

Weeds

Object needed: *A weed!*

Last summer, I went to look at my garden and saw that there was one single weed. I shook my head, shouted at the weed and carried on with what I was doing. A week later I looked at my

garden again and counted over ten weeds. I told myself how unhappy I was with all those weeds in my garden, and then I went for a walk.

A week after that, my garden was fence-to-fence weeds. By this point I was very sad about the state of my garden.

But if, as little as three weeks earlier, I had taken the time to do something about it, instead of just complaining about it, the weeds would have been dealt with. My garden would have been fine if I had just got around to picking some weeds out.

The lesson is simple: Stop complaining and start doing.

The News

Object needed: *A video of the news.*

I used to hate watching the news with my parents. There always seemed to be a news story  that was really sad, maybe an earthquake in a certain part of the world. My parents would shake their heads and make some comments about how terrible it was. Then maybe there would be another story about some floods happening in a nearby town and they would shake their heads and say, "What a shame!"

It was annoying, because the news would then finish and my parents would forget all about it. They never did anything; they just shook their heads and carried on with their daily lives.

This isn't a good thing to do. We need to see the needs and then try and meet the needs.

When someone is crying in the playground, for example, maybe you could go and see what's up. How about it?

We always think it's somebody else's job. It's not. Get involved. Do something about it. Go help some people. Stop just feeling bad, and go and do something about it.

Illustration 3

A Need To Meet

Object needed: *A leaflet or flyer showing a need that can be met.*

Use this slot to advertise a project which the children can get involved in. This could be sponsoring a child, or collecting toys for children in a foreign country. Anything! The aim is to show the children that they need to do more than just be concerned. They need to help; they need to do something.

● STORY – Gladys Aylward (2)

When the China Inland Mission college rejected her, Gladys refused to accept that decision as final. She knew that there were people in China who desperately needed help, and she had no intention of doing nothing while they suffered.

But what could she do? The college had thrown her out and she had no money to get to China. She had no qualifications, no job, no support. But Gladys wasn't a "tut-tut" person; Gladys was a doer, and she was going to *do* something.

She took a job as a housekeeper in South Wales but spent all her spare time working for a rescue service, helping young girls who had run away from home. Gladys was determined that while she waited to go to China she would not waste her time. She would spend her time helping others; she would do something.

She was determined to go to China. So one day she walked down to the travel agent and asked for the cheapest way to China. The travel agent told her the route and then told her the price. Over the next couple of years Gladys regularly brought her money down to the travel agent until eventually she had given in enough money to be able to go. She collected her ticket and was ready to set off. *She* would do something even if nobody else did.

(To be continued…)

Give a prize to any child who can come back the following week and tell you how Gladys intended to get to China. What transport would she use?

③ Who Is Jesus?

	Programme	Item
Section 1	**Welcome**	
	Rules	
	Prayer	
	Praise	
	Game 1	Who Am I? (girls)
	Praise (x2)	
	Fun Item 1	
	Game 2	Who Am I? (boys)
	Fun Item 2	
	Bible Text	Luke 9:20
	Announcements	
	Interview	
	Worship (x2)	
Section 2	**Bible Lesson**	Luke 9:18–21
Preaching	**Illustration 1**	Who Am I?
Time	**Illustration 2**	Messiah, Son Of God
	Illustration 3	Who We Are And Who He Is
	Story	Gladys Aylward (3)
	Prayer	

 **verview** The disciples were asked one of the most important questions of their lives: "Who is Jesus?" Peter knew the answer; he said, "You are the Messiah" – the Saviour.

games

Game 1

Who Am I? (girls)

PREPARATION	Pictures of a man, a girl, a boy, an old woman, a younger woman. Cards with the words "father", "daughter", "son", "grandmother", "wife" written on them.
PLAYERS	Three per team.
SET-UP	The players are lined up at A. The pictures are at B. The words are at A.
OBJECT	The players run to B, collect a picture and return to A. Then the next player goes. When all the parts are collected the players must pair the words and pictures.
WINNING	The first team to pair up all the words and pictures wins.

Game 2

Who Am I? (boys)

PREPARATION	Pictures of a man, a girl, a boy, an old woman, a younger woman. Cards with the words "father", "daughter", "son", "grandmother", "wife" written on them.
PLAYERS	Three per team.
SET-UP	The players are lined up at A. The pictures are at B. The words are at A.
OBJECT	The players run to B, collect a picture and return to A. Then the next player goes. When all the parts are collected the players must pair the words and pictures.
WINNING	The first team to pair up all the words and pictures wins.

Preaching Time

BIBLE LESSON LUKE 9:18–21

"Jesus then asked them, 'But who do you say I am?' Peter answered, 'You are the Messiah sent from God.'"
(Luke 9:20)

When Jesus was alone praying, his disciples came to him, and he asked them, "What do people say about me? Who do they think I am?"

They answered, "Some say that you are John the Baptist or Elijah or a prophet from long ago who has come back to life."

They knew that there was something special about Jesus. They knew that he was a prophet – someone who heard from God and told others. They knew he was powerful, like Elijah who had made fire come down from heaven. But the people didn't really know who he was. Then Jesus decided to ask his disciples what they thought about him. They were the people who had been with him every day of the week, who had worked with him and eaten with him and seen the things that he had done.

So Jesus then asked them, "But who do *you* say I am?"

The interesting thing is this: only one of the disciples really knew the answer. Peter answered, "You are the Messiah sent from God."

The disciples had been with him for such a long time, but they still didn't truly know who he was. Only Peter had realised that Jesus was the Son of God.

Illustration 1

Who Am I?

Objects needed: *A whiteboard or a sheet of paper and a pen.*

"Who am I?" is an important question. Most of us are lots of things. Who am I?

Write down the descriptions as they come up.

Well, to my son and daughter I am a father; to my nephews I am an uncle; to my wife I am a husband; to the people who work for me I am the boss; to you guys I am a leader. I am lots of different things to lots of different people.

Lots of different people look at us and see lots of different things. Some of you are sons or daughters; some of you are nephews or nieces; some of you are cousins; some of you are uncles and aunties. You are lots of different things to lots of different people.

The same thing happened with Jesus. Some people saw him as a good man; some saw him as a teacher; some saw him as a healer; some saw him as a friend. But only Peter saw through all that and worked out that Jesus was the Messiah.

Messiah, Son Of God

Object needed: *A clip from the movie* Superman *(or even better still, do the lesson dressed in a Superman cloak).*

Isn't that Bible lesson very interesting? We found out that even though Jesus had been with the disciples for a long time, they had never really worked out who he was. Isn't that amazing? Imagine spending all that time with Jesus, seeing the amazing things that Jesus had said and done, and yet not understanding who he was!

Only Peter could see that Jesus was the Messiah.

I guess it's a bit like Superman. Every day, people worked with Clark Kent, and nobody guessed that he was really Superman. Every time that Superman appeared, Clark was nowhere to be seen. It was only after some time that Lois Lane worked out who her boyfriend Clark really was.

And now down to us. Some of you have been in church or children's meetings like this for a long time, but maybe you still haven't realised who Jesus is. You haven't realised how special he is. You haven't worked out how much he wants to do through your life.

You see, this whole thing is not a matter of knowing *about* Jesus; it's a matter of knowing Jesus, knowing what he wants to do in our lives, and knowing that he wants to make us spectacular.

Who We Are And Who He Is

Object needed: *Flash paper**

Here we have two separate items: over here we have a lighted match… and over here we have a piece of special paper called flash paper. When this object comes into contact with this object, something very special happens. WHOOSH!!

When one item comes into contact with the other, that other item is changed.

Now let's do the same thing again with the same items, but this time, let's say that the piece of paper is us: plain, simple, not particularly spectacular. Now let's say that this match is Jesus. Look what happens! Our lives get touched by Jesus and… WHOOSH! He changes our lives and makes us spectacular. He changes us from the inside out.

How about you? Has your life been changed by Jesus?

* Flash paper available from
www.tricksfortruth.com

● STORY – Gladys Aylward (3)

On Saturday October 15, 1932, Gladys Aylward left from Liverpool Street Station in London for the long train ride across Europe and Russia.

Gladys Aylward was one of those people whose lives have been touched by God. She knew what it was to have a life touched by Jesus himself. It made her spectacular. She may not have been clever enough to get through college. She may have been told that she would never be able to go to China, but she didn't believe it. She knew who Jesus was, and he had changed her life.

People may have said "no" to her plans to go to China, but she was going anyway.

Gladys worked at other jobs and saved her money. Then she heard of a 73-year-old missionary in China, Mrs Jeannie Lawson, who was looking for a younger woman to carry on her work. Gladys wrote to Mrs Lawson and was accepted, *if* she could make her way to China. So she set off from London with her passport, her Bible, her tickets, and two pounds, to travel to China.

The journey was far from easy. The first difficulty was travelling through Germany, where the officials were not happy with her explanation when they asked her why she was going to China. She simply replied: "God said."

They asked her many questions. They tried to stop her continuing but there was no way this woman was turning back. However, the worst was yet to come.

She travelled on through Russia. The Russians were at war with China and the journey was very hazardous. At one point, at a place called Chita, the train stopped and soldiers came on board. They commanded everyone to get off. Gladys protested; as her ticket showed, her destination was Dairen, a place on the China Sea, and she would not get off until she arrived there. The train continued. But some miles later it was stopped again and this time the conductor announced that the train would not be going any further for several months.

Gladys had no choice but to get off the train and walk back to Chita. It was a long walk and before long, the night had come, and with it the blistering cold. She stopped to rest under a tunnel. In the background she could hear wolves howling in the Russian countryside. The wolves were coming closer, but as it turned out, the morning came before the wolves, and Gladys continued on her way. At Chita she boarded another train and, despite a long argument with another soldier, insisted on being taken to Dairen. This time, the train took her no further than Vladivostok.

In Vladivostok the secret police interrogated Gladys and would certainly have locked her in prison if a stranger hadn't helped her escape to the harbour. At the harbour she tried to get a ship to Japan, but the captain refused to take her because she had no money. She pleaded with him until he agreed to take her.

From Japan she travelled to Tientsin, and then went by train, then bus, then mule, to the inland city of Yangchen, in the mountainous province of Shansi, a little south of Peking (Beijing). Most of the residents had seen no Europeans other than Mrs Lawson and now Miss Aylward.

The Germans said "no" but Gladys kept going because God said "yes". The Russians said "no" but Gladys kept going because God said "yes". The wolves tried to stop her but God said "yes". The secret service tried to stop her but God said "yes". Even the China Sea tried to stand in her way, but this was a life touched by God; this was a life that Jesus had made spectacular. Nothing would or could stop Gladys Aylward.

She was determined to do what God had told her to do. She was a spectacular woman, and God was going to do amazing things through her. What a spectacular life!

And God is looking for some other people whom he can touch. He wants to make their lives spectacular too! I wonder if there are any people in this room tonight who want to say to King Jesus: "I want to be spectacular."

If there are, then maybe we could pray together this evening…

4 It's Rarely Easy

	Programme	Item
Section 1	Welcome	
	Rules	
	Prayer	
	Praise	
	Game 1	How Low Can You Go?
	Praise (x2)	
	Fun Item 1	
	Game 2	How Many Can You Carry?
	Fun Item 2	
	Bible Text	Luke 9:25
	Announcements	
	Interview	
	Worship (x2)	
Section 2	Bible Lesson	Luke 9:22–27
Preaching	Illustration 1	Train In The Tunnel
Time	Illustration 2	Dingo
	Illustration 3	Waste
	Story	Gladys Aylward (4)
	Prayer	

 **Overview** Being a Christian may be tough sometimes – in fact it may be incredibly difficult at times, but at least we will not waste our lives.

games

Game 1

How Low Can You Go?

PREPARATION	A brush handle.
PLAYERS	Three per team.
SET-UP	The players are lined up at A.
OBJECT	The players have to go under the broom handle whilst facing the roof – their hands mustn't touch the ground (limbo style). The players will get a point for each player that attempts to go under. If the player touches the stick they are out, but they still get the point (this is about trying, not just getting under). If they go under, the stick is lowered next time.
WINNING	The team that accumulates the most points wins.

Game 2

How Many Can You Carry?

PREPARATION	As many footballs as you can lay your hands on.
PLAYERS	Three per team.
SET-UP	The players are lined up at A. One is designated as the runner.
OBJECT	The first player runs from A to B and back. When he returns, the two other players hand him a ball. He goes to B and back again with the football. When he returns he's given another ball and goes to B again. He/She keeps going until a ball is dropped. They get a point for every ball they attempt to carry.
WINNING	The team that accumulates the most points wins.

Preaching Time

BIBLE LESSON LUKE 9:22–27

"What will you gain, if you own the whole world but destroy yourself or waste your life?" (Luke 9:25)

Jesus told his disciples, "The nation's leaders, the chief priests, and the teachers of the Law of Moses will make the Son of Man suffer terribly. They will reject him and kill him, but three days later he will rise to life."

Then Jesus said to all the people: "If any of you want to be my followers, you must forget about yourself. You must take up your cross each day and follow me. If you want to save your life, you will destroy it. But if you give up your life for me, you will save it. What will you gain, if you own the whole world but destroy yourself or waste your life?"

There were many leaders in Jerusalem at that time. Many of them were trying to gain followers, trying to get people to join them, but they were doing this very differently from Jesus. You see, to get people to follow you, you usually promise them good things – you tell them all the things they will get if they follow you.

But not Jesus! He told the people who wanted to follow him that they would suffer, that bad things would happen to them and that it wouldn't always be easy. He made it hard for people to follow him, but still they did. In fact, all his disciples, except one, were killed just for being followers of Jesus. Throughout the centuries many people have been killed for being his followers. Even now, many people are killed for simply following Jesus. But still they do it. I think the message must be that it's not easy, but it's worth it.

Train In The Tunnel

Object needed: *A picture of a train.*

Corrie Ten Boom was a very famous woman. She suffered a lot in her life. Even though she loved Jesus very much, things didn't always go particularly well for her. She once made a very important statement. She said: "Just because the train goes into the tunnel, don't try and get off the train."

She wanted us to know that even though times may get hard, and things are not always easy, God will always bring us through.

We need to be clear on this point: being a Christian is not always easy. In fact, it is sometimes very difficult. The important thing is that we keep going and don't "jump off the train" when things get tough.

Being a Christian may be tough sometimes, but at least we will not waste our lives.

Dingo

Objects needed: *Pictures of a koala, a kangaroo and a dingo.*

When there are bush fires in Australia – and these tend to happen most summers – most of the animals run away from the fire. They run as fast as they can, but the wind blows the fire very quickly, so that the animals who are trying to escape (the koalas and the kangaroos) get overtaken by the fire. Sadly, many of them die.

I think this is like us when we try and run away from difficulties. I guess, in Corrie Ten Boom's words, we try and "get off the train". But trying to escape from the problems, trying to run away, never really works. Usually we end up in more trouble.

But there is one animal in Australia that does something a little more interesting – a little more spectacular. This animal is the dingo. The dingo

crouches in the long grass and watches the fire approaching. As the fire gets closer, the dingo waits. When the fire is just a few metres away, the dingo waits. Then when the fire is practically on top of the dingo, he jumps! He leaps over the fire.

The dingo doesn't run from the problem. He faces it and jumps straight through it. We need to do the same. Being a Christian may be tough sometimes, but at least we will not waste our lives.

Waste

Objects needed: *A light bulb, a sheet of paper.*

People are always complaining that we are wasting things. They say, "Turn off the light – you're wasting electricity", or "Use the back of that piece of paper – don't waste paper", or "Don't leave the tap running – you're wasting water."

All these things are important. It's true that we mustn't waste things. But I heard a story once of someone who wasted something even more important. This was an old woman, and she said one of the saddest things I have ever heard. She said that God had told her when she was young that she should be a missionary for him and go to a faraway country. The old woman said that she hadn't gone because she had found something else to do. Now she feels that she has wasted her life.

It's bad to waste money or electricity or paper or water. But it is the saddest thing in the world to waste a life. Being a Christian may be tough sometimes, but at least we will not waste our lives.

● STORY – Gladys Aylward (4)

Most of the residents of Yangchen in China had seen no Europeans other than Mrs Lawson the missionary, and now Miss Gladys Aylward. In fact, they distrusted foreign people. They called them foreign devils and threw stones at them.

But Gladys knew that things don't always go well, so she just kept going.

Yangchen was an overnight stop for mule caravans that carried coal, raw cotton, pots, and iron goods on six-week or three-month journeys. It occurred to the two women that their most effective way of preaching would be to set up an inn. The building in which they lived had once been an inn, and with a bit of repair work it could be used as one again. They laid in a supply of food for mules and people, and when next a caravan came past, Gladys dashed out, grabbed the rein of the lead mule, and pulled it into their courtyard. The mule went willingly, knowing by experience that turning into a courtyard meant food and water and rest for the night. The other mules followed, and the men who owned them had no choice but to follow.

The men were given good food and warm beds at the standard price, and their mules were well cared for. There was even free entertainment in the evening – the innkeepers told stories about a man named Jesus. After the first few weeks, Gladys did not need to kidnap customers – they turned in at the inn by preference. Some became Christians, and many of them (both Christians and non-Christians) remembered the stories, and retold them more or less accurately to other mule drivers at other stops along the caravan trails. Gladys practised her Chinese for hours each day, and was becoming fluent and comfortable with it. Then Mrs Lawson suffered a severe fall, and died a few days later. Gladys Aylward was left to run the mission alone, with the aid of one Chinese Christian, Yang, the cook.

Again, Gladys knew that things don't always go well, and so she just kept going.

Now Gladys was in sole charge of the inn and the thought suddenly hit her, "How am I going to pay the tax on the inn? What will happen now?"

The taxes in the region were paid to the mandarin – the man in charge of the region. Anyone not paying would be instantly thrown into jail. Even as she was pondering this, there came a knock at the door: a small boy announced to Gladys that the mandarin wanted to see her. She was sure she was in trouble; she was sure she would be sent to jail. However, Gladys went to see the mandarin. She approached him slowly with her head held low. He was a nobleman dressed in what looked like a silk dressing gown, and he was surrounded by servants. Gladys thought she was in trouble, but God was there to help her.

"Gladys, I need your help," said the mandarin.

Gladys nearly fell over in shock! This was not what she was expecting! However, she had long learned to trust God, even in the difficult times. She asked the mandarin to explain. He went on:

"In my country, Miss Aylward, it has long been the tradition that Chinese girls have their feet wrapped in bandages when they are very young, to stop their feet from growing. This happened because it was felt that small feet were more attractive. But doing this has made many girls disabled and so our government has now made it illegal. Miss Aylward, I want you to be my foot inspector. I want you to travel from village to village to make sure that the law is being kept and that the little girls' feet are not being bandaged. I will pay you to do the job."

Gladys was excited by the fact that she could now pay the taxes, but she hadn't forgotten why she came. "Can I tell people about Jesus?" she asked.

The mandarin didn't even look shocked. "I don't care what you talk about, as long as you do the job."

Gladys was delighted. Now she had an inn where people could hear about Jesus, and she herself was travelling from village to village sharing the good news of a God of love. Life does get difficult sometimes. But it's worthwhile keeping going. Gladys could have gone home, but then she would never have seen all those people learn about Jesus.

(To be continued…)

⑤ The Power Of God

	Programme	Item
Section 1	Welcome	
	Rules	
	Prayer	
	Praise	
	Game 1	Power People (sit-ups)
	Praise (x2)	
	Fun Item 1	
	Game 2	Power People (push-ups)
	Fun Item 2	
	Bible Text	Luke 9:32
	Announcements	
	Interview	
	Worship (x2)	
Section 2 Preaching Time	Bible Lesson	Luke 9:28–36
	Illustration 1	Asleep
	Illustration 2	Houdini And The Great Escape
	Illustration 3	Electric Lamp
	Story	Gladys Aylward (5)
	Prayer	

 **Overview** The key to this lesson is in the Bible text: the disciples woke up and saw who Jesus was. Jesus doesn't want us to be unaware. He is still saying, "Wake up and see my glory." He wants to reveal himself to us and reveal his power.

games

Game 1

Power People (sit-ups)

PREPARATION	None needed.
PLAYERS	One person per team.
SET-UP	The players are lined up at A.
OBJECT	The players have one minute to do as many sit-ups as possible.
WINNING	The person to do the most sit-ups wins.

Game 2

Power People (push-ups)

PREPARATION	None needed.
PLAYERS	One person per team.
SET-UP	The players are lined up at A.
OBJECT	The players have one minute to do as many push-ups as possible.
WINNING	The person to do the most push-ups wins.

PreachingTime

BIBLE LESSON   **LUKE 9:28–36**

"All at once they woke up and saw how glorious Jesus was. They also saw the two men who were with him." (Luke 9:32)

About eight days later Jesus took Peter, John, and James with him and went up on a mountain to pray. While he was praying, his face changed, and his clothes became shining white. Suddenly Moses and Elijah were there speaking with him. They appeared in heavenly glory and talked about all that Jesus' death in Jerusalem would mean.

Peter and the other two disciples had been sound asleep. All at once they woke up and saw how glorious Jesus was. They also saw the two men who were with him.

Moses and Elijah were about to leave, when Peter said to Jesus, "Master, it is good for us to be here! Let us make three shelters, one for you, one for Moses, and one for Elijah." But Peter did not know what he was talking about.

While Peter was still speaking, a shadow from a cloud passed over them, and they were frightened as the cloud covered them. From the cloud a voice spoke, "This is my chosen Son. Listen to what he says!"

After the voice had spoken, Peter, John, and James saw only Jesus. For some time they kept quiet and did not say anything about what they had seen.

Illustration 1

Asleep

Objects needed: *Possibly a nightcap or dressing gown.*

I like to sleep – I really do. I hate getting up in the mornings. Everyone else in my house likes to get up early and start the day. I like to stay curled up in my bed. I really do like to sleep – except on summer camp. On summer camp I hate to sleep. You see, I have this terrible problem. I think if I go to bed then I might miss something. So I stay awake and stay up talking to everyone else until it gets very, very late. And then because it's summer camp, I get up very early the next day.

The problem with sleeping is that you may miss something. We heard in today's Bible lesson that when the disciples woke up, they saw Jesus shining before them. They nearly missed seeing the glory of God. They nearly missed seeing who Jesus really is.

Many people who love Jesus are also in danger of missing who Jesus is. It is as if they too are asleep. And Jesus is shouting, "Wake up! See how much power I have! See how much power I want to give my followers, so that they can show people how great I am."

Illustration 2

Houdini And The Great Escape

Object needed: *A picture of Houdini.*

Has anybody ever heard of Harry Houdini? He was an amazing magician. He could do tricks with cards, and pull rabbits out of hats. He did lots of tricks. But without doubt, he was most famous not for his ordinary tricks, but because he was able to escape from things. On one occasion they locked him in handcuffs and he escaped; on another occasion they locked him up in a safe and he escaped. On yet another occasion they locked him in a jail and he even escaped from there!

Now those things may seem dazzling, but Jesus did something even more dazzling. On the day we now celebrate as Good Friday, Jesus was taken and nailed to a cross, and all the wrong things anyone had ever done or would do were piled upon him. A crown of thorns had been placed on his head. A spear was stuck into his side. And there he died. He was buried and a huge stone was rolled across his grave.

But this is where it becomes dazzling. Jesus, on the day we now celebrate as Easter Sunday, rose from the dead. Escape from a jail might seem amazing, but escaping from death itself shows how powerful Jesus really is.

Illustration 3

Electric Lamp

Objects needed: *An electric lamp and a power source.*

There are some strange ideas flying around. Some people think that we have power inside us that we can call on to do amazing things. That's a really strange idea. It's like saying that I can place this electric lamp here and it will shine all by itself.

It doesn't matter how long we stare at it. It's just not going to happen – until that is, we plug it into the power supply.

Plug the lamp in and switch it on.

We can never do the amazing things that God wants us to do until we get "plugged in" – not into the electricity socket, because that would just make our hair stand on end and maybe put us in hospital! I mean plugged into God. Then we are able to draw power from God and use it to help others and change other people's lives.

Jesus gave his disciples power to heal people, power to drive out evil from people, and power to tell others about God. We need to learn to ask God to give us his power. This power is not from us, but from God. It is power to change lives, power to show God's power.

● STORY – Gladys Aylward (5)

During her second year in Yangchen, Gladys was summoned by the mandarin. A riot had broken out in the men's prison. She arrived and found that the convicts were rampaging in the prison courtyard, and several of them had been killed.

The mandarin said to her: "You have been telling us that those who trust in Christ have nothing to fear, so we want you to go into the yard and stop the rioting."

"How can I do that?" Gladys stammered. "I am only a very small person and they are going wild in there." The mandarin shrugged, "You told us God would protect you, so show us."

There was nothing else for it. Gladys believed in the power of God, and here was an opportunity to show that power. She walked towards the gate and ordered the guards to let her in. She stepped into the prison yard with her knees shaking. She really didn't know what to do; she was trusting in the power of God. The guards locked the gate behind her. The prison looked like a war zone; bodies were scattered everywhere. Prisoners were attacking each other with knives and other weapons. And then, to Gladys' horror, one of the prisoners saw her and ran towards her with an axe held above his head.

Gladys trusted God, but right now she had to admit to being very afraid. Still, she knew that

God's power was great. She watched as the man came closer and then she spoke. With the authority of God she said: "Give me that axe now!"

The prisoner stopped. He had never been talked to like this before. He looked at this tiny woman, he looked at his axe, and then slowly he lowered the weapon.

Gladys looked around. All the prisoners were staring at her. It was then that she noticed that they were all dressed in rags, that they were all looking cold. She went from feeling afraid to feeling sorry for them. She began to talk to them and ask them why they were rioting and why they were so unhappy. This little woman called Gladys from England, who had been kicked out of college, was now sitting on the ground, talking to murderers and thieves. And she wasn't afraid. She was there in the power of God.

She walked back towards the gates. The guards opened the gates and almost bowed to her. The mandarin had seen God's power for himself, and now the man in charge of the prison was going to get a lecture from Gladys. She told him to get the men proper clothes and proper food and to find them jobs to do.

The prisoners never rioted again and the people of China saw the power of God. They began to call Gladys Aylward by the Chinese name "Ai-weh-deh", which means "virtuous one". It was her name from then on.

(To be continued…)

6 Don't Look Back

Programme	Item
Section 1	
Welcome	
Rules	
Prayer	
Praise	
Game 1	Four-legged Race (boys)
Praise (x2)	
Fun Item 1	
Game 2	Four-legged Race (girls)
Fun Item 2	
Bible Text	Luke 9:62
Announcements	
Interview	
Worship (x2)	
Section 2 **Preaching** **Time**	
Bible Lesson	Luke 9:57–62
Illustration 1	My School Run
Illustration 2	Half-completed Jobs
Illustration 3	Reaching The Destination
Story	Gladys Aylward (6)
Prayer	

 **Overview** This theme comes up again and again. It seems to be one of the defining characteristics of great people – their ability to keep going and never give up.

games

Game 1

Four-legged Race (boys)

PREPARATION	A piece of string long enough to tie up all four people in each team.
PLAYERS	Four per team.
SET-UP	The players are lined up side by side at A. The legs of the inside people are tied to the people next to them in the same manner as the three-legged race but with four people.
OBJECT	The players run from A to B and back again. They do this five times.
WINNING	Don't tell the teams until the end, but each team that finishes receives equal points. The points are for finishing, not winning.

Game 2

Four-legged Race (girls)

PREPARATION	A piece of string long enough to tie up all four people in each team.
PLAYERS	Four per team.
SET-UP	The players are lined up side by side at A. The legs of the inside people are tied to the people next to them in the same manner as the three-legged race but with four people.
OBJECT	The players run from A to B and back again. They do this five times.
WINNING	Don't tell the teams until the end, but each team that finishes receives equal points. The points are for finishing, not winning.

Preaching Time

BIBLE LESSON LUKE 9:57–62

"Jesus answered, 'Anyone who starts ploughing and keeps looking back isn't worth a thing to God's kingdom!'" (Luke 9:62)

Along the way someone said to Jesus, "I'll go anywhere with you!" Jesus said, "Foxes have dens, and birds have nests, but the Son of Man doesn't have a place to call his own."

Jesus told someone else to come with him. But the man said, "Lord, let me wait until I bury my father." Jesus answered, "Let the dead take care of the dead, while you go and tell about God's kingdom."

Then someone said to Jesus, "I want to go with you, Lord, but first let me go back and take care of things at home." Jesus answered, "Anyone who starts ploughing and keeps looking back isn't worth a thing to God's kingdom!"

Jesus wanted these people to know that being a follower of Jesus, being a Christian, was a serious business. If people started to follow Jesus, he didn't want them to turn back. He wanted them to keep going to the end. He wanted them to keep on serving him no matter what. So he made it clear: if you start following me and then you stop and turn back, I would rather you didn't start following in the first place.

Jesus is looking for people who will see the whole thing through and not quit halfway.

Illustration 1

My School Run

Object needed: *A pair of trainers.*

When I was your age I entered a big race in school. It was a 1500 metre race. I entered because, in our school, everyone was put into one of four teams and the teams would compete with each other throughout the year. At the end of the year the team with the most points would have their team name put on the school shield.

It was a long race, much further than I had ever run before: it was four times around the school field. I started really well. At the end of the first lap I was in the top three. At the end of lap two, however, I was in sixth place, and by the end of lap three I was in last place.

I could see everyone else disappearing up ahead into the distance and I was feeling really tired. I wanted to give up. I wanted to quit and go for a shower. There was no way I was going to get anywhere near the front again. But one teacher who was in our school team started to shout at me: "Keep running!" he said. I was really tired but he kept encouraging me to keep going.

The last lap seemed to take me forever. I was sure that people could walk around faster than I was running. I made it to the end eventually, and the man at the finish line asked for my name. What was the point of giving my name? Well, it turned out that you got a point for your team for simply finishing. It may only have been one point, but we could have won the school championship that year with that extra point.

When we start something we need to see it through until the end.

Half-completed Jobs

Object needed: *A saw.*

Some people have a terrible problem that I just don't have. They start doing things in their homes and when the job is only half-finished they stop and start something else.

Now I can't do this. Even if it means not going to bed until the early hours of the morning, I need to finish what I've started. Some people start to paint the radiator and then stop halfway through; some people start to wallpaper their bathroom and then give up, saying they will finish it later, but they never do.

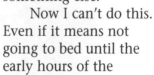

When you visit their homes they are really strange places. Half the lawn is mowed; the other half is tall grass; There are usually ladders left in the hall where some job got started and never finished. Half the bathroom is red while the other half is green.

It's a horrible thing! They are always in the middle of something but never feel the satisfaction of seeing the job done. When we start something we need to see it through until the end.

Reaching The Destination

Object needed: *A suitcase.*

Clearly, as with all these types of story, if you can import your own personal story it will be better.

I had to go on a journey once to a place in the north of the country. I got on a train very early in the morning and was on my way. We hadn't travelled very far when it started to snow. It kept on snowing and didn't look as if it was ever going to stop. When I was halfway there I had to change trains. As I got off at the station, I saw the whole world had gone white. The snow kept on falling and most of the trains were cancelled. There were just a few trains left running; one was going back towards my home and another was going in the direction I was heading but not exactly the right way.

I had to make a decision. It would have been the easiest thing in the world to get on the train that would take me home. But I didn't. I got on the other train. You see, I had friends waiting for me, and I didn't want to let them down. So I got on the other train. In the same way, God is desperate for us to finish the journey we started with him. He doesn't want us to turn back; he wants us to keep going.

The train took me to somewhere near where I wanted to go. Then I had to get into a taxi and travel another 40 miles. The taxi couldn't take me all the way. So in the freezing cold, and well after midnight, I had to walk the last bit. And then to my horror I discovered that the person I was going to stay with wasn't there. I had to phone someone else and eventually found someone to stay with. But I had got there. I didn't turn back. I finished the journey. I reached the destination.

God didn't tell us it would be easy serving

him. In fact, he promised that it would be hard at times. But we must keep going. When we start something we need to see it through until the end.

● STORY – Gladys Aylward (6)

Soon after the prison incident Gladys saw a woman begging by the road, accompanied by a child covered with sores and looking very hungry. Gladys was sure that this woman was not the child's mother but had stolen the child to help her get more money from begging. Gladys offered to buy the child, who was about five years old, for nine pennies. The woman willingly agreed. Gladys was sure she could look after the girl properly and she was also sure that the little girl, whom she named Ninepence, would die if she didn't get help.

This was only the beginning. A year later Ninepence came in with an abandoned boy in tow, saying, "I will eat less, so that he can have something." So Gladys acquired a second orphan. She named him "Less". And so her family began to grow. She became a regular and welcome visitor at the palace of the mandarin. She dressed like the people around her.

Then the war came and the Japanese invaded China. They killed many people in the villages near Gladys' village and they bombed the city of Yangcheng, causing many deaths. The mandarin gathered the survivors and told them to retreat into the mountains for the duration of the war. He also announced that he was impressed by the life of Ai-weh-deh – his name for Gladys – and wished to become a Christian.

Gladys then led many children over the mountains to escape from the soldiers who were intent on killing them. She had more than 100 children to look after as they crossed the mountains. She could have left at any time and returned to England. After all, this was not her war, but she would never desert the cause of Christ. She was determined to lead these children to safety because she was a Christian who never gave in.

Some nights they found shelter with friendly hosts. Some nights they spent unprotected on the mountainsides. Twelve days later they arrived at a river, with no way to cross it. The Japanese would surely catch up and kill them all.

The children wanted to know, "Why don't we cross?" Gladys told them, "There are no boats." But they said, "God can do anything. Ask him to get us across."

They all knelt and prayed. Then they sang. A Chinese officer with a patrol heard the singing and rode up. When he heard their story he said, "I think I can get you a boat." They crossed the river, and eventually reached safety at a place called Sian.

Gladys was exhausted. She collapsed and was diagnosed as having typhoid. But even this could not stop her. She recovered and then started up a Christian church and opened a place to look after lepers. She continued to look after many children.

At the end of her life Gladys wrote of herself: "My heart is full of praise that one so insignificant, uneducated, and ordinary in every way could be used to his glory for the blessing of his people in poor, persecuted China." She never gave in. She lived and died for Jesus. She was unstoppable. She loved God and lived her life for him.

Do we have any people who want to be like that? Who will make a firm decision not to turn their back on Jesus, but to do what he has asked them to do, no matter what?

God's Story

A Series in Five Parts

Introduction

	Title	Themes covered	*Toy Story 2* tie-in
1	Beginnings	God is getting ready to do great things	Woody lives in the perfect world of Andy's bedroom but adventure beckons
2	Broken	Only God can heal broken hearts	Woody is damaged
3	Separated	Sin separates us	The damage leads to Woody being taken away. The damage leads to separation
4	Image	We are wonderfully and fearfully made	Woody realises who he is
5	Rescue	Not only being rescued but also becoming rescuers	Woody is rescued; now he must rescue others

Series Overview

Toy Story 2 was released in 1999 by that great collaboration between Pixar and Disney. The movie, the merchandise and the numerous spin-offs which follow mean it will stand as a firm children's favourite for quite some time to come.

The movie itself has a wonderful theme running from beginning to end that lends itself nicely to our arena of Christian communication. The story of Woody's fall; his redemption; his realisation of who he really is; and finally, his mission to save others – this is purpose-built to allow us to talk of God's story. This is the story of God creating order out of chaos; of the damage that sin caused; of human beings who still bore the image of their Creator; of redemption through God's Son; and ultimately, of our ministry of reconciliation.

This five-part series will follow the journey of *Toy Story 2*, but the movie itself will only form one of the three illustrations on any given day. The Bible lessons will be centred on the dawn of time, before shooting forward to the Crucifixion, the point on which time itself hinges.

① Beginnings

	Programme	Item
Section 1	Welcome	
	Rules	
	Prayer	
	Praise	
	Game 1	Lego 1 – Order Out Of Chaos
	Praise (x2)	
	Fun Item 1	
	Game 2	Lego 2 – Towers
	Fun Item 2	
	Bible Text	Genesis 1:2
	Announcements	
	Interview	
	Worship (x2)	
Section 2	Bible Lesson	Genesis 1
Preaching	Illustration 1	*Toy Story 2*
Time	Illustration 2	Formless And Empty
	Story	Carlos (1)
	Prayer	

Overview It started with God bringing order out of chaos, creating a world of perfection. But God has a flair for the dramatic, and Genesis 1:2 is the build-up before the explosion. The world was empty and dark, with the Spirit of God hovering. Something was bound to happen – God was there. And the same God hovers over the lives of children, waiting to explode.

Games

Game 1

Lego 1 – Order Out Of Chaos

PREPARATION	A pile of Lego for each team, placed at B.
PLAYERS	Four players per team.
SET-UP	Players stand at A.
OBJECT	The players run from A to B, create "something" out of the chaotic pieces of Lego within two minutes and then bring their creation back to A.
WINNING	The team with the best construction wins.

Game 2

Lego 2 – Towers

PREPARATION	As for Game 1.
PLAYERS	Four players per team.
SET-UP	The Lego pieces are placed at B.
OBJECT	The first person races from A to B, collects a piece of Lego (only one piece) and returns. This continues until all the pieces are collected. While the pieces are being collected someone at A attempts to construct the tallest free-standing construction with the pieces.
WINNING	The tallest free-standing construction wins. Remember: free-standing – the towers must not be held.

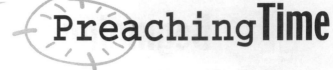

PreachingTime

BIBLE LESSON GENESIS 1:1 – 2:4

"The earth was formless and empty, darkness was over the surface of the deep, and the Spirit of God was hovering over the waters." (Genesis 1:2, New International Version)

Genesis is the very first book in the Bible, and it's where we will be spending most of our time for the next couple of weeks. It has some great accounts of Noah and his ark, of Abraham and Isaac, and of Joseph and his coat of many colours. All these are found in Genesis. But right at the start of Genesis is a very special account indeed. It is the story of creation – of how it all began. It tells of how God created day and night and animals and plants and flowers. Listen as I read you the first verses from the first book in the Bible:

In the beginning God created the heavens and the earth. The earth was barren, with no form of life; it was under a roaring ocean covered with darkness. But the Spirit of God was moving over the water. God said, "I command light to shine!" And light started shining. God looked at the light and saw that it was good. He separated light from darkness and named the light "Day" and the darkness "Night". Evening came and then morning – that was the first day.

God said, "I command a dome to separate the water above it from the water below it." And that's what happened. God made the dome and named it "Sky". Evening came and then morning – that was the second day.

God said, "I command the water under the sky to come together in one place, so there will be dry ground." And that's what happened. God named the dry ground "Land", and he named the water "Ocean". God looked at what he had done and saw that it was good. God said, "I command the earth to produce all kinds of plants, including fruit trees and grain." And that's what happened. The earth produced all kinds of vegetation. God looked at what he had done, and it was good. Evening came and then morning – that was the third day.

God said, "I command lights to appear in the sky and to separate day from night and to show the time for seasons, special days, and years. I command them to shine on the earth." And that's what happened. God made two powerful lights, the brighter one to rule the day and the other to rule the night. He also made the stars. Then God put these lights in the sky to shine on the earth, to rule day and night, and to separate light from darkness. God looked at what he had done, and it was good. Evening came and then morning – that was the fourth day.

God said, "I command the ocean to be full of living creatures, and I command birds to fly above the earth." So God made the giant sea monsters and all the living creatures that swim in the ocean. He also made every kind of bird. God looked at what he had done, and it was good. Then he gave the living creatures his blessing – he told the ocean creatures to live everywhere in the ocean and the birds to live everywhere on earth. Evening came and then morning – that was the fifth day.

God said, "I command the earth to give life to all kinds of tame animals, wild animals, and reptiles." And that's what happened. God made every one of them. Then he looked at what he had done, and it was good.

God said, "Now we will make humans, and they will be like us. We will let them rule the fish, the birds, and all other living creatures."

So God created humans to be like himself; he made men and women. God gave them his blessing and said: "Have a lot of children! Fill the earth with people and bring it under your control. Rule over the fish in the ocean, the birds in the sky, and every animal on the earth. I have provided all kinds of fruit and grain for you to eat. And I have given the green plants as food for everything else that breathes. These will be food for animals, both wild and tame, and for birds." God looked at what he had done. All of it was very good! Evening came and then morning – that was the sixth day.

So the heavens and the earth and everything else were created.

By the seventh day God had finished his work, and so he rested. God blessed the seventh day and made it special because on that day he rested from his work. That's how God created the heavens and the earth.

Toy Story 2

Object needed: *A video clip.*

Play the introductory scenes from Toy Story 2 – *you'll know which part to play and where to stop from the narrative that works with it below.*

That was a small clip from *Toy Story 2*. It is before all the action really gets going and before Woody's adventure really begins. It shows just a quiet, ordinary bedroom. Some of you may live quiet, ordinary lives; maybe the action hasn't got going yet. But for those who will let God be part of their lives, the adventure is yet to begin.

Formless And Empty

Objects needed: *Modelling clay, Flash paper*, matches.*

The whole story of creation is wonderful, but I particularly like the first part: "The earth was formless and empty, darkness was over the surface of the deep, and the Spirit of God was hovering."

"The world was formless and empty." Let's use our imaginations. Imagine "formless and empty". That would be like this modelling clay: no shape, no form, of no real use. How about, "darkness was over the surface of the deep"? *(Turn the lights off and ask for complete silence.)*

Then the Spirit of God was hovering. *(Light a match.)*

You see, when the Spirit of God is hovering, you can be pretty sure that something is going to happen. And the Spirit of God is hovering over your lives tonight, lives that may seem to have no shape or form, lives which are dark because of that stuff called sin – the junk, garbage, rubbish in our lives. But God's hovering. He's about to do something. He wants to do something.

And the Spirit of God hovered over the formless and empty earth and then God said, "Let there be light". *(Light the flash paper.)* And there was light. *(Put the lights back on.)*

God wants to take your life, which you may feel is empty and a bit formless, and make it into something remarkable.

So in a way, we are like modelling clay. It is formless, it has no real shape, like many of our lives. But it is God who puts the shape and form into us. He gives us purpose – we use a big word: destiny. This means becoming what God wants us to become.

* Flash paper is available from Paul Morley Supplies on (0161) 653 6626

● STORY – Carlos (1)

Carlos sat down in his bedroom and looked around the sea of beds in the dormitory. There were fifteen beds in all. It was crowded, but comfortable. All the boys who shared the dormitory had their own cupboard for storing their things – not that Carlos had many things. He had two pairs of trousers that had been given to him, two T-shirts, a jumper and a sprinkling of underwear and socks. Oh, and the coat that one of the older boys had kindly given him because it didn't fit him any longer.

Carlos looked into the mirror fastened to his cupboard. He stared. Two bright blue eyes stared back. He began to dress for bed. He put on his boxer shorts and looked at himself in the mirror one more time. He was hoping that his muscles would arrive soon, but there didn't seem to be any signs yet. He flexed his right arm, but there really was nothing there – nothing, that is, except Carlos' strange mark. On the top of his left arm there was a very curious shape. It looked like a wave splashing into the air. Carlos often wondered what it was, but recently had decided it was just a birthmark. Carlos crawled into bed and lay back on his pillow; he pushed his long, curly blonde hair out of his eyes and stared up at the ceiling. Carlos was nine years old. The place he lived in was not his real home, but it felt like home to him. He grabbed his stuffed rabbit, which by now was looking a bit the worse for wear, snuggled it under his chin and began to drop off to sleep.

Carlos' earliest memories were very happy ones. He remembered being rocked to sleep by his father, and the feel of the cot blankets on his face. His fondest memories were of looking up into his mother's radiant blue eyes as she sang to him a song about cows jumping over moons, and plates running away with spoons.

The little stuffed rabbit was his only reminder of that time now. Somehow that world had vanished away from him, and now he lived with many other boys and girls in an orphanage run by monks. Carlos lay on his bed thinking, little realising that everything was about to change.

(To be continued…)

2 Broken

	Programme	Item
Section 1	**Welcome**	
	Rules	
	Prayer	
	Praise	
	Game 1	Damage 1
	Praise (x2)	
	Fun Item 1	
	Game 2	Damage 2
	Fun Item 2	
	Bible Text	Isaiah 61:1
	Announcements	
	Interview	
	Worship (x2)	
Section 2	**Bible Lesson**	Sin Comes
Preaching	**Illustration 1**	*Toy Story 2*
Time	**Illustration 2**	Broken (Bones)
	Illustration 3	Broken (Hearts)
	Illustration 4	Broken (Relationships)
	Story	Carlos (2)
	Prayer	

 **Overview** One of the inevitabilities of living and breathing is that we will get hurt. The key to not allowing that hurt to cause permanent damage is dealing with it straightaway.

games

Preaching Time

Game 1

Damage 1

PREPARATION A pile of blocks assembled two metres past B. (Tin cans can be used instead of blocks.) A table tennis bat and a bucket of table tennis balls.

PLAYERS Four players per team.

SET-UP Players stand at A. A leader stands at B with the table tennis bat.

OBJECT The players run from A to B in relay formation, throw their table tennis ball at the blocks and return. If the leader bats the ball away, they win no points. If the ball hits the wall, one point is scored.

WINNING The team with the highest score after two minutes wins.

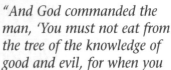
BIBLE LESSON SIN COMES

"And God commanded the man, 'You must not eat from the tree of the knowledge of good and evil, for when you eat of it you will surely die.'" (Genesis 2:17, New International Version)

Genesis tells us of a perfect world, a world of plenty, a world where everything which human beings needed would be provided. God placed Adam and Eve into his perfect garden, but they would soon damage it. Something was about to get broken. See if you can guess what it is.

Show the creation and fall clip from the video Noah, *in the Bible Society video series* Testament. *End the clip at the point where Adam and Eve take the fruit from the tree. We will use the remainder of the video, where God sends them away from the garden, for the next lesson.*

If for some reason you don't have access to this resource, retell Genesis 2 – 3 using another creative technique.

Game 2

Damage 2

PREPARATION As for Game 1, but this time the leaders throw the balls, and a member of each team defends.

PLAYERS One player per team.

SET-UP As for Game 1.

OBJECT As for Game 1 but with the roles reversed. This time the teams score a point for every table tennis ball they hit.

WINNING The team with the most points at the end wins.

Illustration 1

Toy Story 2

Object needed: *A video clip.*

Play the scenes from Toy Story 2 *where Woody is damaged and placed on a shelf – you'll know which part to play and where to stop from the narrative that works with it below.*

Woody is damaged. Through no real fault of his own Woody is damaged; he feels rejected, he is placed on a shelf out of the way, he feels unloved, he feels a whole load of things which some of you may have felt at some point in your life – which some of you may be feeling right now. Sometimes we get damaged and it is our

fault. Maybe we deliberately did things that we knew were wrong and got hurt through it.

God wants to heal the hurts that weren't your fault and also the hurts that were your fault. He wants you to come close to him. God can heal actual broken bones, but more importantly tonight, God wants to heal broken hearts.

Broken (Bones)

Objects needed: *A picture of a skeleton (or a real skeleton if possible). Alternatively, if you have the technology, show a clip from Dorling Kindersley's* Human Body *CD ROM.*

Has anyone ever broken a bone? I have! I broke my collar bone. *(Substitute personal details.)* My dad has broken most of the bones he has. Bones usually mend over time, but sometimes they don't mend properly, they don't join properly. Usually bones heal most quickly and effectively when a doctor examines them as soon as the damage happens. The doctor can tell if a bone needs to be moved to fit properly.

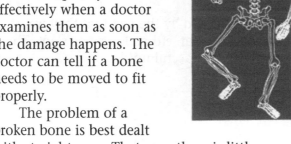

The problem of a broken bone is best dealt with straightaway. That way, there is little or no long-term damage.

Broken (Hearts)

Object needed: *A picture of a heart.*

When we damage a bone it's usually fairly obvious. It hurts and shows on the outside. When we hurt our hearts – when our feelings and emotions are hurt – it's not so easy to tell, but it can hurt every bit as much and can sometimes hurt a whole lot more.

Has anyone ever damaged their heart? I'm sure there are lots of people who have. But listen now! There aren't many doctors who can heal our feelings and emotions. In fact I don't know of any. Only King Jesus can do that. The Bible says of Jesus that he came to "bind up the broken-hearted". He came to fix broken hearts. He came to fix our hurts and emotions.

But just as it's best to get a physical hurt sorted out by a doctor as soon as it happens, so with our emotions it is very important to come to King Jesus as soon as the hurt happens. We need to come to him and pray and ask him to heal the hurt.

Broken (Relationships)

So what do you think was broken in our video clip? (The answer that is usually given is "rules"). Rules have certainly been broken, but something more than that, something much deeper, has been broken. Relationships have been broken. Our relationship with God has been broken.

When relationships are broken, we get hurt. When a boyfriend and girlfriend break up, people get hurt. When a husband and wife break up, more people get hurt. When it's our mum and dad, then we get hurt as well.

Always, when relationships are broken we are hurt. But remember, it is God who can bind up broken hearts. God can begin to heal the hurt and pain of broken relationships. It may not be completed today, but God can start to heal if we let him.

● STORY – Carlos (2)

Carlos lay on his bed thinking, little realising that everything was about to change.

Carlos often thought about where he had come from. The monks had told him of how they

had found him on the steps outside the home, wrapped in a blue woollen blanket with the word "Carlos" embroidered on it and clutching his stuffed rabbit. He was about 18 months old. Carlos celebrated his birthday on January 1st, but he wasn't quite sure how the monks knew when his birthday was. Whenever he had asked them he was told that they had guessed, but Carlos felt that they were hiding something. Carlos had always felt that they were hiding something.

Carlos thought about his parents often. He asked himself again and again why they would leave him on the steps of the monastery. He remembered when he was little how he had thought that it must have been his fault. Maybe it was because they thought he was ugly; maybe he had done something to upset them; maybe they had never really wanted him. He remembered the agonising times when his mind was full of the question "Why?" He had spent many tearful nights and still more tearful days trying to work it out. But he had discovered something: when he explained how he felt to God in prayer – as the monks had taught him –

he did feel better. And slowly but surely he had begun to realise that it couldn't possibly have been his fault – after all, he was so young. And another thing, every time he remembered his times with his parents he could only remember happy times. He was sure his mother and father loved him dearly.

Eventually Carlos let all the bad feelings he had fade away. He asked God to help him and he tried to remember the happy times. So now when Carlos lay thinking about those times, he only felt happy feelings and, of course, curiosity too. He wondered who he really was and where he had really come from. He couldn't help feeling that maybe he was a bit special. His eyes became heavy and eventually he dropped off to sleep.

It was New Year's Eve and the day before Carlos' birthday. Birthdays weren't a big thing at the orphanage; too many of the boys there had no idea when they were born, so the whole thing was played down. Nobody seemed

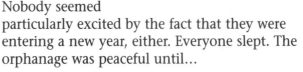

particularly excited by the fact that they were entering a new year, either. Everyone slept. The orphanage was peaceful until…

(To be continued…)

③ Separated

	Programme	Item
Section 1	Welcome	
	Rules	
	Prayer	
	Praise	
	Game 1	Separate 1
	Praise (x2)	
	Fun Item 1	
	Game 2	Separate 2
	Fun Item 2	
	Bible Text	Romans 8:35
	Announcements	
	Interview	
	Worship (x2)	
Section 2 **Preaching** **Time**	Bible Lesson	The Gateway To Eden
	Illustration 1	*Toy Story 2*
	Illustration 2	One Man And His Dog
	Illustration 3	Lost
	Story	Carlos (3)
	Prayer	

 **verview** It is an inevitable consequence of sin that it separates us from God.

Game 1

Separate 1

PREPARATION	A container with multi-coloured pieces of Lego at B and an empty container per team at A.
PLAYERS	Four players per team.
SET-UP	Players stand at A.
OBJECT	The players run from A to B in relay formation, collect a red piece of Lego and return to A, placing it in the box. This continues for two minutes.
WINNING	The team with the most red pieces after two minutes wins.

Game 2

Separate 2

PREPARATION	As for Game 1.
PLAYERS	Four players per team.
SET-UP	Players stand at A.
OBJECT	The players run from A to B in relay formation, collect a blue piece of Lego and return to A, placing it in the box. This continues for two minutes.
WINNING	The team with the most blue pieces after two minutes wins.

PreachingTime

BIBLE LESSON **THE GATEWAY TO EDEN**

"Who shall separate us from the love of Christ?" (Romans 8:35, New International Version)

Show the creation and fall clip from the video Noah, *in the Bible Society video series* Testament. *Start at the point where you ended last time and end it where Adam and Eve are expelled from the garden. And then continue the narrative below.*

If for some reason you don't have access to this resource, retell the Genesis 2 – 3 account using another creative technique and focusing on the fact that a fiery angel was now placed at the gateway to Eden. Adam and Eve were separated from God.

This is what sin always does. Now remember, sin is the wrong things we do, the junk, garbage and rubbish in our lives. In this case Adam and Eve's sin was that they disobeyed God. When we sin, when we disobey God, when we fill our lives with bad things, we separate ourselves from God.

Illustration 1

Toy Story 2

Object needed: *A video clip.*

Play the scenes from Toy Story 2 *where Woody is abducted by Al from the garage sale – you'll know which part to play and where to stop from the narrative that works with it below.*

It isn't enough that Woody has been damaged and left behind, he has now ended up at the garage sale and is about to be abducted by Al. He will soon find himself separated from the other toys, separated from his best friend Buzz Lightyear, and, worst of all, separated from Andy.
Sometimes separation comes through no fault of our own: someone leaves, and we are left

behind. Sometimes we end up separated because of things that we do. When we are unkind to our friends and they don't want to play with us any more, we become separated and it is our own fault. The Bible too talks about separation. It is the separation which comes when we sin – do wrong things – the worst separation of all. It separates us from God.

One Man And His Dog

Object needed: *A video clip of this amazing programme! (Alternatively just talk about it.)*

There is a programme that used to be on television that lots of people watched, but didn't really know why they did! The programme was called *One Man And His Dog* and was all about sheepdog trials. Basically, a sheepdog had to do certain tasks with sheep. He had to round them up and lead them around the course, and the shepherd would direct him with whistles. The dogs usually did their job very well, but the task they always struggled with was separating two sheep from the other sheep. This part of the job was very difficult. The sheep didn't want to be separated. There was a certain safety in being together. In the same way, there is a certain safety when we are not separated from God. The Bible talks about God protecting us under the shadow of his wing. We need to learn never to be separated from God.

The sheepdog would move around the sheep until he had separated them. The sheep that had been separated looked worried. They were very troubled, even alarmed, and they almost looked relieved when the dog allowed them to rejoin the other sheep.

Lost

Object needed: *A picture of a huge shopping centre.*

Has anyone ever been lost? I remember being lost once. It was in a huge shopping centre. *(Substitute personal story.)* I was separated from my mum and dad and I didn't like it. I had wandered down the fruit and vegetable aisle and when I turned around they had gone. I remember racing back up the aisle and searching around the tins of beans and then running over to the clothes section and looking there, but I still couldn't find them. So, I did what any four-year-old would do. I stood in the middle of the clothes aisle and burst into tears. I cried and cried. It seemed that everyone in the shop came to look at me.

Then a very kind shop assistant came and took my hand. She led me through the shop until I saw my mum and dad in the distance. I pulled away from the lady and ran towards them at full speed. My mum and dad hadn't even noticed I was missing. It had only been a couple of minutes. But I felt that it was hours and hours. I felt separated, I felt alone, I felt lonely.

That is what sin does to us. It separates us from the one whose very desire is to look after us and care for us. It's maybe time to ask God to forgive those sins and to come close to the Creator again. Maybe we need to come close to Jesus once more. Nobody likes being separated.

● STORY – Carlos (3)

It was New Year's Eve and the day before Carlos' birthday. Birthdays weren't a big thing at the orphanage; too many of the boys there had no idea when they were born, so the whole thing was played down. Nobody seemed particularly excited by the fact that they were entering a new year, either. Everyone slept. The orphanage was peaceful until...

It sounded like an explosion. There was fire sweeping up the walls of the orphanage. Carlos opened his eyes and all around there was chaos. There were men walking around the dormitory with masks on, asking the boys questions. They were searching for somebody. They were looking for Carlos. Carlos heard one of the men asking Tom where Carlos was. Carlos rolled off the bed and scampered underneath. He waited until one of the men had walked past and then he scurried into his cupboard and closed the door. He could just make out the proceedings through a small crack. The orphanage was clearly on fire, but the men weren't trying to leave. They had lined all the boys up beside their beds and were asking them where Carlos was. Then the monks were brought in and were asked the same question. They all answered truthfully: "We don't know. He should have been in his bed."

But the men weren't satisfied. They began shouting that the monks were hiding him. One of the monks was knocked to the ground. Carlos thought the monks would be shot but the man who was clearly the leader grabbed the gun. He ordered that all the monks and all the boys be removed and taken to the castle. Then one by one they were marched out. By now the flames had engulfed most of the orphanage and Carlos felt that he would be burned alive.

Carlos waited as long as he could, then, coughing and spluttering, he burst out of the cupboard. He didn't really know why, but he made a special point of grabbing his old stuffed rabbit. He rushed out of the room and down the stairs to the ground floor, but ahead of him the front door seemed obliterated by flames.

(To be continued...)

 **Image**

	Programme	Item
Section 1	Welcome	
	Rules	
	Prayer	
	Praise	
	Game 1	Clay Words
	Praise (x2)	
	Fun Item 1	
	Game 2	Clay People
	Fun Item 2	
	Bible Text	Psalm 139
	Announcements	
	Interview	
	Worship (x2)	
Section 2 **Preaching** **Time**	Bible Lesson	Creation
	Illustration 1	*Toy Story 2*
	Illustration 2	Remembered
	Illustration 3	Mirror Man
	Story	Carlos (4)
	Prayer	

**verview** We often try to be something we're not! We very rarely try to be something we are!! We are created in the image and nature of God, yet we act as though we are nothing. It's time to see ourselves as God sees us.

Game 1

Clay Words

PREPARATION	A ball of modelling clay per team.
PLAYERS	Four players per team.
SET-UP	Players stand at A.
OBJECT	The players run from A to B and make the words GODS STORY out of the clay. When they are satisfied with the result they return to A.
WINNING	The team that completes first and whose words are legible wins.

Game 2

Clay People

PREPARATION	A ball of modelling clay per team.
PLAYERS	Four players per team.
SET-UP	Players stand at A.
OBJECT	To construct a clay person.
WINNING	The best clay person constructed after 90 seconds wins.

PreachingTime

BIBLE LESSON

CREATION

Psalm 139 – Read the whole psalm using a modern translation.

We use a big word to describe God. The word is omnipotent. This word means that God is all-powerful. The account of creation in Genesis shows us how powerful God is. He spoke a word and things happened. He said, "Let there be light" – and light flooded into the entire universe. Can you imagine what that would be like? You could say anything and it would come into being. You could say, "Chocolate" – and the room would fill with chocolate. You could say, "Toys" – and the room would fill with toys.

I wonder what you would say. *(Ask some of the children.)*

God spoke and it happened. But the really exciting thing is this: when it came to making you and me, when it came to creating people, God knelt in the dust and began to form and shape it. *(Hold up some of the clay people from Game 2.)* God thinks that we are so special that he took his time to make us, to create us, to put us together. That's how much God loves you.

Illustration 1

Toy Story 2

Object needed: *A video clip.*

Play the scenes from Toy Story 2 *where Woody finally discovers who he is and how special he is.*

Woody thinks he is no good. He thinks that he isn't wanted by anyone. Then he sees a video. This video shows him that actually he is a priceless toy. He is very valuable. So are we. We are so valuable that somebody actually died for us. Jesus, the Son of God, died for us.

Then Woody looks at his foot and sees Andy's signature written on it. Not only is Woody very valuable – he actually belongs. We need to understand this. We are valuable and we belong.

Illustration 2

Remembered

Object needed: *Write the word "milk" on the palm of your hand.*

How's your memory? Mine's not so great. Sometimes I walk into rooms and forget why I went there. Very often I go to the supermarket and come back with the wrong things, and at least once a week I go to the office and leave something important at home. I forget birthdays and I forget anniversaries. But I learned this great idea from God: when I need to remember things I write them on my hand. Look, I know I need some more milk, so I've written "milk" on my hand. So, how did I learn this from God? Well, the Bible tells me that God has written my name on the palm of his hand. He's written it there so that he will never forget me. Your name is there too. Doesn't that make you feel good? How good it is to know that God loves and cares for you so much that he has written your name on his hand so that he will never forget you!

Mirror Man

Object needed: *A mirror.*

Invite some people to play the part of the various people groups. Ask some children to act the friends, some others to act as teachers, etc.

Scientists and other very clever people tell us that we never see ourselves as we really are. We usually see ourselves as others see us. Let me show you what I mean.

I look in this mirror and I see a reflection of me. But that is not what is the most important thing to me. I don't care very much what the mirror says I'm like. I care more about what I look like to people who I think are important.

So, my friends say to me, "You are so uncool! We're embarrassed to be with you." But I've just looked in the mirror. I know I look OK. I know what they say isn't right. But who do I believe? The person I saw in the mirror, or my friends? I have to tell you – most of you will believe your friends.

Let's try another example: I know I'm good at mathematics, but my teacher says to me, "You are so stupid." But I know I'm

good at mathematics. Who do I believe? Again, most of you will believe the teacher.

One more example: I know that God loves me and thinks I am very special. I know he thinks I'm so special that he allowed his Son Jesus to die on a cross for me so that one day I could be with him in heaven. I know all this. But the devil or one of his friends whispers in my ear: "God doesn't really love you!"

Who do you believe? It's time we learned the truth. God really does love us and we really are special.

● STORY – Carlos (4)

Carlos waited as long as he could, then, coughing and spluttering, he burst out of the cupboard. He rushed out of the room and down the stairs to the ground floor, but ahead of him the front door seemed obliterated by flames.

Carlos hesitated, then, covering himself with a blanket, he ran towards the front door and burst through it into the garden area. He rolled on the ground to make sure all the flames were out and then pulled the blanket off. He was unharmed, but very shaken.

Carlos turned to see the burning orphanage behind him. It lit up the night sky. He stood astounded. This was the second time that a place that he had come to know as home was taken away from him. He didn't know what to do. He was alone; the monks had been taken away.

Carlos felt deserted yet again. All the old feelings came back. He began to feel that maybe this was all his fault. After all, it was definitely him that the men were looking for. His mum and dad had deserted him, and now the orphanage had been destroyed. Maybe Carlos made bad things happen.

Then Carlos stopped himself thinking that way. He knew that it wasn't true. He was special, he was important, and even though he felt separated and alone right now, he knew it wasn't his fault. He would have to sort all this out. He would have to find the monks, and maybe in doing so he might find out who he really was. The monks' trail wouldn't be difficult to follow – there were lots of footprints going into the desert. He would track them down.

As the sun set Carlos set out, determined to set the monks free if it was the last thing he did. He walked into the night with countless thoughts flying through his head. On he went, following the tracks of the masked men, until finally he could see lights in the distance. It was a village, almost in the heart of the desert. He knocked on the first door, intending to ask if the masked men had come this way, but the events of that night were beginning to affect him. He fell through the door as it opened, and lay exhausted on the floor.

The next thing he knew he was gazing up into the eyes of a very kind-looking woman. She was offering him soup, which he willingly took. He was beginning to feel that he had no chance of rescuing the others. And anyway, who did he think he was to be able to rescue his friends and the monks from such a strong force of masked men?

Carlos finished his soup. He felt better. His rabbit still lay beside him. He stood up and walked to a wash basin nearby. He poured some water into the bowl and splashed it onto his face. He took off his top and began to wash himself. The woman returned, collected his bowl and was about to leave when she saw the birthmark on his arm, shaped like a wave splashing onto the shore. She let out a scream and dropped the bowl onto the floor. It smashed and brought the rest of the family running in. Two men and two teenage boys stood staring at Carlos. Then they dropped to their knees. Carlos didn't understand. He didn't know what was going on. He stood and stared. Then the oldest man looked up at Carlos and proclaimed:

"You are Carlos! You are the son of the king who was killed by the masked men."

(To be continued...)

5 Rescued

	Programme	Item
Section 1	Welcome	
	Rules	
	Prayer	
	Praise	
	Game 1	Stuck In The Mud 1
	Praise (x2)	
	Fun Item 1	
	Game 2	Stuck In The Mud 2
	Fun Item 2	
	Bible Text	John 10:10
	Announcements	
	Interview	
	Worship (x2)	
Section 2 **Preaching** **Time**	Bible Lesson	God's Big Plan
	Illustration 1	*Toy Story 2*
	Illustration 2	Amy Carmichael
	Illustration 3	Lifeboat
	Story	Carlos (5)
	Prayer	

Overview There are many people in our world who have no understanding of the Christian message. The vast majority of people who become Christians do so before their 18th birthday. Children telling children is a very important form of evangelism.

Game 1

Stuck In The Mud 1

PREPARATION	None needed.
PLAYERS	Six players per team.
SET-UP	Three players stand at A and a further three players stand at B.
OBJECT	A player runs from A to B, collects a team mate from B and returns with them to A. When they return, the next player leaves from A.
WINNING	The first team to "rescue" all its players from B wins.

Game 2

Stuck In The Mud 2

PREPARATION	None needed.
PLAYERS	Six players per team.
SET-UP	Three players stand at A and a further three players stand at B.
OBJECT	As for Game 1 except the players at B must be carried back!
WINNING	The first team to "rescue" all its players from B wins.

PreachingTime

BIBLE LESSON **GOD'S BIG PLAN**

"The thief comes only to steal and kill and destroy; I have come that they may have life, and have it to the full."

(John 10:10, New International Version)

From the very beginning of time when man and woman sinned against God, God has worked to make a way for human beings to come back to him. He made a way by sending Jesus to the cross.

It would be useful to show a clip of the Crucifixion here.

Because Jesus died on the cross, everyone everywhere has the chance to come to Jesus, to ask him to forgive their sins, and to become Christians. However, not everyone knows this. There are many people who would probably love to become Christians, but they don't know about Jesus and what he did for them. People in faraway countries, people in our country, old people and young people, rich people and poor people – all these people may not know about Jesus. They may never even have heard about him.

And that's why we, as Christians, must tell others.

Toy Story 2

Object needed: *A video clip.*

Play the scenes from Toy Story 2 *where Jessie is rescued – you'll know which part to play and where to stop from the narrative that works with it below.*

This is a very exciting part of the movie. Woody has been rescued by the other toys, but now he is desperate to rescue Jessie before she is forced onto the aeroplane and sent to Japan. Woody fights hard to rescue Jessie. Woody has been rescued and now he is going to rescue others.

That's what we should all be doing. We have been rescued – if we are Christians, we have been rescued – so now we must go and rescue others.

Illustration 2

Amy Carmichael

Objects needed: *Flowers.*

Amy Carmichael was a missionary in India. She went to India to tell children there about Jesus. But before she went, Amy had a dream. She dreamt that she was on the edge of a cliff and lots of people were rushing towards the edge of the cliff and were dying on the rocks below. Amy tried her best to stop as many people as possible from falling off the cliff, but she wasn't fast enough to rescue them all. Amy saw some people on top of the cliff picking flowers. She shouted to them to come and help her, but they looked away, saying that they were too busy. Amy kept rushing back and forth but still couldn't reach all the people.

Amy woke up and asked God what the dream meant. God told her that she was rescuing people from toppling into hell. The people who were picking flowers were those people who had been rescued but refused to become rescuers. Amy decided there and then that she wouldn't just be rescued – she would also become a rescuer to tell others about Jesus. What will *we* do? Will we just be rescued or will we become rescuers?

Illustration 3

Lifeboat

Object needed: *A picture of a lifeboat.*

Have you ever tried to pull someone into a boat? It's actually very difficult. It's even more difficult if the person is in trouble, maybe drowning, or in very deep water. The most difficult way to do it is to be in the water with the person. It becomes practically impossible, as the person kicks and screams and splashes and scratches. The only way to be able to do it properly is to actually be in the lifeboat ourselves first. If we have been rescued then we can rescue others.

It's actually impossible to help people become Christians if we are not Christians ourselves. It's impossible to show someone the way to heaven if we are not going there ourselves.

● STORY – Carlos (5)

The next couple of hours became a blur for Carlos. Very soon the whole village seemed to be standing outside his door. Then even more people came, then others. Word was spreading to the surrounding villages that the new king had come. Carlos was dressed in the finest clothes and many people were clamouring to bring him gifts. They were bowing low and bringing him present upon present. It was quite a new experience for someone who had never received a present in his life – apart, that is, from his stuffed rabbit.

The elders of each of the villages were called and came to stand before Carlos. They all agreed that he was the rightful king. They could not deny the birthmark, and furthermore, most of them remembered the old king and said that Carlos looked just like him. They were prepared to make Carlos king in an official ceremony. He could live in the best houses – they apologised for not being able to let him live in the castle, but the masked men had captured it the same night that Carlos' parents were killed.

Carlos listened carefully. He knew that he would be able to live the rest of his life having whatever he wanted, with servants and gifts and nice clothes and lovely food. But he also remembered the monks had taken care of him, and also his friends. And of course there was the fact that these masked men had killed his parents

and were now living in his castle. He had been rescued, but he was going to become the rescuer.

He told the elders of each village what he wanted to do. They looked very nervous, but how could they disobey their king? They each summoned their fighting men and made their way to fight against the masked men. They marched all day and camped outside the castle at dusk. The night was spent listening to the jests and jokes from the masked men who stood on the battlements. Clearly they didn't think Carlos' army was a threat at all.

The following morning, Carlos' men prepared for battle. They stood in battle formation and awaited orders. The masked men, instead of staying in the castle and waiting for the attack, opened the drawbridge and charged! Carlos was amazed – the masked men were so confident of victory they didn't even fight from their castle. Carlos gave the order to charge, but the masked men were indeed superior warriors. They chopped men down from their lofty camels;

they devastated Carlos' army. Then, after wiping out more than 100 men, they returned to their castle and once again stood on the battlements, laughing and joking about Carlos' men.

Carlos didn't know what to do. He became angry with himself. How could he have thought that he could gain the victory over such superior forces? How could he have been so full of pride? He picked up his little stuffed rabbit and hurled it at a nearby rock. But instead of thudding, the rabbit toy made a rattling sound. Carlos walked over and examined the rabbit more closely. He felt deep inside and, sure enough, there was something hard in there. He cut a small hole at the bottom of the stuffed rabbit and rummaged until he pulled out an iron key. He stared at it. He could see that some of the others were staring at it too. One of the eldest men walked up and looked at the key. He smiled: "Carlos, you have the key to the castle."

Carlos couldn't believe it. He prepared his men for ambush, and deep into the night they crept into the castle. The masked men were brave warriors but were so sure of their safety inside the castle that they slept without guards. Carlos' men took them all without a fight. His friends were freed. Many of them stayed and lived in the castle with Carlos, while the monks returned to their monastery.

The rescued had become the rescuer.

Code Breakers

A Series in Three Parts

Introduction

Title	Themes covered
1 Ask	The gospel
2 Search	Looking for God
3 Knock	God wants to speak

 **Series Overview** This series deals with Matthew 7:7 and the keys to developing a relationship with God based on asking, searching and knocking.

The stories involve a group of young teens who have formed a band with a view to megastardom. The Bible lessons deal with one of Israel's youngest ever kings – Josiah.

1 Ask

	Programme	Item
Section 1	Welcome	
	Rules	
	Prayer	
	Praise	
	Game 1	Code Breaker 1
	Praise (x2)	
	Fun Item 1	
	Game 2	Code Breaker 1
	Fun Item 2	
	Bible Text	Matthew 7:7
	Announcements	
	Interview	
	Worship (x2)	
Section 2 Preaching Time	Bible Lesson	Josiah *2 Chronicles 34-35*
	Illustration 1	Enigma
	Illustration 2	The Sphinx
	Illustration 3	Christianity
	Story	Justin And The Band (1)
	Prayer	

 **Overview** Some people think that the Christian message is difficult to understand; they somehow have the idea that you have to solve some difficult puzzle to become a Christian. The gospel is very simple, if we only ask God.

games

Game 1

Code Breaker 1

PREPARATION Sheets of paper per team with the following code:

3, 15, 4, 5

2, 18, 5, 1, 11, 5, 18.

PLAYERS Three per team.

SET-UP The players line up at A with the three sheets at B. The players are also told that A = 1, B = 2, right through to Z = 26.

OBJECT The team members run in relay from A to B, collect the sheet of paper, and return to A. When they are all back, they must decode the message.

WINNING The first team with all the sheets decoded wins.

Game 2

Code Breaker 1

PREPARATION Sheets of paper per team with the following code:

19, 5, 1, 18, 3, 8

1, 19, 11

11, 14, 15, 3, 11.

PLAYERS Three per team.

SET-UP The players line up at A with the three sheets at B. The players are also told that A = 1, B = 2, right through to Z = 26.

OBJECT The team members run in relay from A to B, collect the sheet of paper, and return to A. When

they are all back, they must decode the message.

WINNING The first team with all the sheets decoded wins.

PreachingTime

BIBLE LESSON **JOSIAH**

"Ask, and you will receive. Search, and you will find. Knock, and the door will be opened for you." (Matthew 7:7)

Josiah was only eight years old when he became king of a whole nation. From the very start he was a good king. Can you imagine that – being the king of a whole nation and only being your age? It would be very exciting and probably a little scary. But Josiah was determined to do right and to serve God well.

This is even more amazing when you remember that Josiah's father had been a very wicked king who had set up all sorts of strange statues and forced the people to pray to them. He had also commanded that all sorts of terrible things be done to please these strange statues that he called gods.

Josiah asked God for help, and God wanted to help him. Josiah simply had to ask God, and at the age of eight that is exactly what he did. God helped Josiah. He was about to become one of the best kings that there would ever be in Israel.

Illustration 1

Enigma

Object needed: *A picture of a computer.*

Codes can be a lot of fun, but breaking codes can do more than just win us points in a game.

The Enigma machine was a device developed

by the Germans during the Second World War. It produced a virtually unbreakable code – nobody thought it could ever be broken. Germany used the Enigma code to coordinate strategy

during World War 2. But in 1939 a team of very clever people, led by William Winterbotham of MI6, cracked the code using one of the first computers. The result was that at the height of the war, Britain was intercepting and decoding 2,000 German signals daily.

Enigma produced a very complicated code indeed, but some people think that Christianity is very complicated too. They think it is like a code that only a few people know.

The Sphinx

Object needed: *A picture of the sphinx.*

Many years ago, according to an ancient legend, the city of Thebes was terrorised by a monster that took over the main road. It was called the sphinx. It had the body of a lion and the upper part of a woman. It lay crouched on the top of a rock, and stopped all travellers who came that way. It asked them to solve a riddle, with the condition that those who could solve it would pass safely, but those who failed would be killed.

Not one person had yet succeeded in solving the riddle; everyone had been killed. But the king's son Oedipus was not daunted by these alarming accounts; he boldly advanced to face the sphinx. The sphinx asked him, "What animal is that which in the morning goes on four feet, at noon on two, and in the evening upon three?"

Oedipus replied, "It is Man, who in childhood creeps on hands and knees, in manhood walks erect, and in old age walks with the aid of a staff."

The sphinx was so angry that the riddle had been solved that she threw herself down from the rock and died.

Some people think that Christianity is a

riddle that has to be solved. They think Christianity is a riddle and that only a few people know the answer. But if they asked someone who is a Christian, then they would find out that Christianity is for everyone.

The Bridge

Object needed: *A picture of Jesus on the cross.*

The truth is that Christianity is neither a code to be broken nor a riddle to be solved. It is very simple indeed. It simply says that Jesus was born in a stable in a place called Bethlehem, lived a perfect life without doing anything wrong, was nailed to a cross for the wrong things that we had done or would ever do, was buried in a borrowed grave, three days later came back to life and then ascended back to his Father in heaven where he sits at the right hand of God waiting for the time when he will come back again.

There is no hidden message; there is no code. Jesus came to give us life; he came because God loved the people of the world so much.

There is no code or riddle in Christianity, just a God who loves people and who wants us to love others in the same way.

● STORY – Justin And The Band (1)

"1, 2, 3, 4!", shouted Russell – and the band began to play. They weren't the greatest musicians in the world: Russell on drums, Stuart on electric guitar, Claire on keyboards, Susie on bass, Tim on the sound desk and of course Justin on lead vocals. They all had a say in what the band played and how it all sounded, but there could be no doubt that it was Justin who made the final decisions. There could be no doubt that this was Justin's band. They played rock music and pop music, but Justin was never happier than when he had his baseball cap turned the wrong way around and he was rapping. He loved to rap.

Hey guys, I am the man,
I'm Justin the leader of this band.
They play the tunes, I shout the words,
They say that it scares the birds.
But I don't care what they say –
This is Justin's band and we're here to stay!

Justin was very, very cool! He dressed well, his blond hair was never out of place, he was one of the cleverest in school and of course he was the lead singer in a band. For a thirteen-year-old, he had a lot going for him.

Justin still felt sad sometimes. He spent holidays with his mum but mainly he lived with his dad. Some nights he lay on his back looking at the ceiling, wishing that his parents were still together. He'd spent a lot of time thinking recently. Why am I here? What am I going to do with my life? Is there a God? Is there a God? That question had kept coming back to him a lot recently. He'd spent quite a few nights thinking about that, and if there *was* a god, then what did he think of Justin? So last night, Justin had said a prayer. Justin would never have called it a prayer; he would have called it asking. He just asked God to show him if he was real. Then he went to sleep.

That was last night, but right now his mind was clear, right now all seemed well. His band was sounding great. They had a gig lined up in a couple of days' time at the end-of-school party, and also he was fairly sure that the Valentine card he had received had come from Susie – he liked Susie. Tonight, playing in the old garage

behind Stuart's house, they sounded better than they ever had before; everything was perfectly balanced, thanks to Tim. Justin was just about to break into his rap routine when suddenly all the instruments stopped and the lights went out.

There were some sighs, and some clanging as Russell fell off his drum stool, and then Justin took control: "Everyone keep still. I'm sure it's nothing serious." And sure enough, before he could properly finish the sentence, the lights came back on.

"No problem, everyone! It was just a passing power surge. Let's get back to practice." But, as he turned back towards the band, they all stared at him.

"What's on your T-shirt?" Susie asked.

Justin looked. Sure enough, his plain white T-shirt now had some strange shapes on it. What was going on? Then, as the band looked at each other, they saw that they all had the same pattern on their shirts:

Justin had asked God to show him if he was real, and now maybe God was giving him an answer. But what could it mean?

(To be continued…)

2 Search

	Programme	Item
Section 1	Welcome	
	Rules	
	Prayer	
	Praise	
	Game 1	Code Breaker 2
	Praise (x2)	
	Fun Item 1	
	Game 2	Code Breaker 2
	Fun Item 2	
	Bible Text	Matthew 7:7
	Announcements	
	Interview	
	Worship (x2)	
Section 2 **Preaching** **Time**	Bible Lesson	Josiah
	Illustration 1	Archaeologists
	Illustration 2	The Brain
	Illustration 3	Christianity
	Story	Justin And The Band (2)
	Prayer	

 **Overview** Some people think that asking God is enough. But God adds a further dimension and tells us that he will reward us if we seek his face. We need to be searchers after God and not just askers.

games

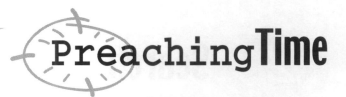

Preaching Time

Game 1

Code Breaker 2

PREPARATION	Several balloons in different colours – red, yellow, blue. The balloons are allocated a point value: red = 3, yellow = 5, blue = 7.
PLAYERS	Three per team.
SET-UP	The players line up at A.
OBJECT	The team members in relay run from A to B, collect a balloon and return to A. They must collect balloons to the value of 25.
WINNING	The first team to get to 25 points wins.

Game 2

Code Breaker 2

PREPARATION	Several balloons in different colours – red, yellow, blue. The balloons are allocated a point value: red = 3, yellow = 5, blue = 7.
PLAYERS	Three per team.
SET-UP	The players line up at A.
OBJECT	The team members in relay run from A to B, collect a balloon and return to A. They must collect balloons to the value of 29.
WINNING	The first team to get to 29 points wins.

BIBLE LESSON ## JOSIAH

"Ask, and you will receive. Search, and you will find. Knock, and the door will be opened for you."
(Matthew 7:7)

Even after being king for ten years Josiah kept asking God to help him, but there is something else we can do to find out about God that involves more than asking. Not only do we need to ask; we need to search.

Josiah knew this and constantly searched out the things of God. Someone else was also searching. This was one of the priests who worked for Josiah and who served God. He had been searching in the temple. Eventually he found what he was looking for: *The Book of the Law.* This was a very special book which told how God wanted his people to live.

The book was to have a powerful effect, but nobody would ever have known about it if someone hadn't done a lot of searching. Searching is a very important part of the process.

Illustration 1

Archaeologists

Object needed: *A clip from the movie* Jurassic Park.

Lots of people use shovels. Some people are builders and use shovels for digging holes and mixing sand and cement. Some people are miners and use them for digging coal and other materials from the ground. But there is another job which involves people using shovels. It's quite an interesting job. It's called archaeology.

Archaeology involves digging in the ground looking for objects left by people who lived hundreds of years ago. The clip we just saw is from a film called *Jurassic Park.* In the film some archaeologists dug in the ground and found a fossil of a dinosaur. They searched. They probably didn't find what they wanted straightaway – they had to search until they found it. If we go in search of God and genuinely want to find him, then we will.

Illustration 2

The Brain

Object needed: *A picture of a brain.*

Here's a picture of a brain. Believe it or not, we all have one! Some of us use our brains more than others, but we all have them. Brains are there to help us do all sorts of things, but one of the main things they help us do is make decisions.

We are supposed to use our brains to make decisions. We use them to decide which things are right and which things are wrong, which things are good and which things are bad. We make these decisions by searching through the evidence. When we take the time to search for things, then we very often find the answer.

Illustration 3

Christianity

Object needed: *A magnifying glass.*

This magnifying glass helps us to look at things closely. You see, Jesus didn't say, "Just believe everything I say and don't ask any questions." On the contrary, Jesus told us to search, to examine. I personally spent much time looking at the claims of Jesus before I decided to become a Christian. I assure you that the claims of Jesus are true.

There really is a God, he really did send Jesus to die on the cross, he really did rise from the dead and he is alive right now and loves you very much.

● STORY – Justin And The Band (2)

The band stared at the strange symbols on each other's T-shirts, but nobody could work out what they were or what they meant:

🖊⑥ඎ   ③⑥❷⤳⑩   ❺⑥❶

They were completely mystified. They looked at each of the numbers and then at each of the letters, but they couldn't make any sense of them. They decided that they would meet up the next morning at the library and look through some books to see what they could find.

Justin walked Susie to her house and then he went home as well. He undressed, drank a milky drink and went to bed. But as he slept he had a strange dream. He could see a huge throne with a figure sitting on it. There was a bright white light shining all around and a voice was saying: "You asked, Justin. Now search for me and you will find."

Then the throne was gone, and the next thing Justin saw, very clearly, was a church. He didn't know the name of this particular church but he knew where it was. It was in the city centre. Then the vision was gone. Justin spent the rest of the night turning this way and that before eventually he woke up. It was morning. He rushed to the phone and called Susie. "Susie, meet me opposite the music shop in an hour. We're going to church."

An hour later, there they were, standing opposite the church. St Michael's was the name written on the wooden sign outside. Susie asked lots of questions, but Justin simply said, "Come on; we need to look at this place." When Susie asked how he knew, he just shrugged. They went in.

The church was very quiet. It was quite an old church with wooden pews and cold stone walls. They walked around looking here and there – and then they saw it, etched into the brickwork:

❺⑥❶   ②❺⑥❸   🖊⑥ඎ   ③❶❷⤳⑩

Justin was sure that these were the same type of letters and numbers that he and his friends had seen on their T-shirts. But what could they mean?

"Ah, I see you're looking at the ancient engraving. Interesting, isn't it?" They spun around. There behind them was an old man wearing a priest's outfit. He smiled at them and they smiled back. "Yes, it's very interesting," Susie replied, "but what does it mean?"

"Oh, it simply means, 'You know God lives'," the old man replied.

Justin pulled out his notebook and began to copy down the shapes. The engraving wasn't the same as the message on the T-shirts, but there were some common letters. He finished scribbling, then grabbed Susie and said, "Come on, let's get to the library and show the others!" They turned and began to run for the door. Susie shouted, "Thanks!" as they rushed towards the door. Just then, a young priest walked in.

"Oh!" he exclaimed. "Can I help you?"

"No," Justin responded. "The old priest has helped us."

"Sorry! I'm the only priest here."

Susie and Justin glanced at each other. "But he helped us translate that strange writing on the wall," Susie answered. The priest looked confused and then added: "I think you're mistaken. Firstly,

I really am the only priest here and secondly, nobody knows what the writing says – it's been there ever since the church was built."

Susie and Justin didn't know what to say, so they nodded and walked out. This was becoming quite a mystery, but they were sure that they did have the translation and were keen to get to their friends and show them the letters. They hurried to the library, where the others were waiting. They pulled out the code and wrote the translation underneath:
Then they picked out the letters which matched the ones on the T-shirts and started to write down what the T-shirt message meant.

Give the children a week to see if they can work it out – display the code and translation shown below beneath the original code.

(To be continued...)

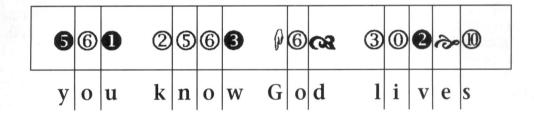

3 Knock

	Programme	Item
Section 1	**Welcome**	
	Rules	
	Prayer	
	Praise	
	Game 1	Code Breaker 3
	Praise (x2)	
	Fun Item 1	
	Game 2	Code Breaker 3
	Fun Item 2	
	Bible Text	Matthew 7:7
	Announcements	
	Interview	
	Worship (x2)	
Section 2 Preaching Time	**Bible Lesson**	Josiah
	Illustration 1	Knock, Knock
	Illustration 2	Ignored
	Illustration 3	Christianity
	Story	Justin And The Band (3)
	Prayer	

 **verview**   God is wanting to speak to us. He is desperate to communicate with us. We mistakenly think God isn't speaking, when in reality we're not listening.

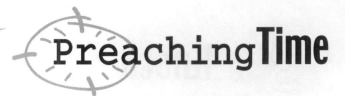

Game 1

Code Breaker 3

PREPARATION	Place the above on an acetate or copy it onto a sketch board.
PLAYERS	One leader.
SET-UP	The acetate is displayed.
OBJECT	All the children try and decipher the original message. The first child who can do it must run to his or her team leader with the answer.
WINNING	The first team to work out the code wins.

Game 2

Code Breaker 3

PREPARATION	Several sheets of paper and several paint brushes placed at B.
PLAYERS	Three players per team.
SET-UP	The players line up at A.
OBJECT	The teams all together run from A to B and try and copy the original design shown above onto the sheets of paper. They have one minute.
WINNING	The team that produces the best design wins.

BIBLE LESSON **JOSIAH**

"Ask, and you will receive. Search, and you will find. Knock, and the door will be opened for you."
(Matthew 7:7)

King Josiah and his priest had searched in the temple and eventually they had found a book. You may not think that a very special occurrence, but it was to change things greatly. The book was called *The Book of the Law*. Immediately, Josiah commanded his people to obey it and live by it. He ordered a special gathering so that all the people could come and listen as he read out this book of God's law.

Asking for God was a part of the process, searching for God's book was also very important, but there came a point when God showed the priest the book and he had to walk through the door and take it.

God tells us that if we knock, the door will be open to us. We need to walk through the door and come close to God – not just asking, not just searching, but coming through the door to Jesus.

Illustration 1

Knock, Knock

Object needed: *None needed.*

Does anyone know any "Knock, knock" jokes? You know, jokes where I say:

"Knock, Knock… "
Now you say, "Who's there?"
I say, "[blank]"
Now you say, "[blank] who?"
And I say, "[blank]"

You see, if you don't say, "Who's there?", then the joke doesn't work. I do the "knock, knock" part and you do the response part. Without a response there's no point.

Ignored

Object needed: *None needed.*

When I was younger there were lots of things that really annoyed me. I didn't like being called names; I hated it when people were nasty to me; but the thing I hated most of all was if people ignored me.

My sister used to do it all the time. She would pretend I wasn't there. When I asked her a question she would pretend it was a mouse going "squeak". It was seriously annoying.

I think I would rather have people shout at me than ignore me. It's quite mean when people ignore you.

Christianity

Object needed: *A picture of Jesus on the cross.*

Today's part of the Bible text is "Knock and the door will be opened for you." When we knock on the door and the door is opened, the next thing we have to do is step inside. If the door opens and we don't go inside it's quite a waste of time knocking.

When we ask if God is real, he shows himself to be real. When we search for God we find him. But there comes a point when we know that God exists and that he wants to forgive the wrong things we've done and become our leader. At that point, the choice is down to us. Do we give our lives to Jesus? Do we ask him to forgive the wrong things we've done? Do we ask him to become our leader? Or do we ignore him?

● STORY – Justin And The Band (3)

Justin sat in the library with the rest of the band. They were all wearing their special T-shirts and were all staring at the bits of paper on the table.

Slowly but surely, using the translation they

had found in the church, they began to put all the bits of paper together. They constructed the first word… "God"; then the second… "loves"; and then the final word was put in place. The message said:

GOD LOVES YOU

Susie read it out loud and then looked at the rest of the band wearing their T-shirts. They looked very confused; nobody knew what to say for some time. But Justin knew what was going on. He remembered the night he had asked God if he was really there.

Now it all made sense. He had asked, and God had shown himself to them. Now the question was: What should happen next? Again Justin knew. He asked the band to meet him that evening back at Russell's.

That evening they all gathered at Russell's garage waiting to hear what Justin had to say. They didn't have to wait long. Justin walked in with a Bible in his hand. He began to read. He read the verse that we've been looking at over the last couple of weeks: "Ask and you will receive. Search and you will find. Knock, and the door will be opened for you." Then he began to explain.

"Asking is the first thing this verse talks about. I asked God if he was really there and if he was, to show himself to me. And then the strange signs appeared on our shirts. The next bit is about searching, so I searched for what the strange signs meant. The third bit is about knocking and the door being opened." The band just sat and listened.

"I think God really is there and wants us to come to him. I think he wants us to be a band made up of people who have asked Jesus to forgive the wrong things we have done and who have asked him to be our leader. The last bit means we have to make a response. We have to decide now. Are we going to go through the door and be what God wants us to be?"

The band was very quiet for ages. Justin was just beginning to think that he may have made a fool of himself when suddenly Susie spoke up and said: "Justin, I am going to ask God to be my leader and to forgive me. I want to be a part of this band and sing for God."

Then Russell followed, and so did Tim, and then one by one they all said that they wanted to serve Jesus. The band would do whatever God wanted.

(Now maybe give the children an opportunity to give their lives to Jesus.)

The BEE Attitudes

A Series in Nine Parts

Introduction

Title	Themes covered
1 Being Before Doing	An introduction
2 Poor In Spirit	Trusting God
3 Those Who Mourn	It's not wrong to be sad
4 The Meek	Humility
5 Hunger And Thirst For Righteousness	Longing for what is right
6 The Merciful	Mercy
7 Pure In Heart	Purity
8 Peacemakers	Peace
9 Persecuted Because Of Righteousness	Doing right, no matter what

Series Overview

Over the next nine weeks we will be looking at the Beatitudes. For Jesus, character always precedes works. What we are is more important than what we do, for what we are will ultimately colour what we do.

Jesus' exhortation to right behaviour is summarised at the start (in typical Jewish teaching style) of the Sermon on the Mount. We will look at each of the eight sayings in turn, and at the same time we will discover the story of Bernard, Bellamy and the other bees, as it parallels the lessons that Jesus presents.

The Bible lessons will look at each of the disciples and how their lives match up to the Beatitudes.

1 Being Before Doing

	Programme	Item
Section 1	**Welcome**	
	Rules	
	Prayer	
	Praise	
	Game 1	Honey Pot
	Praise (x2)	
	Fun Item 1	
	Game 2	Honey Pot Revisited
	Fun Item 2	
	Bible Text	Matthew 12:33
	Announcements	
	Interview	
	Worship (x2)	
Section 2	**Bible Lesson**	Judas
Preaching	**Illustration 1**	Trees
Time	**Illustration 2**	"Be" Attitudes
	Illustration 3	What's Inside?
	Story	Bernard The Bumbling Ladybird-Bee
	Prayer	

 **Overview** As we begin this look at the Beatitudes we will be making the statement that being precedes doing. What we are will ultimately affect what we do.

games

Game 1

Honey Pot

PREPARATION	An empty bucket at B representing the honey pot. A bucket at A full of balls.
PLAYERS	Four players per team.
SET-UP	The first player stands at A, takes a ball, runs to B, deposits the ball in the bucket and returns. Then the next player goes.
OBJECT	To deposit as many balls in the bucket as possible within two minutes.
WINNING	The team with the most balls wins.

Game 2

Honey Pot Revisited

PREPARATION	None if Game 1 is still set up.
PLAYERS	Four players per team.
SET-UP	Players stand at A, run to B, take a ball from the bucket and return.
OBJECT	The reverse of Game 1: to return as many balls to A as possible.
WINNING	The first team to empty its bucket at B wins.

Preaching Time

 **BIBLE LESSON** **JUDAS**

"Make a tree good and its fruit will be good, or make a tree bad and its fruit will be bad." (Matthew 12:33, New International Version)

Judas was a disciple chosen by Jesus. He walked with Jesus, the Son of God. He ate with Jesus, the Son of God. He worked with Jesus, the Son of God. He pretended to be a friend of God; on the outside he looked like he was the best disciple.

But when it came to the night of the Last Supper, Judas showed himself to be something completely different. He betrayed Jesus. He showed Jesus' enemies where he was hiding. He handed over Jesus, the Son of God, for thirty pieces of silver.

Judas was not what he appeared to be. He appeared to be a disciple. He did the things that followers of Jesus should do. But deep down inside, he wasn't a disciple of Jesus.

What we are like deep down inside always comes out in the end.

Illustration 1

Trees

Objects needed: *An apple, an orange and a pear.*

Hold up the apple and ask... What sort of tree did this come from? Of course, an apple tree.

Hold up the orange and ask... What sort of tree did this come from? Of course, an orange tree.

Hold up the pear and ask... And how about this one? I know, these are ridiculously easy questions!

However, before the fruit appears on the branches, unless you're an expert on trees, it's not really that easy to tell what sort of tree it is. It's by the type of fruit that comes out that we can tell what sort of tree it is. And how nice the fruit is tells us how good the tree really is.

If the tree produces apples and it has good strong roots that go deep into the ground, we can be pretty sure that it is a good apple tree. But if it produces apples and its roots are not very good, we could probably guess that it's a bad apple tree. If it doesn't produce any fruit, it's a very bad apple tree.

We don't produce fruit, do we? We'd look a little strange walking around with a bunch of bananas hanging from our noses. However, we do have something that is called "character". Our character is basically what we are really like, not what we pretend to be. Character is what we are like inside. Now, our characters do show. If we spend all our time telling lies and swearing, there's a fair chance that our character is not good. We are producing bad fruit. If we say that we are Christians and yet our character is bad, then we probably are not very good Christians.

Good trees have roots that go deep into the ground and find water. Good Christians, with good character, are those who spend time talking to Jesus – what we call prayer. When we learn to do that, it's as if our roots also go deep and we become strong.

"Be" Attitudes

Object needed: *Display a picture of an old woman and then display the Beatitudes as shown in Appendix 2, p. 279.*

Some of us think that what we do is the most important thing. That's actually not true. Who we are is much more important than what we do. You see, you may help an old woman across the road, but if you are doing it just to impress your girlfriend, then that isn't so great. If you volunteer to wash your dad's car, but you're just doing it because you know that you might get some extra pocket money for

doing it, then you aren't doing it for the right reasons at all. We need people who *are* kind, not just pretending to be kind. We need people who *want* to help and who are not just helping because they want to get something back.

Eventually, what we are like on the inside will come out. If we are kind on the inside, then we will be kind on the outside. But even if we pretend to be kind on the outside, but inside we're not, eventually the inside will come out and we'll stop being kind and *be* what we really are.

Over the next couple of weeks we are going to look at one of the most famous speeches that Jesus ever made. It is called the Sermon on the Mount. In it he talks about the Beatitudes. Five of them talk about what we should *be*; it is only three that talk about what we should *do*. Jesus knew that what we are is more important than what we do. Being is more important than doing.

What's Inside?

Object needed: *An apple.*

Doesn't this apple look great? It's shiny and green. It reflects the light, it's so shiny. It really does look the part. But I'm sure you can tell me the best way to find out what this apple is really like. Yes, you got it. I'll have to eat some. *(Bite into the apple, then pull all sorts of nasty faces.)*

Oh! That's really horrible! I don't understand. It looked lovely. I was really looking forward to eating it. I guess, yet again, we proved that what is on the inside is a whole lot more important than what appears on the outside.

What are you really like on the inside? Jesus wants to help you to be good on the inside, so that you can become good on the outside.

● STORY – Bernard The Bumbling Ladybird-Bee

Bernard was not a very happy bee. For one thing, every time he came near to anyone, they started jumping about shouting, "Shoo, shoo!" Bernard

was only trying to be friendly, after all. He didn't understand it. Other insects didn't have these problems. Butterflies, for example, didn't have these problems. Every time someone saw a butterfly, they would say things like, "What a beautiful butterfly!" Yet Bernard only got "Shoo, shoo!" And those jolly ladybirds – they seemed to be the most popular creatures of all. Everyone loved ladybirds. They were allowed to land on people's arms and the people told them poems about how they should fly away home. But if Bernard tried landing on someone's arm, the person tried to bash him and then there would be more "Shoo, shoo!"

Bernard was not a happy bee. He had complained to his friends, Bellamy and Betsy. But they had told him to just be himself! He would always be a bee at the end of the day! But Bernard was not happy.

After several more weeks of "Shoo, shoo!", Bernard was getting very annoyed. And then he had an idea. Bees weren't that different-looking from ladybirds. He had legs and wings a bit like a ladybird. And that little girl Lucy had been painting again and, as usual, had left her paints out. All Bernard would need to do would be to roll about in the right colours and he would be a ladybird.

So Bernard rolled this way and that in the paint until he was red with black spots. Bellamy and Betsy didn't recognise him at first, but when they did they just started to laugh. They couldn't stop laughing. "You look ridiculous!" chortled Bellamy. "You may look like a ladybird, but you're not a ladybird. It'll all end in tears." But Bernard was determined. He started to fly around with his wings flapping. Sure enough – no more "Shoo, shoo!" Bernard was enjoying his newfound popularity.

"I knew it was better to be a ladybird," Bernard hummed to himself. Then he saw Lucy

in the garden. He flew down towards her. She didn't run away or say "Shoo!" He landed on her arm. She didn't seem bothered; she started the rhyme that she used for the ladybirds, the one about flying away home. But Bernard didn't want to fly away home. And then Bernard got a strange feeling. It began to rise inside him. He couldn't stop himself.

"No! I'm a ladybird!" he shouted. But the feeling wouldn't go away. And then, almost without him knowing, his stinger came up and stuck straight into Lucy's arm. Lucy screamed and threw Bernard into the air. Bernard felt quite bad. Lucy was crying now. But Bernard couldn't have stopped himself. He was after all a bee, no matter what he looked like on the outside. You see what I mean. What we are really like on the inside will always come out eventually.

2 Poor In Spirit

	Programme	Item
Section 1	Welcome	
	Rules	
	Prayer	
	Praise	
	Game 1	Carry Together
	Praise (x2)	
	Fun Item 1	
	Game 2	Pudding Mix
	Fun Item 2	
	Bible Text	Matthew 5:3
	Announcements	
	Interview	
	Worship (x2)	
Section 2 **Preaching** **Time**	Bible Lesson	Matthew
	Illustration 1	Dependent
	Illustration 2	Independent
	Illustration 3	Interdependent
	Story	Bernard And The Flower
	Prayer	

 **Overview** The first Beatitude talks about being poor in spirit. This is best defined as being totally reliant on God.

Games

Game 1

Carry Together

PREPARATION	None.
PLAYERS	Four players per team.
SET-UP	Three players must carry the fourth player.
OBJECT	The three players must carry the fourth in whatever fashion they think best from A to B and back again three times.
WINNING	The team that completes the game first wins. If a player being carried touches the ground the team is disqualified.

Game 2

Pudding Mix

PREPARATION	A jar of currants, some flour, a glass of milk, and a mixing bowl per team.
PLAYERS	Five players per team.
SET-UP	The items at A. The players in relay formation at A.
OBJECT	The first player takes the mixing bowl to B and returns to tag player two, who takes the currants to B and returns. He or she tags player three, who takes another ingredient. This continues until player five runs to B, collects the bowl and returns.
WINNING	The first team to bring back the pudding mix wins.

Preaching Time

 **BIBLE LESSON** **MATTHEW**

"Blessed are the poor in spirit, for theirs is the kingdom of heaven." (Matthew 5:3, New International Version)

Matthew was a tax collector – then as now, being a tax collector was not a very popular job – but Matthew was also a dishonest tax collector.

It was very hard for Matthew to become "poor in spirit". "Poor in spirit" doesn't mean that we don't have any money or any things. It means that we become totally dependent on someone else. Matthew had been invited by Jesus to become his disciple.

It would not be easy for Matthew. People would laugh at him. He would have to repay all the money he had taken dishonestly. He would have to trust Jesus for his next meal. But Matthew swallowed his pride. Pride is the opposite of being "poor in spirit". Matthew became a follower of Jesus.

 **Illustration 1**

Dependent

Objects needed: *Display three pieces of card, one saying "dependent", one saying "independent" and one saying "interdependent".*

Line three boys up side by side. These will form the basis of each of the three illustrations today.

I'm going to talk about three key words. *BOY 1* will help us understand the first word; it has nine letters. *BOY 2* will help us understand the second word; it has eleven letters. And *BOY 3* will help us with the third word, which has a staggering fourteen letters. Remember, we're talking about whether it is a sign of weakness to ask for help. Let's begin.

Let me use *BOY 1* to talk about the first

word. It has nine letters; the word is "dependent". Let me show you what it means. Babies are dependent, and *BOY 1* is going to play the part of a baby this morning. Now, if you go to the local toy shop you may find baby dolls and this is what you do with them: if you pull the string on their backs, the baby dolls say, "Mama, Mama", and if you squeeze their tummies they say, "Feed me, feed me". This morning, *BOY 1*, you are going to play the part of that baby doll. When I pretend to pull the string on your back, you need to say in a high-pitched voice, "Mama, Mama". And, when I pretend to squeeze your tummy, I need to hear the words "Feed me, feed me".

You see, babies really are this nine-letter word: you have to feed them, you have to wash them, and you even have to change their nappies. They are dependent. Now, when you are six months old it's OK to be dependent, but when you're nine or ten it really would be wrong to be dependent. *(Be careful if there are disabled children in the group.)*

Jesus doesn't want us to be unable to do anything for ourselves. He wants us to look to him and trust him all that we do, but not to be babies.

Independent

Object needed: *Continue from illustration 1.*

Most of you are more like *BOY 2* – you're the eleven-letter word "independent". Now, this is definitely better than *BOY 1*. *BOY 2* knows how to wash himself; he knows how to feed himself, and he even knows how to change his own nappy! He can do most things himself.

However, the problem with being independent is that we tend to think we can do *everything* ourselves. We think we don't actually need anyone to help us. When we're in the playground and somebody picks on us, we never go to the teacher and tell her the problem, because we think we can handle everything ourselves. We never ask for help. When we are in class and we can't solve a problem our teacher has given us, if we are independent people we will never put our hands up and ask for help. Independent people think it's weak to ask for

help. Obviously, being independent is better than being dependent, but I think it's also obvious that being independent isn't the *best* way to be.

God really doesn't want us to be independent. When we try to be independent we show that we are proud. Remember, pride is the opposite of being "poor in spirit".

Interdependent

Object needed: *Continue from above.*

Finally, the fourteen-letter word "interdependent". Let's have a quick recap. What was the nine-letter word? And what was the eleven-letter word? And who can remember this one, the fourteen-letter word?

"Interdependent" is like "independent" in that we can do most things ourselves, but it's better, because a person who is interdependent can do most things themselves, but knows that they will be better and stronger if they learn to ask for help when they need it.

This is what God wants us to be like. He wants us to be strong, but also to be totally reliant on him. The Bible says that if we learn to be "poor in spirit" we will see the kingdom of heaven. That means we get to see heaven one day and to see God's work done on earth.

● STORY – Bernard And The Flower

Bernard had finally realised that he was a bee and not a ladybird, but he was still a very proud bee.

He loved to fly around showing off his lovely wings. He loved to boast about his lovely yellow and black stripes and he liked to tell everyone that he was the coolest bee in the whole world and that he didn't need anyone. He was just the coolest there was.

Bellamy and Betsy used to make fun of him; they used to do impressions of him. They also told him that everyone needs friends, but Bernard wouldn't listen.

"One day," he would say, "you'll see that I am the coolest bee ever. I'll probably be the king of the bees."

Bellamy and Betsy would just smile to themselves and leave Bernard to his boasting. You see, Bernard liked to boast, but he really wasn't very clever and he always made mistakes. Today was going to be no exception. Bernard had

been out looking for nectar to make into honey. He was clever enough to realise that nectar came from flowers, but he always got a bit confused over which flowers were which. He went looking for roses and ended up in the daisies, and he went looking for daffodils and ended up in the weeds. All these things were a little embarrassing, but nobody saw him, so there was no real problem.

Today, however, the next "flower" that he saw was going to get him into all sorts of trouble.

It looked like the most amazing flower of them all. He was sure that it would be perfect to make into honey. He flew close to it and could smell the sweet smell of pollen. He hovered closer and then descended into the flower. He was covering himself in pollen when suddenly the flower snapped closed. Bernard was trapped! This was a special type of flower. It was literally going to let Bernard rot inside it and then digest him! It was a nasty process.

Most bees would have been shouting for help straightaway, but not Bernard. He wasn't like the "poor in spirit" who know that they are reliant on God. Bernard didn't want to be reliant on anyone. After all, he'd told everyone that he wanted to be king. So Bernard was trapped and beginning to die.

The next day Bernard heard a bee humming outside, but he didn't make a sound. He was too proud. He just began to rot. The next day and the day after that, bees flew past and Bernard stayed quiet. By day four he wasn't so proud any more. He was very hungry and was feeling very squashed, but on day four, no bees went past. Day five came and went, and still no bees came past. It was on day seven that Bernard next heard a bee and by then he was desperate. He began to scream and kick and cry. It was Bellamy that flew past. He heard the sound and stopped. Bellamy pulled open the flower and found Bernard, but it was too late – Bernard was already dead.

When the queen of the hive asked the bees why Bernard hadn't called out for help straightaway, Bellamy simply answered that Bernard was too proud. Bernard was not "poor in spirit" – he was proud. And being proud is not a good thing.

3 Those Who Mourn

	Programme	Item
Section 1	**Welcome**	
	Rules	
	Prayer	
	Praise	
	Game 1	Feelings
	Praise (x2)	
	Fun Item 1	
	Game 2	Blind Feelings
	Fun Item 2	
	Bible Text	Matthew 5:4
	Announcements	
	Interview	
	Worship (x2)	
Section 2	**Bible Lesson**	Jude (Also Called Labbaeus)
Preaching	**Illustration 1**	The First Of The "Do's"
Time	**Illustration 2**	Spring Harvest Boy
	Illustration 3	Our World
	Story	Bellamy Bee Mourns
	Prayer	

Overview As we look at the first of the "do" Beatitudes – "Blessed are those who [do] mourn", it is interesting to see that our "do" list begins with something we wouldn't normally expect God to tell us to do.

games

PreachingTime

Game 1

Feelings

PREPARATION	Eight paper plates with different expressions drawn on them: one happy, one sad, etc.
PLAYERS	Four players per team.
SET-UP	Players stand at A. The plates are positioned at B, preferably blu-tacked to a wall or display board. The first player of each team is positioned at A, ready to run.
OBJECT	The games master will call out a feeling, e.g. "sad". The first player on each team then runs from A to B, collects a plate which they think matches the emotion, and then returns. The games master notes who has the correct plate and adds a point to their score – he doesn't tell them who is right. The plates are returned to the display and player two prepares to run. This is repeated until all the players have gone twice.
WINNING	The team with most faces wins.

Game 2

Blind Feelings

PREPARATION	As for Game 1, but this time the plates are turned so that the faces face inwards.
PLAYERS	Four players per team.
SET-UP	As for Game 1.
OBJECT	As for Game 1.
WINNING	As for Game 1.

BIBLE LESSON JUDE (also called Labbaeus)

"Blessed are those who mourn, for they will be comforted." (Matthew 5:4, New International Version)

Some people are called by names different from the one they were first given. Some of you have nicknames; some of you have changed your names; and some of you go by your middle name. Your name might be Steven Harry Smith, but you like to be called Harry. Today's disciple is called Jude, but he is also known by a different name: Labbaeus.

Labbaeus means "man of the heart". The heart is the place that we talk about when we talk about feelings. Some people think that God doesn't have any feelings. Some religions in our world believe that we need to stop our feelings altogether, that we should be able to go through life without feeling anything. God doesn't want us to be like this. The Bible shows us that God himself laughs, cries and can be pleased. We are created in God's image. We are like God. So we too should learn to feel. Sometimes we feel happy, sometimes sad; but it is good to feel.

Illustration **1**

The First Of The "Do's"

Object needed: *A sad face.*

As we look at the first of the "do" Beatitudes – "Blessed are those who [do] mourn" – it is interesting to see that our "do" list begins with something we wouldn't normally expect God to tell us to do. "Blessed are those who mourn." This means that God will bless us when we are sad. Those who mourn get God's favour. Literally, God smiles on them.

You wouldn't expect it to be the case, would you? You'd expect God to want us to be happy, to be jolly, to be constantly smiling. But God doesn't want people who are smiling constantly. Yes, he wants us to be full of joy, but there are some things which make God very unhappy, and these things should make us unhappy as well. It is not wrong to feel sad about some things. God himself feels sad about some things.

It's OK to feel sad sometimes.

Spring Harvest Boy

Object needed: *A picture of a little boy.*

I once went to a conference to work with a large group of children. Most of the children were very good and very well behaved – all in fact, except one. I forget what his name was, but I'll never forget how naughty he was. When he was told to sit, he stood; when he was told to stand, he sat; when he was told to be quiet, he talked; and when he was asked to talk, he went silent. He was hard work. I looked after him for the whole week and couldn't work out what was wrong.

It wasn't until very close to the end of the week that I eventually got to find out the truth. I was praying for him and the whole group, when God told me to ask him about his grandfather. (God tells us things sometimes, if we're listening.) So I asked the boy. He told me that his granddad had died two months before and that he had loved his grandfather very much. Then he added this statement: "But I didn't cry. Something told me not to cry, so I didn't."

This little eight-year-old boy had been holding in all his feelings for two whole months. I don't know who or what had told him not to cry, but I told him, "God thinks it's OK for you to cry. God doesn't mind." The little boy began to cry. He cried and cried. Later he felt much better and started behaving much better.

It's OK to feel sad sometimes.

Our World

Objects needed: *Pictures from newspapers or television.*

There are lots of things in our world which are not good. If you have been watching the news recently you will have seen all those people fighting in Jerusalem. *(Update each time you use this illustration.)* You see people being murdered and others badly hurt in all sorts of situations.

It's OK to feel sad about some of these things. God himself looks down from heaven and feels sad about some of these things. The important thing is that we don't get depressed – that means: so sad we stay sad for ages. It is important that we remember how much God loves us; that always makes us feel better. Still, there *are* things which make us feel a bit sad.

It's OK to feel sad sometimes.

● STORY – Bellamy Bee Mourns

Bellamy was very quiet for many days. He had never seen a bee that was dead before and wasn't sure how to respond. Bernard may have been a very proud bee and a very silly bee at times, but Bellamy still missed him.

But Bellamy too was proud. He didn't want anyone to think that he was unable to cope with the death of his friend. He flew around as he always had done. He collected pollen as he always had done, but his heart wasn't in it. He was feeling very bad inside. On the outside, however, Bellamy still tried to look as if everything was fine. He didn't want his friends to see how he really felt.

It was a shame that Bellamy didn't show them. They were feeling the same way. Everyone missed Bernard – but most of the bees were prepared to show it. Betsy burst into tears every now and then, and some of the other bees held a special service to say goodbye to Bernard. But Bellamy didn't go; he was trying to deal with it by himself.

It wasn't going to work. Soon Bellamy became very moody and angry with everyone. He wouldn't come out to play, he didn't want to mix with others and he was getting more and more miserable. You see, it is not wrong to feel sad sometimes. We mustn't walk around looking miserable all the time, but we also don't need to pretend to be happy when actually we're sad.

Bellamy just got worse and worse. He stopped eating, he stopped talking and he even stopped flying. The whole thing could have ended in disaster, except that one day, the queen of the hive, Queen Belinda Bee, summoned Bellamy to her rooms. Bellamy was feeling terrible, but he didn't dare refuse to go.

He walked into the queen's room and sat down. The queen looked him straight in the eyes and then began to shout at him: "You have been a very foolish bee, Bellamy! You are sad. You feel bad. You miss Bernard. So do we all."

Bellamy began to cry, and when the queen mentioned the name Bernard, Bellamy began to sob uncontrollably. He cried and cried for some time, and then after he had cried, he felt better.

It's OK to feel sad sometimes.

4 The Meek

	Programme	Item
Section 1	**Welcome**	
	Rules	
	Prayer	
	Praise	
	Game 1	Between The Obstacles
	Praise (x2)	
	Fun Item 1	
	Game 2	Bucket Ball
	Fun Item 2	
	Bible Text	Matthew 5:5
	Announcements	
	Interview	
	Worship (x2)	
Section 2	**Bible Lesson**	Peter
Preaching	**Illustration 1**	Meekness (Word Challenge)
Time	**Illustration 2**	Power Out Of Control
	Illustration 3	Weak And Strong
	Story	Betsy Goes Berserk
	Prayer	

 **Overview** Blessed are the meek. What is meekness? We will look at the word and conclude that meekness is not weakness, but instead it is power under control.

games

PreachingTime

Game 1

Between The Obstacles

PREPARATION	Set up sets of two chairs in a slalom fashion.
PLAYERS	Four players per team: two large and strong, two small and light.
SET-UP	Players stand at A. The first player piggy-backs the second through the slalom obstacles, to B and back.
OBJECT	To negotiate the obstacles without touching them, in the fastest time.
WINNING	The team to complete the game in the fastest time without touching the obstacles wins. This game is about accuracy, not just speed – any team touching an obstacle is disqualified.

Game 2

Bucket Ball

PREPARATION	A bucket and six tennis balls per team.
PLAYERS	Three players per team.
SET-UP	The buckets are placed two metres past B, and the balls placed at A.
OBJECT	The players run in turn from A to B with a tennis ball. They pitch the ball towards the buckets and return. They continue until all the balls are gone.
WINNING	The team with the most balls in the buckets wins.

BIBLE LESSON PETER

"Blessed are the meek, for they will inherit the earth." (Matthew 5:5, New International Version)

Peter couldn't really be described as meek. When Jesus found him he was a fisherman on the Sea of Galilee. He was brash and outspoken. He was constantly doing things he shouldn't and constantly saying things he shouldn't. Jesus had to tell him off on many occasions.

On the very night before Jesus was crucified, Peter had cut off a guard's ear to protect Jesus. He was strong, he was bold, but he wasn't particularly meek.

What *is* meekness? Many people think it is the same as weakness, but it's not. After Jesus had risen from the dead and spent some time with Peter, Peter really was meek. Does that mean he had lost his strength? Does that mean he wasn't bold any more? Absolutely not! Peter preached in front of a huge crowd, and 5,000 men responded. Peter spoke to a crippled man and saw him healed. He was still bold.

You see, meekness isn't weakness; it's power under control. Peter hadn't learned to be weak – he had learned to control his strength.

Illustration 1

Meekness (Word Challenge)

Objects needed: *A set of words: "weak", "caring", "strong", "bold", "timid", "powerful", "helpful", "shy", written on cards.*

Here is a set of cards. Each card has a word written on it. All you have to do is tell me which words could be used to describe a meek person and which couldn't. So, if I hold up the first card that says "weak" and you think a meek person is weak, then you must nod your heads; if not, you must shake your heads. Remember, no sounds, just nod or shake your heads.

Hold up the cards in turn. Some may need explanations such as, "You can be powerful and be meek." The only words not describing a meek person are "weak", "timid", and "shy".

Power Out Of Control

Object needed: *A picture of a car.*

I have a friend who has a fast car, a sports car. He also has a daughter. When this incident happened she was about four years old.

The car was fast – incredibly fast, but this was not a problem, because my friend was a safe driver and always had the car under control. He knew how to drive. His daughter liked the car very much because it was red. She liked red. One day she decided she'd like to drive this red car. So, she took her daddy's keys off the table and went to the garage. She opened the car door and got in. She put the keys in the ignition just like she'd seen her dad do, countless times before. She'd seen her dad drive and it didn't look particularly hard. She was in the car. The car was very powerful.

We're about to see what is so special about this word "meekness".

She turned the ignition key. Her dad had left the car in gear. The car shot forward at tremendous speed and crashed through the garage door which the little girl had forgotten to open. The car stalled just outside the garage and the little girl was found crying her eyes out.

Meekness is power under control. It's not weakness and it's not just power. It's power under control.

Weak And Strong

Object needed: *A picture of a weightlifter and a picture of a weak-looking person.*

We often get this silly idea that meekness is like this: *(Display the picture of the weak-looking person.)* This is not meekness; this is weakness.

But we would also be mistaken if we thought meekness looked like this: *(Display the picture of the strong person.)* Yes, he looks strong! But he may have a terrible temper; he may get worked up easily and hit out at people – maybe like some of you! Meekness isn't weakness, and meekness isn't power.

Meekness is power under control.

● STORY – Betsy Goes Berserk

Betsy Bee thought of herself as very meek indeed. She always tried to be kind to people, she was very sympathetic towards Bellamy when his friend Bernard died, and she worked very hard every day collecting pollen to keep the queen happy and of course to make lots of honey. Betsy did her best to get along with all the other bees. She was kind and considerate, gentle and compassionate. Most of the bees agreed that Betsy was very meek indeed.

But some of the bees, Bartholomew and Basil Bee, for example, weren't so convinced. They knew about meekness. They knew it was power under control and while they were convinced that Betsy knew how to be gentle, and while they were also convinced that Betsy was actually a very strong bee – you couldn't argue with the huge amounts of pollen she brought back every day – they had also seen what had happened one day when little Lucy had tried shooing Betsy away from her garden. They had seen how angry Betsy had become – and how quickly. They saw how aggressive she became. This was power, but it didn't look like it was under control. However, Betsy had managed to calm down and fly away from that garden.

For most of the time, Betsy collected pollen from the wild flowers that grew on the far side of Farmer Smith's farm. They were good flowers and they smelled very sweet. But always on the way back Betsy would fly over Lucy's flowers and smell how much sweeter they were – how much she had enjoyed those flowers before! But Betsy kept flying, because she remembered what had happened last time she was there. She knew that the queen would be very unhappy with her if she stung a little girl.

Towards the end of summer, the flowers at the far side of the farm started to die off. Try as Betsy could, she just couldn't find any more flowers to collect pollen from… except from little Lucy's garden! There were still lots of flowers there. Lucy and her mum and her little brother Andy had spent much time watering and looking after those flowers.

Betsy tried to fly past, but she couldn't resist. Anyway, she thought there wouldn't be a problem – all the bees said that she was a very meek bee. She dived into the flower patch just as Lucy was starting to water the flowers. Betsy was

just beginning to get herself covered in pollen when suddenly she was soaking wet. She was furious! How dare someone pour water on her! She flew out of the flower and headed straight towards Lucy. The little girl started to shoo Betsy away. Then Lucy hit Betsy's wing with her hand. Betsy was now out of control: she pulled out her stinger, dived at Lucy, and stung her on the arm. Lucy burst into tears and began to call her mum. Lucy's mum rushed out, but by now Betsy had gone berserk! She flew at Lucy's mum and stung her, and then she stung Andy, and then she flew at Lucy's mum again. Lucy, Andy and their mum retreated inside quickly.

Betsy was still angry when she got back to the beehive. But that wasn't the worst of it. Lucy, Andy and their mum would be just fine – they had some special cream to fix bee stings. But Basil had seen the whole thing and had told the queen. Betsy wasn't meek at all. Meekness was power under control; Betsy was out of control.

The queen summoned Betsy, and Betsy knew she was in trouble!

(I'll tell you what happens to Betsy soon.)

5 Hunger And Thirst For Righteousness

	Programme	Item
Section 1	Welcome	
	Rules	
	Prayer	
	Praise	
	Game 1	Reach
	Praise (x2)	
	Fun Item 1	
	Game 2	Guided Reach
	Fun Item 2	
	Bible Text	Matthew 5:6
	Announcements	
	Interview	
	Worship (x2)	
Section 2	Bible Lesson	Simon The Zealot
Preaching	Illustration 1	The Arabs
Time	Illustration 2	Desire
	Illustration 3	Righteousness
	Story	Bellamy The Lazy Bee
	Prayer	

Overview "Hunger and thirst for righteousness." With these words Jesus is trying to show us the intensity involved in this longing for what is right. This lesson will try to communicate the longing for what is right.

Games

 PreachingTime

Game 1

Reach

PREPARATION	Write the letters of the word RIGHTEOUSNESS on separate cards. Each time has a set. A chair per team.
PLAYERS	Four players per team.
SET-UP	Players stand at A. The letters are placed at B but at a height that the players cannot reach without climbing onto the chair.
OBJECT	The teams go in relay formation, collect a letter and return to A. They keep going until they have all the letters and then they assemble them to form the word.
WINNING	The team with the word completed first wins.

(Note: the players have to reach high for the letters.)

Game 2

Guided Reach

PREPARATION	As for Game 1, but this time no chair is included.
PLAYERS	Four players from each team.
SET-UP	As for Game 1.
OBJECT	As for Game 1 but the players go in twos and help each other to reach the letters.
WINNING	As for Game 1.

BIBLE LESSON **SIMON THE ZEALOT**

"Blessed are those who hunger and thirst for righteousness, for they will be filled." (Matthew 5:6, New International Version)

Simon the Zealot was one of Jesus' disciples. But what is a zealot? *(Allow the children to answer.)*

Simon was given the name Zealot because he belonged to a group or a gang of people called Zealots. They used aggression and violence to fight for what they thought was right. They attacked the Roman soldiers with whatever weapons they could find.

Simon hadn't really understood that Jesus came in peace. He probably went to see Jesus because he thought he was a great soldier who was ready to lead the people to fight against the Romans. But as he followed Jesus he soon began to learn. Even though he learned, his zeal (other words for zeal would be "strong desire" or "passion") never changed – he was still determined to do what God wanted at any cost and he was willing to do anything to serve Jesus. It must have taken Jesus some time to teach Simon that he was to be zealous for righteousness – doing the right thing – and not zealous to kill anyone who didn't agree with him. But once he learned, he would do all he could to ensure that the right thing was done.

Illustration 1

The Arabs

Object needed: *A picture of an Arab.*

Jesus told us that we are to hunger and thirst for righteousness. He meant that we should desperately want the right thing. In this country we probably don't really understand what Jesus meant by "thirst for righteousness" because we've probably never been really thirsty. It's very easy for us at the end of our football match to take a drink of water from the tap. But the people Jesus spoke to thoroughly understood thirsting. In that part of the world the people wear special head coverings *(show the photograph)*, but they don't do

it to try and look nice; they do it for a very special reason.

Sometimes in the deserts which the Arabs have to travel across, there is a storm. It is not the sort of storm that we are used to, where the rain beats down on us and we get wet. This is a *sandstorm*, where the wind swirls around the person and the sand stings his face. The storm is too strong for a person to continue on his journey, so he has to wrap himself up in his head covering, wrapping it around his head and allowing only a small space for his eyes to see out as he turns away from the storm.

He will stand like this until the storm passes. Some storms may last several hours and he will feel the sting of the sand on his face, the suffocating effects of the sand up his nose and the terrible taste of sand in his mouth. His mouth will be dry and gritty, but still he will stand. This man understands what it is to be *really* thirsty. So he would understand what Jesus meant about thirsting for righteousness.

Desire

Object needed: *A picture of a computer.*

Have you ever wanted something really badly? Have you ever wanted something so much that all you ever did was think about it? You would lie awake at night, thinking about it. Maybe you really wanted to go out with that girl and couldn't stop thinking about her, or you really wanted to be in the school football

team and you would sit in school, dreaming about it. Maybe you wanted something for your birthday or Christmas so much that you couldn't think of anything else.

I was like this once. I was fifteen and I wanted a computer. I dreamt about this computer. I would stand at the shop window and look at this computer. I even had a picture of this computer that I would pretend was real; I would type onto it and pretend that things were coming up on the screen. The computer cost £200 and I had asked for it for Christmas. Now £200 in those days is probably worth a lot more now, so it was a lot of money. I had never had anything that cost so much before. I had asked and begged my parents for it every single day. I had offered to do jobs around the house to get it. I was doing my best. I really wanted this computer.

Christmas Eve was a terrible time. My mum told me that there were no computers left in the shop and so I wouldn't be able to have one. You would not believe how badly I wanted this thing! Thinking about how I felt helps me to understand what Jesus meant when he told us that we should hunger and thirst for righteousness. He meant that we should really want it, desperately want it, just as I really wanted that computer.

And then Christmas Day arrived. I came downstairs, not particularly excited. After all, the computer I wanted was sold out. Then I walked into the living room and there it was: the computer! I was so pleased!

Righteousness

Object needed: *None.*

Jesus wasn't talking about hungering and thirsting for computers, was he? He was talking about hungering and thirsting for righteousness. So what is righteousness? Righteousness means doing what is right. It means living right before God and before each other. It means to do the right thing.

- It means when we have the chance to take something that doesn't belong to us and we know we'll never get caught, we still do the right thing.

- It means when we have a chance to cheat in a test, we don't, because we want to do the right thing.
- It means when we think we can get out of trouble by telling a lie, we don't, because we always do the right thing.

● STORY – Bellamy The Lazy Bee

Bellamy Bee was not happy. He knew what he should be doing. He should be doing his job: collecting pollen. That was the right thing for him to do. But, as most of us know by now, doing the right thing sometimes takes effort. It takes energy, and Bellamy was not happy about making the effort to do the right thing. After all, his friend Bernard was gone and his friend Betsy was still waiting to see the queen because she was in big trouble. It seemed to Bellamy that nobody else was out there collecting pollen, so why should he be? The whole thing seemed seriously unfair to him.

So instead of going to collect pollen, he put his feet up and did nothing. He relaxed. He knew what the right thing was, but he didn't want to do it. In the morning he relaxed; in the afternoon he relaxed. He didn't do what he should have been doing.

At the end of the day all the other bees started to return. Bartholomew and Basil came back loaded with pollen and so did most of the other bees – not as much as Basil and Bartholomew, but certainly a lot of pollen. When the other bees saw Bellamy they were confused. He didn't seem to have any pollen at all. He didn't even look tired. They asked him

how this could be and he told them plainly enough: "I didn't do any work today. I decided not to do the right thing, so I stayed in and relaxed. And furthermore, I think I'll stay in and relax tomorrow as well. Relaxing is a whole lot better than working."

The other bees couldn't believe what they were hearing. They always worked hard; they always did the right thing. They decided to say no more about it and made their way instead to the dining room. Bellamy was hungry; in fact, all that relaxing had made him very hungry. Not to worry, tonight was his favourite: honey on toast followed by honey cake and custard.

All the bees ate together in a huge dining room. They all stood as usual, as the queen entered and took her seat. She had left Betsy waiting; she hadn't decided what she would do with her yet. The queen said grace. Bellamy's tummy rumbled. Then the bees began to sit down.

The queen ordered that the food be served and then she added: "But no food is to be given to Bellamy!"

Bellamy protested, "But, Your Majesty, I'm hungry! I need food!"

The queen looked at Bellamy and slowly added: "Bees that do the right thing get the blessings for doing the right thing – in this case, honey cake and custard. Bees that don't want to do the right thing don't get the blessing."

Bellamy slumped back in his chair. He wished he'd done the right thing. In the same way, God made us a promise: when we hunger and thirst for righteousness, we will be blessed.

6 The Merciful

	Programme	Item
Section 1	Welcome	
	Rules	
	Prayer	
	Praise	
	Game 1	Marshmallow From Beans
	Praise (x2)	
	Fun Item 1	
	Game 2	Mercy Find
	Fun Item 2	
	Bible Text	Matthew 5:7
	Announcements	
	Interview	
	Worship (x2)	
Section 2 Preaching Time	Bible Lesson	John
	Illustration 1	Sheep And Goats
	Illustration 2	Forgiving Debts
	Story	Betsy And The Queen
	Prayer	

Overview The ability to show mercy demonstrates a quality of greatness; handing out punishment can be done by anyone. The ability to forgive is rooted in the very heart and nature of God himself.

games

PreachingTime

Game 1

Marshmallow From Beans

PREPARATION	Four marshmallows per team. A plate of beans per team.
PLAYERS	Four players per team.
SET-UP	Players stand at A. The plates of beans are positioned at B with four marshmallows in each.
OBJECT	Players run from A to B in relay formation, take a marshmallow out of the beans, using their mouths only, then return to A.
WINNING	The team to complete the game first wins. Give a bonus for the player with the most bean sauce on his face.

Game 2

Mercy Find

PREPARATION	Place the letters of the word MERCY on cards stuck onto various walls around the hall.
PLAYERS	Four players per team.
SET-UP	The players stand at A.
OBJECT	Players collect the letters and form the word MERCY.
WINNING	The first team to complete the game wins.

BIBLE LESSON **JOHN**

"Blessed are the merciful, for they will be shown mercy." (Matthew 5:7, New International Version)

If any disciple could be described as the closest to Jesus, it would be John. John has been described as the disciple of love. All his writings (he wrote three letters and the gospel of John) talk about love and especially the love of God. It was John who wrote: "God is love."

Towards the end of his life, John actually made an amazing statement. He said: "Love God and do what you like."

You see, John understood something. When we really love God, all the other things will be easy for us. If we really loved God we would have no problem with this thing called mercy. We would be merciful because we would want to please God, who is merciful to us.

Illustration 1

Sheep And Goats

Objects needed: *A storybook; a picture of a sheep and a goat.*

This is a storybook. I like to read stories. Today we're going to look at two stories that Jesus told. The first involves two sorts of animals: sheep and goats.

Jesus said that at the end of time, all the nations will be gathered together and will stand before God as he sits on his royal throne. God will divide up the people into two groups, in the same way as a shepherd divides up the sheep and the goats. One group he will place on the right, and the other group on the left.

To those on his right he will say: "Come, you who are blessed, into the kingdom prepared for you before creation."

The people on the right are confused, however, for although they are delighted to be placed in God's kingdom, they don't really know why. So they ask: "Lord, why did we get chosen?"

And God answers: "When I was thirsty, you gave me something to drink; when I was a stranger, you invited me in; when I was in need of clothes, you clothed me."

But try as they might, the people cannot remember doing these things for God. Then God adds: "When you did these things for the least person, you did it for me."

So when we show mercy to the least person, sometimes even to the most undeserving person,

we do it as if we're doing it to God. That's a reason to be merciful.

To those on his left Jesus will say: "Come, you who are cursed, go to that place where there will be crying and anguish."

The people on the left become angry and say: "God, we have never done anything wrong! We don't deserve this."

And God says: "When I was thirsty, you gave me nothing to drink; when I was hungry, you left me to starve; when I needed clothes, you ignored me."

But try as they might, the people cannot remember not doing these things for God, so they ask God and he replies: "When you didn't do these things for the least person, you didn't do them for me."

So when we refuse to be merciful, it's as if we show no mercy to God.

Forgiving Debts

Objects needed: *Pictures of a king and a man – alternatively invite some people to play the parts.*

Jesus told another story about a man who owed a lot of money to a king. The king was sorting out all his paperwork and summoned the man into his throne room.

"Now, sir! Let me see. Ah yes, you owe me £1 million. Would you like to give me the cash or would you like to write me a cheque?"

The man began to sob uncontrollably. He knew what kings did to people who didn't pay up and he really didn't want to have his head chopped off. Through his tears he sobbed: "Your Majesty! I'm sorry, but I can't pay you."

The king looked at the man hard and then felt merciful. "Sir! This is your lucky day. I will let you off."

The man was overjoyed! He ran through the palace, dancing and celebrating and singing. Just as he was about to leave, he bumped into the king's butler. The man stopped dead, and then, looking at the butler, he said: "Sir! You owe me £20, don't you? Pay me now or I'll have you thrown in jail."

But the butler didn't have any money; he wasn't going to be paid until the end of the month. He sobbed and sobbed but the man would not show mercy. He had the butler thrown in jail.

Soon after this, the king found out and was furious. He called for the man and pronounced: "I showed you mercy over £1 million and you can't show mercy over £20. You are an unfair man and, as such, you must go to jail and the butler will be freed."

Jesus told us this story to teach us something special: if we want to be shown mercy, we must be merciful. God forgave us, so we must forgive others.

● STORY – Betsy And The Queen

Betsy had been waiting to see the queen for several days. The queen was a very busy bee and had decided not to put herself out for somebody as naughty as Betsy who went around stinging children. But eventually, when all her schedule was complete, she summoned the shaking Betsy to come and stand before her.

"Now, Betsy!" she began. "I think we have a problem."

Betsy was shaking like a leaf. She had never been so close to the queen before and she certainly appeared to be larger and more frightening than Betsy ever thought she was. The queen towered over Betsy and stared at her.

"So you are the bee that likes to sting little children, are you?" the queen asked.

Betsy gulped! The queen's voice was soft, yet it carried an unmistakable authority. Betsy

nodded her head.
The queen
continued: "Do you
think it's a good
thing to go around
stinging people,
Betsy?"

Betsy shook
her head. It seemed
as if all her powers
of speech had left
her.

"What if I were
to sting you?" demanded the queen.

Now Betsy was paralysed with fear. If the
queen were to sting her, she would die. She
didn't know what to do. She knew that the queen
was very frightening indeed, and if she wanted
to, she could sting her right now.

"No!" said the queen. "This time I will let
you go."

Betsy couldn't believe what she had heard,
but the queen knew what she was doing. Anyone
can punish people, but it is a sign of true
greatness if we can forgive and be merciful. The
queen was wise: she knew that Betsy would never
do it again. She had met the queen, and the
queen had shown her mercy. Out of respect and
maybe fear of the queen, Betsy would never do
this wrong thing again.

When we meet King Jesus, he too could
punish us for the wrong things we have done.
But he also shows mercy. And if we've really met
the King of all kings, out of respect and maybe
fear, we try never to do wrong again.

In the same way, when people wrong us, we
must learn to follow King Jesus' example. It
shows more strength to forgive and have mercy
than it does to punish.

Betsy could hardly walk as she left the
queen's presence; her legs were still trembling
with fear; but she was also overjoyed. She was
overjoyed that the queen had been merciful.

7 Pure In Heart

Programme		Item
Section 1	Welcome	
	Rules	
	Prayer	
	Praise	
	Game 1	Water Walks
	Praise (x2)	
	Fun Item 1	
	Game 2	Water Interchange
	Fun Item 2	
	Bible Text	Matthew 5:8
	Announcements	
	Interview	
	Worship (x2)	
Section 2 **Preaching** **Time**	Bible Lesson	Bartholomew
	Illustration 1	Word Challenge
	Illustration 2	Boiling
	Illustration 3	Why Can't I See God?
	Story	Jam
	Prayer	

Overview Today's Beatitude tells us that the pure in heart will see God. What an exciting proposition – to see God! This lesson will look at the benefits – seeing God; and the responsibility – being pure.

Games

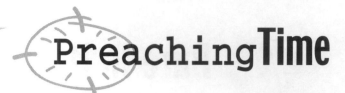
Preaching Time

Game 1

Water Walks

PREPARATION	A glass of water per team, filled to the brim.
PLAYERS	Four players per team.
SET-UP	Players stand at A in relay formation.
OBJECT	Players run from A to B and back again while holding the glass of water on their heads without spilling any.
WINNING	The team to complete the relay with the most water left wins.

Game 2

Water Interchange

PREPARATION	Two buckets per team, one at A and the other at B. A cup per team.
PLAYERS	Four players per team.
SET-UP	As for Game 1.
OBJECT	Players bring as much water as possible from the bucket at B to the bucket at A in two minutes.
WINNING	The team with the most water in their bucket wins.

BIBLE LESSON ## BARTHOLOMEW

"Blessed are the pure in heart, for they will see God."
(Matthew 5:8, New International Version)

Bartholomew, who was also known as Nathaniel, was one of the first disciples that Jesus called. He doubted that Jesus really was the Son of God, until he met Jesus. Then everything changed. As soon as Bartholomew saw Jesus he changed his mind. There was something about Bartholomew that meant he could recognise God. Jesus knew what it was when he said to him: "Here is an Israelite with no guile."

Guile is the bad things inside us. Jesus was telling people that Bartholomew had no bad things in him; he was pure in spirit. And, because he was pure in spirit, he could see God – he knew that Jesus was God. If we want to be able to see God, we need to be pure.

Illustration 1

Word Challenge

Objects needed: *A whiteboard or large piece of card, pens.*

So, what does this word "pure" mean? What words can you think of that may be associated with this word "pure"? *(Allow the children to think this through – words like "clean", "clear", "unmixed", "holy".)*

Let's look at our list. So if people want to see God they must be… *(Read through the list.)*

Boiling

Object needed: *A cup full of mud – water and earth.*

It is fairly obvious that this cup may contain some water, but the water is far from pure; it's full of all sorts of stuff. It's got earth in it. Now the question is this: How do you get pure water out of this? *(Allow the children time to answer.)*

There may be several ways to do this, but the only way I know is this. *(Light a flame under the glass.)* This way, the water will boil and turn to steam. I'll then catch the steam by putting this other glass above, and then let the steam cool back down to water. You get pure water by boiling the dirty water.

God sometimes does the same thing to us to make us pure. He allows difficulties to happen to us so that we become more pure.

Why Can't I See God?

Object needed: *A scarf with the word "sin" written on it.*

Some people may never see God. That's a very sad statement, but it's true. There may be a million different reasons why they don't see God: they don't believe in God; they are too busy stealing and cheating; maybe they just don't want to be pure. But it all comes down to one word. We don't see God because of…

Invite a volunteer up, and tie the scarf around his eyes. The word "sin" needs to be displayed on the outside.

This person can't see anything. The reason people can't see God is because of this thing called sin. Sin is the junk, the garbage, the rubbish in our lives. It is the thing that stops us being pure.

● STORY – Jam

Bees love honey! At least, most bees love honey. For some strange reason that nobody was quite sure about, Bellamy loved jam. His favourite was strawberry jam. He loved the stuff; he just couldn't get enough of it. He would deliberately fly into people's kitchens to sneak it off their toast. He loved jam. And strangest of all, Bellamy only really liked strawberry jam.

Now that wouldn't be a problem, except that jam makes bees very, very sticky. It gets onto their wings and stops them from flying. It stops them from doing what they should be doing – collecting honey.

Time and time again, the queen had sat Bellamy down and explained to him that he shouldn't go near jam; if he kept going near things which he knew he shouldn't touch, then eventually he wouldn't be able to do what he should do.

This is just like us. If we remain pure, then we will see God one day. If we don't remain pure, then we never will see God. We must stay away from the things which stop us being pure.

Bellamy tried very hard. He went for three whole weeks without looking at any jam. He even flew past Lucy, who was eating a sticky jam trifle. He really was doing well. Then Lucy's granny, who lived at the bottom of Lucy's street, started making strawberry jam for the playgroup. She made it every morning. And, what was worse, she would always leave her toast to cool in the window. Every morning, Bellamy had to fly past on his way to collect pollen. He could smell the jam, he could see the jam, but he knew that if he went near it, it would stick to his wings.

Every morning he flew past, until that morning five days ago when he'd missed breakfast – oh, the smell of that jam on the toast! He flew over and looked. He smelled it and then he climbed on top of the toast and started to nibble. Just then, Granny came to get her toast and jam, and there on the jam was a bee. She took her rolling pin and brought it down… BANG! But Bellamy was too fast. He flew away, but not as fast as usual. He had jam on his wings.

The next day Bellamy couldn't resist. Now he had a taste in his mouth for jam. This happens to us too. Once we do something that makes us impure once, we find it hard not to do it again and again. It becomes a bad habit.

Bellamy again flew over to the jam. And again he started to eat. This time Granny crept up quietly. She lifted her rolling pin and… BANG! Again Bellamy was too fast for her, but only just.

All that jam on his wings was slowing him down. The jam was beginning to stop him doing what he should be doing.

Things that make us impure stop us serving God and stop us seeing God.

Sure enough, the next morning Bellamy was back in the jam again. But this time when Granny lifted up the rolling pin, Bellamy could hardly move. He managed to take off, but hadn't got very far before he heard… BANG!!! He thought his head had exploded. He became dizzy and lost control. He could feel himself falling… and then nothing. Bellamy thought he was dead.

Messing about with things that stop us being pure can get us into lots of problems.

Bellamy lay on the ground all yesterday. He wasn't moving. His eyes were closed. And that's where Betsy found him this morning, unconscious on the ground. I don't know what will happen to him.

We must be pure in heart, and not fill our heart with bad things. The pure in heart will see God.

(Next week I'll tell you what happens to Bellamy.)

8 Peacemakers

	Programme	Item
Section 1	**Welcome**	
	Rules	
	Prayer	
	Praise	
	Game 1	Honey Cake
	Praise (x2)	
	Fun Item 1	
	Game 2	Honey Eaters
	Fun Item 2	
	Bible Text	Matthew 5:9
	Announcements	
	Interview	
	Worship (x2)	
Section 2 Preaching Time	**Bible Lesson**	Disciples
	Illustration 1	Peace And Quiet
	Illustration 2	Peacemakers
	Illustration 3	Not Just Men
	Story	Bellamy Bee
	Prayer	

 **Overview**　Our world is full of warmongers. Wouldn't it be great if, instead, our world was full of peacemakers?

games

Game 1

Honey Cake

PREPARATION	A plain cake per team, a small jar of honey, and some sweet decorations at B.
PLAYERS	Four players per team.
SET-UP	Players stand at A.
OBJECT	Players run from A to B together. They make a face on a cake at B. When the players are happy with the result, they return to A.
WINNING	The cake with the best face wins.

Game 2

Honey Eaters

PREPARATION	The cakes made above placed at B.
PLAYERS	One leader per team.
SET-UP	One leader per team stands at A.
OBJECT	The leader runs from A to B, eats the cake – totally – and returns.
WINNING	The leader who gets back first wins.

PreachingTime

BIBLE LESSON ## DISCIPLES

"Blessed are the peacemakers, for they will be called sons of God." (Matthew 5:9, New International Version)

One day Jesus and his disciples got into a boat, and he said, "Let's cross the lake." They started out, and while they were sailing across, he went to sleep. Suddenly a storm struck the lake, and the boat started sinking. They were in danger. So the disciples went to Jesus and woke him up, "Master, Master! We are about to drown!"

Jesus got up and ordered the wind and waves to stop. They obeyed, and everything was calm. Then Jesus asked the disciples, "Don't you have any faith?"

But they were frightened and amazed. They said to each other, "Who is this? He can give orders to the wind and waves, and they obey him!"

The disciples were amazed. They hadn't yet learned that Jesus is the only one who can bring calm to the storm, the only one who can bring peace into chaos.

But it wasn't always to be that way. Jesus was preparing his disciples so that they too could be people who would bring peace. Where there was trouble and chaos, where there were homes where nothing except arguments and rows took place, where there were estates where people spent all their time shouting, where there were schools where people spent all their time fighting, Jesus was, and is, teaching his disciples to bring peace.

"Blessed are the peacemakers."

Illustration 1

Peace And Quiet

Object needed: *A drum or tambourine or loud horn.*

Someone walks onto the stage banging their drum, or shaking their tambourine, and singing in their loudest voice: "I love noise, I love riot, I love the sound of the big bass drum." If you don't know the tune, make it up.

Some people think that peace is when there is…

The drummer continues until he is tapped on the shoulder and spoken to.

Excuse me! I'm trying to talk. Yes, that's much better. Now, where was I? Yes, some people think that peace is when there is no noise. But it's really quite amazing. Even when it's very quiet people don't feel peace inside. That's where real peace needs to be – inside.

The drummer walks off singing the song he came on to.

Illustration 2

Peacemakers

Object needed: *The following table.*

Over the past 100 years several people have won a very special award. It is called the Nobel Peace Prize. Here's a list of some of those people and why they won the award.

1998 **JOHN HUME** and **DAVID TRIMBLE** for their efforts to find a peaceful solution to the conflict in Northern Ireland.

1993 **NELSON MANDELA**, the man who would become the president of South Africa.

1989 The fourteenth **DALAI LAMA (TENZIN GYATSO)**, the religious and political leader of the Tibetan people.

1988 **THE UNITED NATIONS PEACEKEEPING FORCES**, New York, USA.

1984 **DESMOND MPILO TUTU** of South Africa, for insisting that all people should be treated the same, no matter what the colour of their skin.

1979 **MOTHER TERESA** of Calcutta, India, leader of the Order of the Missionaries of Charity.

The list is very impressive. It includes people from all sorts of backgrounds who tried to help others: people who worked hard to bring peace to South Africa, people who worked hard to bring peace to Northern Ireland, people who worked exceptionally hard to bring peace to various parts of the world. Mother Teresa is on the list for the work she carried out in India.

This is an exciting list. I know that these people are children of God. How do I know this?

Because God said: "Blessed are the peacemakers, for they will be called sons of God."

We may never win the Nobel Peace Prize, but we too are called to be peacemakers, to do our best to end conflict between people.

There is a person whose name is missing from the list, but he has often been mentioned by the people who have taken the prize. His name is Jesus. The Bible tells me that he is the Prince of Peace. And he did not come to bring peace to just one area. He came to bring peace to all areas. He came to bring peace to the whole world.

Illustration 3

Not Just Men

There has been fighting between men and between women ever since the start of history. There has been conflict, there have been wars, there have been numerous battles, two world wars and countless deaths. But I need to tell you this: these wars will never stop and the fighting will never end until we make peace. But not peace with each other. That will come automatically. We need to make peace with God. When we all acknowledge God for who he is, the King of kings and Lord of lords, the Prince of Peace – then, the wars will stop.

And Jesus made a way so that we could have peace with God. He did this *(show a picture of the crucifixion)*:
Jesus died so that we could have peace with God.

● STORY – Bellamy Bee

Bellamy's eyes slowly began to focus. For a couple of seconds he thought that he had died and gone to heaven. But the throbbing coming from the top of his head assured him that he was still very much alive. He looked around and saw Betsy standing over him.

Eventually he remembered what had happened. He'd been hit over the head by Granny's rolling pin. He'd been knocked unconscious and Betsy had rescued him from underneath the window – all because he couldn't keep away from strawberry jam. He wanted to get up and thank Betsy for saving him, but he really couldn't move very far. It was a full three weeks before he was eventually well enough to get up and wander around the hive again.

When Bellamy did start wandering around, the other bees surprised him. He thought they would be glad to see him, but instead they talked about him; they said how stupid he was, and how bad he had been in making Betsy – a girl bee – get into danger rescuing him. Bellamy knew that he had been stupid, but he was also very sure that he didn't deserve all the hassle he was getting from the other bees.

The other bees started refusing to work with Bellamy. They refused to go near him. Before long, Bellamy felt very sad indeed. But to cover up his sadness, he just became angry and started to pick fights with the other bees. The hive was a mess, nothing was getting done, everyone was arguing and everyone was fighting.

We get like this sometimes. Someone does something wrong and we refuse to forgive them. Instead we begin to argue with them and call them all sorts of horrid names. We refuse to be their friends any more.

The amazing thing about bees is that every single one of them needs the other ones. Every single one, from the queen down to the worker bees, has a special job to do. They all have a special function to fulfil and they all need each other.

The amazing thing about people is that they sometimes are not as clever as bees. We also need each other, we also all have special jobs to do and we also all have a function. We all have a destiny to fulfil for King Jesus, but we just don't realise it.

Eventually the queen had to get involved. She called all the bees together in a huge bee meeting and she began to talk: "Bellamy has been silly; there is no doubt of that. He put Betsy in danger; there is no doubt of that. But let me say this to you: if you are the bee who has never done anything wrong, then you can be the bee to ignore Bellamy. But if you *have* done things wrong, then you must know how bad Bellamy feels, and you had better make friends very quickly."

Everyone was deadly quiet. Betsy was remembering the time she stung little Lucy; other bees were remembering the times that they stayed out too long and nearly got lost. Other bees remembered the pollen that they had been too lazy to collect, or the pollen they had dropped on the way back to the hive. One by one they all started to apologise to Bellamy.

We too need to think before we start fighting with people. We've all done things wrong. Maybe we need to be peacemakers and not split people up. Maybe we need to spend more time making friends than making enemies. Maybe it's time to sort some things out with other people.

Maybe, just maybe, it's time to make peace with God. Maybe it's time to ask God to forgive all those wrong thoughts and wrong actions. Maybe it's time to become a friend and not an enemy of God.

Persecuted Because Of Righteousness

Programme	Item
Section 1	
Welcome	
Rules	
Prayer	
Praise	
Game 1	Stones
Praise (x2)	
Fun Item 1	
Game 2	Stones Reversed
Fun Item 2	
Bible Text	Matthew 5:10
Announcements	
Interview	
Worship (x2)	
Section 2 **Preaching** **Time**	
Bible Lesson	Disciples
Illustration 1	Fox's Book Of Martyrs
Illustration 2	It Still Happens Today
Illustration 3	Seeds
Story	Hive Tragedy
Prayer	

**verview** "Come to Jesus and all your problems will seem insignificant." This statement is probably true. Some of the situations that Christians have faced throughout church history and even today make most of our problems seem insignificant. But if we mean by this statement that if we become Christians everything will be great, then maybe that's not so true.

games

Game 1

Stones

PREPARATION	Several buckets full of newspapers rolled into balls.
PLAYERS	Four players per team.
SET-UP	Players stand at A in relay formation. Leaders stand at B with the buckets of newspaper.
OBJECT	Each team starts with 100 points. They run from A to B and back. The leaders throw balls at them. If the players are touched, they lose a point.
WINNING	The game plays for two minutes. The team with the most points at the end wins.

Game 2

Stones Reversed

PREPARATION	As for Game 1.
PLAYERS	Four from each team.
SET-UP	As for Game 1, but the children and the leaders swap roles.
OBJECT	The team scores a point every time they hit a leader.
WINNING	The team with the most points after two minutes wins.

Preaching Time

BIBLE LESSON — DISCIPLES

"Blessed are those who are persecuted because of righteousness, for theirs is the kingdom of heaven."

(Matthew 5:10, New International Version)

The Bible doesn't really give us a whole lot of information about the fate of the disciples after Jesus ascended. We hear about Peter and the miracles he did. We hear of John being sent to an island called Patmos. But for more details, we have to turn to history to find out what happened to them.

You may be forgiven for thinking that since the disciples were Christians they would live happy lives and die as old men, surrounded by their grandchildren. After all, they served Jesus, the Prince of Peace. Surely, everything would go well for them.

The truth is not like that. In fact, church history tells us something different. Now, if I'm trying to get you to be a disciple of Jesus, to be a real Christian, maybe I shouldn't tell you this stuff. But I guess you should know the truth.

All the disciples were beaten, put in jail, thrown out of town, called names. In fact, only John died of natural causes. All the others were killed for being Christians. When Peter was quite old, according to church history, he was crucified just like Jesus. But because he didn't think himself good enough to die the same way that Jesus died, he was crucified upside down. Some disciples were beheaded; some were thrown to lions.

Hey! It's not easy being a disciple for Jesus.

Illustration 1

Fox's Book Of Martyrs

Object needed: *A book with "Fox's Book Of Martyrs" written on it.*

This is not the nicest book in the world. It is full of some of the terrible things that were done to people who did nothing other than tell people about Jesus. This is a book about the way Christians were treated, just for being Christians.

It has some frightening accounts. It talks of people being thrown to the lions, of others being killed by gladiators, of others being used as burning human torches to light the way to the Roman emperor's palace. It talks of Christians who were beheaded and of even worse things than these.

It Still Happens Today

Object needed: *A world globe.*

It doesn't just stop there. People are still being persecuted for being Christians today. Not so much in this country, but in other parts of the world, terrible things happen to people just for being Christians.

In India recently, Christians were burned alive just for telling others about God. In China many have been imprisoned for telling others about Jesus. In countries where there are a lot of Muslims, Christians have suffered all sorts of horrible things.

Sometimes we think it's hard to be a Christian in school when people make fun of us, or laugh at us, but imagine what it's like to be dragged out of your home and have stones thrown at you until you are unconscious.

It's important to know that even though we live in a country where there are no real problems in being a Christian, this wasn't always the case. Many people are still giving their lives, so that people in different parts of the world can learn about being Christians.

Seeds

Object needed: *A packet of seeds.*

So why do people do it? Why do they allow themselves to be killed and hurt? It's because they know something very special, something which not many people understand. Certainly the devil, who is the enemy of God, doesn't understand.

When you plant one of these seeds, something will grow. Somebody once said this: "The blood of the martyrs is the seed of the church."

That's the secret! It means this: whenever a Christian's blood is shed for Jesus, that person's blood falls to the ground and there, right there, the church begins to grow. God claims the ground where the blood flows, for himself and for his servants. It's a story that's being repeated all over the world. Remember all those people who were killed in India for Jesus? Well, thousands upon thousands of people are now becoming Christians there. It's the same in China and in many parts of the world.

Sometimes being a Christian is incredibly hard. But it is always worth it.

● STORY – Hive Tragedy

The hive was on the far side of a piece of farmland. It was high up in a tree and was very safe and secure – or so the bees thought. They had deliberately built it there to be out of people's reach. Anyone who climbed the tree got stung. Everything seemed excellent – but only seemed! The bees didn't have the full story.

Far away from the hive a discussion was taking place: "So do we take this new road around the edge of the woods or do we take the road straight through the middle?"

The two men scratched their beards, looked at the woods, then looked at the army of diggers, cement mixers and steamrollers backed up behind them. "Let's go through the middle."

The other man nodded and the decision was made. The hive's destiny was set.

The following morning the bees were awoken by the sound of banging and crashing. The hive began to sway from side to side and panic erupted. The bees flew to the edge of the hive and looked out. There, trundling towards them, was the biggest pile of machinery they had ever seen. Trees fell in its path; birds were flying; animals were running.

The bees had less than two minutes before this huge vehicle squashed their tree, their hive and possibly them. Then, almost as one, they stopped panicking and stood still. They began to think. The queen was the future of the hive. If she survived, there would be more bees and more hives. If she died, it was all over. Bellamy shouted above the machines: "Get the queen!"

Several worker bees went to the centre of the hive and began to bring the queen to the surface, but there was barely enough time left. The machines were already upon them. Bellamy jumped from the hive and flew towards the vehicles. Other bees followed his example. A swarm of bees descended on the machines. The drivers were being stung, but they were fighting back. First one bee was swatted, then another and another. Bees were being killed all around Bellamy, but still he flew in and stung, again and again. He would not let up. He was determined to make enough time for the queen to escape. Then he felt a bang on his head and he fell to the ground.

As he looked up he saw the queen and her entourage flying into the distance. They had escaped. The hive would survive. There would be more bees. Bellamy blacked out.

Bellamy didn't mind what happened to him as long as the hive survived. Christians, true Christians, will do anything to proclaim Jesus. Some are even prepared to die.

Bellamy looked up. All was calm. There was a huge road where the tree once was. Everything was still now; the machines had stopped for the night. Bellamy stood up. He was alive and able to fly. He would soon track down the rest of the bees. They had survived.

Like A Little Child

A Series in Five Parts

Introduction

Title	Themes covered
1 O Jerusalem, Jerusalem	Security
2 Never Will I Leave You	Time
3 Come, Follow Me	Example
4 Surely I Am With You Always	Encouragement
5 Love Your Neighbour As Yourself	Love

Series Overview

Over the next five weeks we will look at five statements that Jesus made and see how they relate to the fundamental needs of every child. The object of this curriculum series is to show how simple the words of Jesus really were, yet how profound. The games will all be simplified relays.

The life application story looks at "Mrs Thompson's Class", a classroom full of rather interesting children.

1 O Jerusalem, Jerusalem

	Programme	Item
Section 1	Welcome	
	Rules	
	Prayer	
	Praise	
	Game 1	Running
	Praise (x2)	
	Fun Item 1	
	Game 2	Hopping
	Fun Item 2	
	Bible Text	Matthew 23:37
	Announcements	
	Interview	
	Worship (x2)	
Section 2	Bible Lesson	Matthew 23:37
Preaching	Illustration 1	A Hen Protects Her Chicks
Time	Illustration 2	Hugs
	Illustration 3	Umbrellas
	Story	Mrs Thompson's Class – Kelly
	Prayer	

Overview We all need to feel secure. We work better and function better in a secure and caring environment. What better security can there be than knowing that the God who created the whole universe is looking after us?

games

Game 1

Running

PREPARATION	None.
PLAYERS	Six players per team.
SET-UP	Players line up in relay formation at A.
OBJECT	The first person runs from A to B and back. The next person then goes.
WINNING	The first team complete and sitting down wins.

Game 2

Hopping

PREPARATION	None.
PLAYERS	Six players per team.
SET-UP	Players line up in relay formation at A.
OBJECT	The first person hops from A to B and back. The next person then goes.
WINNING	The first team complete and sitting down wins.

Preaching Time

BIBLE LESSON **MATTHEW 23:37**

"O Jerusalem, Jerusalem, you who kill the prophets… how often I have longed to gather your children together, as a hen gathers her chicks." (Matthew 23:37, New International Version)

Jerusalem had once been one of God's favourite places. All the people who lived there used to worship God and pray to him every day. But by the time Jesus had come to earth, Jerusalem wasn't such a nice place. It had a very bad history.

God had sent many prophets – people who heard what God was saying and came to tell others – to Jerusalem to warn the people to turn back to God. But instead of listening to these prophets, the people of Jerusalem had killed the prophets, sometimes by throwing stones at them until they were dead.

But Jesus showed how much he loved the people of Jerusalem by telling them that even though they had hurt his servants, he still wanted to protect them and love them.

Even though we haven't always been good, God still wants to look after us and protect us. It's a wonderful thing to know that God wants to protect us and keep us safe.

Illustration **1**

A Hen Protects Her Chicks

Object needed: *None.*

Once there was a certain barn and in that barn there was a hen. One day something tragic happened and the barn caught fire. The flames engulfed the entire building, and all the straw quickly caught fire. But the hen didn't move from her position; she refused to come out of the barn.

Soon the flames were so high the farmer saw them from a nearby field. He rushed to his blazing barn and after much hard work with a bucket and a tank full of water, he eventually put out the flames.

When he came to examine what was left of the barn he saw the poor dead hen, but from where she lay he could hear a "cheep, cheep" sound. He moved the hen and there beneath her body were three tiny yellow chicks going "cheep". The hen had refused to leave the barn because she was there protecting her chicks.

When Jesus says he longs to look after us like a hen looks after her chicks, it's a very serious thing. Jesus really does want to make us secure. He really does want to look after us.

Hugs

Object needed: *A picture of people hugging.*

It's wondrous
What a hug can do,
A hug can cheer you
When you're blue.
A hug can say, "I love you so"
Or "I hate to see you go."
A hug is "Welcome back again!"
And "Great to see you!" or
"Where've you been?"
A hug can soothe a small child's pain
And bring a rainbow after rain.
A hug delights and warms and charms,
It must be why God gave us arms.
Hugs are great for
Fathers and mothers,
Sweet for sisters, even for brothers,
And chances are some favourite aunts
Love them more than potted plants.
Kittens crave them,
Puppies love them,
Heads of state are not above them.
A hug can break the language barrier,
And make the dullest day
Seem merrier.
No need to fret
About the store of 'em,
The more you give
The more there are of 'em.
So stretch those arms without delay
And give someone a hug today.

(*Author unknown*)

Illustration 3

Umbrellas

Objects needed: *An umbrella, a watering can and a paddling pool or big bowl; two boxes, one with the word "sadness" written on it and the other with the word "loneliness".*

The narrator stands in the bowl. Another person stands above the narrator on a chair with a watering can and begins to pour. The narrator begins to speak.

When it's raining we have two choices. We can either stand under the rain and get wet, or we can do something about it. I like to put my umbrella up. It keeps me protected.

The umbrella is put up.

There we go – protected from that nasty rain. It's a bit strange that it's raining indoors though!

Sometimes we need protecting against other things. When it's raining, usually the worst thing that can happen is that we get wet. Other things don't so much get us wet, but hurt our feelings. What do we do when someone shouts at us and upsets us? What happens when we just feel sad, or lonely, or our mum and dad argue and make us sad?

What do we do when things like sadness and loneliness land on us?

The water has now stopped and two boxes labelled "sadness" and "loneliness" are thrown on.

What do we do then? The Bible says something amazing. In a part of the Bible called the Psalms, it says: "Under the shadow of your wings I find security."

It's God talking. Obviously, God doesn't have wings, but what he's saying is this: When you feel upset and sad, then if you come to God and talk to God – and remember, praying is just talking to God – then he protects you and makes you feel better.

It's a good thing to do. To find security in God is a smart thing to do.

● STORY – Mrs Thompson's Class – Kelly

Mrs Thompson was a Christian. She loved God very much and prayed to him every day. But with all her prayers and all her experience, she was still having a rough year. Her new Year Six class had arrived in September and it was now January. They were still hard work. They seemed to have so many problems between them that needed constant attention. Timothy was a nightmare, Clara was always sad, Harvey couldn't stop climbing on top of things, Jodi was always quarrelling and Kelly... Well, Kelly just kept crying recently. Mrs Thompson had tried to be nice to her, but she just cried even more.

Mrs Thompson had tried to work out what was wrong with Kelly. She knew Kelly's dad had left home and Kelly now lived with her mum, but she didn't understand why Kelly was so upset. Lots of other children in the class lived with just mum or just dad, but they didn't seem to cry all the time like Kelly did. They seemed OK.

The weeks went by and Kelly didn't get any better. She would be halfway through her science lesson and she would burst into tears and run off. She seemed afraid of everything. She would cry if the boys shouted too near her; she would cry if she got her sums wrong; she would cry if it rained. Kelly really was very, very upset.

Mrs Thompson had tried to talk to Kelly, but every time she tried to help her Kelly would burst into tears and shout: "I'm just fine, leave me alone!"

Mrs Thompson had tried to work out what to do. She had spoken to some of the other boys and girls whose dads had left. She had explained to them that even though their real father may have left, God also wanted to be their Father and would look after them. Mrs Thompson thought that maybe she should try and explain this to Kelly. She waited until it was gym day. She knew that Kelly would be the last to get changed and go into the hall – she always was. Mrs Thompson waited until everyone else had left and then she began to explain to Kelly: "Hey, Kelly! You do realise that even though your father has left you, you still have another Father. God wants to be your Father and look after you."

Mrs Thompson thought this might work, but instead of it making things better, Kelly burst into tears and started crying hysterically. She started to shout: "I don't want another father, please, no!"

And with that Kelly ran out of the classroom. Mrs Thompson was very upset. She tried to run after her, but she couldn't keep up. Mrs Thompson phoned her house every hour during that day, but there was no answer until she phoned at 5 p.m. Kelly's mum answered: "Hi, Mrs Thompson! I think we need to talk."

And so an appointment was made; Mrs Thompson went to see Kelly and her mum. What Mrs Thompson heard when she went to visit shocked her. Kelly's mum tried to explain: "Mrs Thompson, Kelly's dad wasn't very nice. He was quite nasty to me and to her, and now he isn't allowed to see Kelly or to come near her."

Mrs Thompson couldn't believe what she was hearing. She kept listening: "So Mrs Thompson, when you told Kelly that God would be her Father she was frightened. Every time Kelly thinks of a father, she sees someone who is mean and nasty."

Mrs Thompson understood.

Lots of people struggle with seeing God as their Father, because their idea of a father is someone mean and nasty. I know lots of you have great fathers, but not everyone does.

Mrs Thompson decided she would spend some extra time with Kelly. She asked Kelly to write down all the things she thought of as being the perfect father. Kelly wrote: kind, caring, loving, giving, gentle, helpful, there for me, keeps me safe and doesn't harm me, supporting...

Mrs Thompson waited until Kelly had reached the bottom of her list, and then she said, "When I told you God wanted to be your Father, it was a father like the one you just described. God is the perfect Father."

It took a long time before Kelly really understood. But eventually she came to understand that God wanted to look after her and make her secure.

God wants to be your Father too. God searches over the whole world for those who have been hurt or upset, wounded or bruised, and he looks for those he can take care of, those who will let him be their Father. He also looks for those who have good parents but who still want God to be their Father as well.

God wants to be your Father, to keep you safe and secure, to look after you.

Mrs Thompson also had to deal with a little girl called Jodi. But that can wait until next week.

2 Never Will I Leave You

	Programme	Item
Section 1	**Welcome**	
	Rules	
	Prayer	
	Praise	
	Game 1	Frogs
	Praise (x2)	
	Fun Item 1	
	Game 2	Crabs
	Fun Item 2	
	Bible Text	Hebrews 13:5
	Announcements	
	Interview	
	Worship (x2)	
Section 2 Preaching Time	**Bible Lesson**	Hebrews 13:5
	Illustration 1	Cat's In The Cradle
	Illustration 2	Shundi's Girlfriend
	Illustration 3	Grannies
	Story	Mrs Thompson's Class – Jodi
	Prayer	

 **Overview** Last week we learned that God will keep us secure, and that he protects us. This week we find out that God wants to spend time with us as well.

games

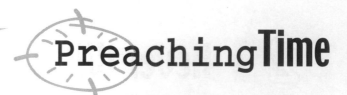

Game 1

Frogs

PREPARATION	None.
PLAYERS	Six players per team.
SET-UP	Players line up in relay formation at A.
OBJECT	The first person crouches down and frog-jumps from A to B and back. The next person then goes. There are some serious rules for frog jumping, primarily that hands must land before legs each time.
WINNING	The first team complete and sitting down wins.

Game 2

Crabs

PREPARATION	None.
PLAYERS	Six players per team.
SET-UP	Players line up in relay formation at A.
OBJECT	The first person crab-walks from A to B and back. The next person then goes. There are rules for crab walking. The children's tummies must be facing upwards, they must use hands and feet and they must move sideways.
WINNING	The first team complete and sitting down wins.

Preaching Time

BIBLE LESSON HEBREWS 13:5

"Never will I leave you; never will I forsake you." (Hebrews 13:5, New International Version)

Promises from some people mean nothing at all. "I'll meet you after school," they say, and then forget to show up. "We'll go swimming when I finish work," then they forget. "I'll come and watch you take part in the sports" – but no one comes.

God made a promise. When God makes a promise, it really does happen. God never breaks a promise. God promised: I will never leave you or forsake you. God promised that he would always be there for us. God never breaks his promises.

"I feel all alone right now!" You're not alone; God is with you.

"I feel really upset." God promised that he would never leave you.

"Where's God now? I feel so hurt." God is always there. He never leaves you or forsakes you.

Illustration 1

Cat's In The Cradle

Object needed: *CD or music video of "Cats In The Cradle" by Harry Chapin – also by Ugly Kid Joe.*

Play the CD or music video as you speak, but make sure it stays background – speak slowly so that much of the song can play.

This is a song called "Cat's in the Cradle".

- It tells the story of a little boy. *(Have a big pause between each statement.)*
- Every day the little boy asked his dad to spend time with him.
- But his father was a busy man.
- "There are bills to pay and planes to catch," he would say.

- But the boy would keep saying:
- "Thanks for the ball, Dad. Come on, let's play."
- But even though the dad bought the boy many things, he never had time to be with him.
- The little boy longed for his dad's company.

- The song's last couple of verses are about what happens when the boy grows up.
- Now the dad wants to spend time with his boy, but it's too late.
- The son isn't interested. He hasn't got time.

- The song is trying to teach us to spend time with the people who are important to us while we can.

Shundi's Girlfriend

Objects needed: *Girlfriend, a sofa, a boy.*

Shundi and his girlfriend sit side by side on the sofa. Shundi is very confident, very cool, but not very smart.

GIRLFRIEND: Oh, Shundi, it's so nice to spend time with you.
SHUNDI: It's cool to be with you too... What was your name again?
GIRLFRIEND: Sandra! You knew that.
SHUNDI: Oh, yes! Of course, just bluffing.
GIRLFRIEND: Anyway! As I was saying, it's good to spend time with you.

Shundi jumps up and gets into his car.

SHUNDI: Oh, well, got to go; I've got to take my car for a quick drive.
GIRLFRIEND: But you were supposed to be spending time with me tonight!
SHUNDI: See you later...

Shundi drives off. A day passes.

GIRLFRIEND: Hi, Shundi. *(Sounds a bit cold.)*
SHUNDI: Hi, Sandra, sorry about last night. I had to... do stuff.
GIRLFRIEND: Well, I suppose I can forgive you.
SHUNDI: Cool!

GIRLFRIEND: I'm looking forward to us spending time together tonight.
SHUNDI: Of course.
GIRLFRIEND: So what have you been doing today?
SHUNDI: Lots! Anyway, I must go...
GIRLFRIEND: But you said you'd spend time with me tonight!
SHUNDI: Sorry, got to go...

Shundi drives off in his car. A day passes.

SHUNDI: Hi, Sandra. *(Sandra ignores him.)* Look, Sandra, I'm sorry, I had to go... out!
GIRLFRIEND: But we were supposed to spend time together.
SHUNDI: Well, let's spend time together now.
GIRLFRIEND: OK then, but this is your last chance.
SHUNDI: Thanks, Sandra. You won't regret it. Look, I've brought you a flower.
GIRLFRIEND: Wow! Thanks, Shundi. You're lovely!
SHUNDI: I know. Anyway, I'm just off...
GIRLFRIEND: What do you mean? You can't leave again!
SHUNDI: I've got to go.

Shundi drives off in his car. A day passes.

SHUNDI: Hi, Sandra. *(Sandra ignores him.)* Sandra, I'm sorry!
GIRLFRIEND: *(Silence)*

Another boy walks on.

SHUNDI: Who are you? *(Looks at the boy.)*
GIRLFRIEND: Shundi, meet Shishkebab! He's my new boyfriend.
SHUNDI: But I thought I was your boyfriend.
GIRLFRIEND: I need a boyfriend who spends time with me.
SHUNDI: Oh!

Girlfriend and boy walk away hand in hand.

SHUNDI: I guess time is more important than I thought. Spending time with people is obviously very important. I wish someone had told me.

Illustration 3

Grannies

Object needed: *A clock or a picture of one.*

This little poem was written by a nine-year-old girl about her granny.

Grandmothers don't have to do anything except to be there. If they take us for walks they slow down past things like pretty leaves and caterpillars, and they never say "Hurry up".

Usually grandmothers are fat but not too fat to tie shoes.

They wear glasses and funny underwear and they can take their teeth and gums out.

Grandmothers don't have to be clever, just be able to answer questions like "Why isn't God married?" and "Why do dogs chase cats?"

Grandmothers don't talk baby-talk to us like visitors do because they know it's hard for us to understand it.

When they read to us, they don't skip pages, or mind if it's the same story over and over again.

Everybody should have a grandmother especially if you don't have television

… because they're the only grown-ups that have time.

● STORY – Mrs Thompson's Class – Jodi

The children in Mrs Thompson's class were bad. That was an understatement. They were really bad. Today we'll meet another member of the class with her own list of problems. This one's called Jodi.

Jodi's dad was very rich. Jodi used to think he was a lorry driver, but recently she had found out that he owned the lorry company. This meant he had over 100 lorries, employed 120 people and was very, very rich. Jodi liked being rich. She liked her enormous house. She liked the fact that she could have anything that she

wanted. She liked the fact that she could do whatever she wanted. She had three horses, an enormous bedroom, and her very own bathroom attached. She liked being rich. Everything in her life was good, except for one thing. She didn't seem to have any friends and she couldn't understand why.

I wonder if you can work out why she didn't have any friends. Here's a typical day in the life of Jodi the rich kid.

She was dropped off at school in her black sports car. It was Monday. She felt a bit tired; she'd had a hectic weekend. She walked into the playground and everyone ignored her. She marched over to Kelly. "Hi Kelly, do you want to play with me?" Jodi enquired.

Kelly stared at her for a couple of minutes and then blurted out, "No, I don't want to play with you. I stood outside the cinema for an hour waiting for you on Friday night. Where were you?"

Jodi stammered and stuttered and then eventually said, "I went horse riding with Virginia instead. Sorry!"

"But you didn't let me know – you just left me standing there by myself! Why didn't you call?"

Jodi thought for a moment and then answered, "Forgot, I suppose! Anyway, there's Clara – I'll go play with her instead."

Kelly almost shouted: "Well, you better had, because I'm not playing with you. You left me standing outside the music shop last week and you didn't turn up, and the week before, I stood outside the café and you didn't turn up. I've had enough."

Jodi walked over to Clara. "Hi, Clara. Want to hang out with me?"

Clara turned and was clearly annoyed: "Do you know how long I waited for you on Saturday morning? 'I'll come around, and we'll go shop.' But you never came, did you? Three hours I waited in for you. I went with Kelly in the end. You are *so* not my friend."

And with that she turned and walked away. Jodi tried to talk to Harvey, but he only said, "Forget it, Jodi. I waited for you outside the roller rink all evening. Go away!"

So Jodi walked off. It was the same with everyone she came to. Jodi had no friends. I wonder why? *(Invite the children to answer.)*

The thing is, we do the same thing so often – not to our friends, but worse, we do it to God. "Hey God," we say. "I'll pray to you every night before I go to bed. I'll talk to you [because praying is only talking to God] every

night before bedtime." So God comes to listen to us – and we've gone straight to sleep and ignored him.

"Hey God, I'll talk to you every morning, and read my Bible." So God comes – and we sleep late and ignore him. It's important to spend time with God, because God wants to spend time with us.

At the end of the day, Jodi was picked up from school in her sports car. She was taken back home. She had so much money, but no friends. She just didn't spend time with them, and she made promises she didn't keep.

By the end of the week, Jodi will probably have friends again. But I wonder what she'll do next weekend. Will she forget her friends again?

The thing is this: if we have friends, we must spend time with them; if they want us to be their friend, they must spend time with us. If we want to be God's friend, we must spend time with him. God wants to be our friend and wants to spend time with us. So every morning this week, how about just sitting and praying to God for a couple of minutes, or maybe before bed? Spend time with God; he wants to spend time with you.

Last week we learned that God will keep us secure, that he protects us. This week we found out that God wants to spend time with us as well. Mrs Thompson's girls were bad, but that was nothing compared to the boys. Next week we are going to meet the first boy, Harvey.

③ Come, Follow Me!

	Programme	Item
Section 1	**Welcome**	
	Rules	
	Prayer	
	Praise	
	Game 1	Crawling
	Praise (x2)	
	Fun Item 1	
	Game 2	Wheelbarrow
	Fun Item 2	
	Bible Text	Matthew 4:19
	Announcements	
	Interview	
	Worship (x2)	
Section 2	**Bible Lesson**	Matthew 4:19
Preaching	**Illustration 1**	George Washington
Time	**Illustration 2**	Lemmings
	Illustration 3	Bananas
	Story	Mrs Thompson's Class – Harvey
	Prayer	

Overview An old Zulu parable says: "I can't hear what you're saying because what you are is screaming in my face." While it is important to learn from the example of Jesus, it is also important that we learn whose example we should and shouldn't follow. And also, do *we* set a good example or not?

games

Game 1

Crawling

PREPARATION	None.
PLAYERS	Six players per team.
SET-UP	Players line up in relay formation at A.
OBJECT	The first person crawls on their hands and knees from A to B and back, making sounds like a baby. The next person then goes.
WINNING	The first team complete and sitting down wins.

Game 2

Wheelbarrow

PREPARATION	None.
PLAYERS	Six players per team.
SET-UP	Players line up in relay formation at A.
OBJECT	Person one wheelbarrows person two from A to B. They then swap roles: person two wheelbarrows person one back. Then the next pair go and so on.
WINNING	The first team complete and sitting down wins.

Preaching Time

 **BIBLE LESSON** **MATTHEW 4:19**

"Come, follow me!"
(Matthew 4:19, New International Version)

When someone says to us, "Follow me", it's important that we don't just follow anyone. It's important that the people we follow can be trusted.

This request, "Follow me", written in a Bible book called Matthew, was spoken by someone who can always be trusted, someone who loves you and me very much. None other than Jesus himself said it.

Jesus was looking for disciples – a disciple is someone who follows – and he turned up on the shores of the Sea of Galilee and saw some fishermen. "Follow me," he said.

They dropped their nets and followed Jesus. It was a good decision. We must be careful who we follow, but we will always be OK if we follow Jesus. Jesus sets us a good example to follow.

"Come, follow Jesus."

 **Illustration 1**

George Washington

Object needed: *A picture of George Washington.*

Once, during the American War of Independence, an accident happened as several of the American troops were travelling along a muddy path. A wagon they were using overturned and blocked the road. The captain of the troops lined up several of the men and shouted at them to push and push and push, to try and turn the wagon back over.

When the wagon wouldn't budge, the captain got even more annoyed. He shouted louder at his men to push. After some time a man on horseback arrived at the place where the wagon had turned over and asked: "Captain, why don't you help these men rather than just shout at them?"

But the captain was amazed at the request. "I am their captain," he replied. "I should not dirty my uniform in such a manner."

With that, the man got off his horse. His uniform was already dirty. He walked over to the men and said, "I will help! Let's push again."

Now with the help of this stranger, the wagon was pushed upright. The captain was glad that the wagon was restored but annoyed that this stranger should interfere. As the stranger got back onto his horse the captain demanded: "Who are you, sir? What gives you the right to interfere in my affairs?"

The man, now on horseback, smiled. "I am General George Washington and I interfere because you are in my army. And from now on, Captain, you will lead by example."

The captain didn't know how to answer. So he simply said, "Yes, sir!"

That day the captain learned the importance of leading by example. Do we give a good example for others to follow or not?

Lemmings

Object needed: *A copy of the computer game "Lemmings", if possible. Show the box, or, if possible, project the game onto a large screen.*

I don't know if any of you have ever played this game. It's a lot of fun and really hard to stop playing. I used to play this for hours and hours. It's all about a really strange animal called a lemming. The lemmings follow each other no matter what. If the one at the front runs off the edge of a cliff, then all the other lemmings do

exactly the same – until you have hundreds of these lemmings jumping off cliffs.

It's crazy, really. But some of you are just as crazy! You follow people who really are not very good examples at all. I follow Jesus, because he always gives me a good example. You follow people who smoke, or who get drunk, or who damage things, or who are always in fights. If you are one of those who follow people like that, then you are as crazy as these lemmings. You must learn to follow Jesus; he will always give you a good example.

Bananas

Objects needed: *Bananas and blindfolds.*

(This illustration is also used in the Ultimate Curriculum, Volume 1.)

Choose one person from each team to stand at the front (make sure they like bananas). Blindfold the three volunteers. Ask the three teams to cheer for the three people. Inform all your cheering groups that no matter what happens they must keep cheering for their team member.

Give each of the volunteers a banana and tell them that when you shout "Go!" they are to eat the banana as fast as they can, but one of their hands must be kept behind their backs. When they finish they are to rip the blindfold off.

Shout "Go!" Now quickly remove the blindfolds of the two end people and return them to their seats leaving the middle person to race against himself while the rest laugh a lot, but also keep cheering for the three people. (It works best if you stand at the side as soon as the momentum starts. So when the victim eventually rips off his blindfold he is left standing alone looking a bit lost.)

You see, if we do things just because our friends are doing them, or even because we *think* our friends are doing them, we can look very silly indeed.

Ask the volunteer to return to his seat – thanking him for being such a good sport. You've dented his ego so make sure you re-inflate it!

As soon as the game is finished remind the

children that this is preaching time and, although you appreciated their help in the little game, it is quiet time now.

● STORY – Mrs Thompson's Class – Harvey

Mrs Thompson prayed every day for all the children in her class, but she prayed especially hard for Harvey.

Harvey wasn't really bad. But he was the class leader. He was the person who set an example for everyone else and most of the rest of the class followed him. When the class made a visit to Salisbury to see Stonehenge he was the person who jumped over the fence to get a better look at the stones – and the rest of the class had followed him. There was nothing wrong with Harvey being the leader, but Mrs Thompson prayed that Harvey would learn to be a good example.

Mrs Thompson knew that God always heard her prayers, but she didn't realise that God had decided to show Harvey just how important it is to set a good example. God would let Harvey see for himself how sad it could be when he set a bad example. It happened one weekend.

Harvey had rushed home from school on Friday evening and had spent the entire evening sorting out his bag, his rod, his bait, his nets, his sandwiches... Tomorrow he was going fishing. He heard the weather man say it was going to be sunny, so he was going down to the river and he was going to catch fish, lots of fish. He was going to lie in the sun and have a nice time. He went to bed after the weather forecast and slept very well; he was up at 8 a.m. and ready for fishing. Then it happened – the disaster hit. He was just finishing his breakfast when his mum came down and asked, "Where are you going so early, Harvey?"

"Fishing, Mum. It's a perfect day for it," he replied.

"Oh no you're not! We told you months ago that your father and I had a trip to London planned for today and you were to look after Sophie."

Harvey couldn't believe it. He knew his mum was right, but he'd forgotten about it. This had been going to be such a good day, and now he was going to spend it trapped in the house with his little whirlwind sister. It wasn't that he didn't love his sister. He really did. But she was such a pickle; she was always sneaking into his room and playing with his computer or messing up his books or hanging around behind him like a shadow.

Sophie didn't mean to be a nuisance; she just loved her brother and wanted to be with him all the time. Several times, Mrs Thompson had to send her back to her own classroom because she wanted to stay in Harvey's class. Of course Sophie couldn't stay in Harvey's class – she was only four and was supposed to be in the nursery class. But she did so love her brother.

Well, there it was. Whether Harvey liked it or not, he was looking after his sister for the day. Sophie didn't get up until 9 a.m., by which time their parents had left. But she was looking forward to having a fun day with her brother. She was dressed in her favourite yellow T-shirt, her dungarees with the picture of Chuckie from *Rugrats* on the front and her little pink trainers.

"Hi, Harvey! What are we going to do today?"

It was then that Harvey had the idea. Maybe he didn't have to stay in the house. Maybe he could take Sophie fishing too. He knew she'd scare the fish, but at least it was better than being in the house all day.

"Eat your breakfast, Sophie. We're going fishing."

Sophie crinkled up her face: "Are you sure, Harvey? Mummy says that I shouldn't go near the river."

"She means by yourself! You'll be OK with me. Come on, eat up."

And so just after 10 a.m. Harvey and little sister Sophie set off for the river, Harvey carrying the fishing rods and Sophie carrying a really heavy bucket. She didn't know what was in the bucket; Harvey wouldn't tell her. He hadn't told her because if Sophie had found out she was carrying a bucket full of worms she would never have agreed to carry it.

At 11:30 a.m. they arrived at the river bank. Harvey put down the big blanket, opened the bucket (much to Sophie's horror), and began to get his fishing rod ready. Sophie didn't have a fishing rod, but she so wanted to be like her brother that she got a stick and put some string on the end and pretended to fish as well. It really was going very well. By 1 p.m. Harvey had caught five fish, and Sophie hadn't scared any of them away.

But by 2 p.m. Sophie was getting hot. It was a beautiful day – the sun shone down, the birds sang in the trees, and butterflies flew past. But Sophie was thirsty and although Harvey had brought sandwiches (which they'd eaten before 12 noon), he'd forgotten about pop.

By 2:30 p.m. Sophie was unbearable. Harvey knew that he'd have to get something to drink.

There was a shop not too far away, only about 500 metres, except it was on the other side of the river. There was a bridge, but that was a long way upstream. There was another way across – there was an old water pipe which stretched across the river. It wasn't very thick, but Harvey had balanced across it before. He told Sophie to stay where she was, to sit and watch the rod and not to go anywhere until he came back.

Then he set off. Sophie watched in amazement as Harvey balanced across the pipe. She was so proud of her brother: he could do anything. Harvey balanced across to the other side and went to the shop. The sign on the door said, "Back in five minutes."

Harvey waited. Sophie waited as well, wondering where her brother was. Ten minutes later the shopkeeper finally came back and Harvey bought the cans of pop. But Sophie had got tired of waiting. She had walked over to the pipe and looked across.

"Surely I can do this," she thought to herself.

It must be OK – after all, Harvey had done it. She put one foot onto the pipe and then the other foot. She was balancing on the pipe. She began to walk…

Harvey hurried back from the shop. He didn't like leaving his sister alone for so long. But he wasn't ready for the sight that greeted him when he arrived at the pipe. There in the middle of the pipe was Sophie, balancing. She lifted up her head and saw Harvey coming and shouted, "Harvey! Look at me! I'm doing what you did. I'm just like you, Harvey!"

But just then, to Harvey's horror, Sophie lost her balance, screamed… and Harvey's little four-year-old sister tumbled head first into the river and was immediately pulled downstream. Harvey dropped the pop and ran down the side of the bank, shouting.

God watched. He watched as a young boy called Harvey learned what happens when we set a bad example. That's why Jesus gave us a good example to follow.

Sophie disappeared under the water.

"Sophie, where are you?" Harvey screamed.

It seemed like forever before her head popped back up. "Harvey, help me!" Sophie shouted.

Harvey dived in. He swam with all his might towards his little sister. "Hold on, Soph!" he cried. "I'm coming!"

Harvey swam like he'd never swum before, until he eventually grabbed his little sister. He pulled her head out of the water and held on tight. He hadn't thought what he would do next. He just wanted to save his sister. Anything might have happened if an old fisherman hadn't seen them rushing towards him. He quickly grabbed a round life preserver from the side of the river and threw it towards Harvey. "Catch this!" he shouted.

Harvey grabbed. He missed. He tried again and again. Then he had it. He held tight as he and Sophie were pulled to safety. The fisherman drove them straight home, just in time to meet their parents on the driveway. They had a lot of explaining to do, but at least they were safe.

Mrs Thompson had prayed hard for Harvey. Today he had learned how really important it was to set a good example. God smiled – it was important that Harvey learned how to set a good example. One day he would be a great leader for God.

So far we've learned that…
- **God wants to keep us SECURE.**
- **God wants to spend TIME with us.**
- **God is our EXAMPLE to do right.**

There are only two parts left. Next week we'll find out about something called ENCOURAGEMENT. And next week Mrs Thompson has to deal with Clara, a girl who just can't do anything.

Surely I Am With You Always

	Programme	Item
Section 1	**Welcome**	
	Rules	
	Prayer	
	Praise	
	Game 1	Three-legged Race
	Praise (x2)	
	Fun Item 1	
	Game 2	Sack Race
	Fun Item 2	
	Bible Text	Matthew 28:20
	Announcements	
	Interview	
	Worship (x2)	
Section 2 **Preaching** **Time**	**Bible Lesson**	Matthew 28:20
	Illustration 1	Lifting The Whole Block
	Illustration 2	Gauntlet
	Illustration 3	It Takes The Whole Village
	Story	Mrs Thompson's Class – Clara
	Prayer	

Overview God never intended us to live our lives alone and in isolation. He surrounded us with other people: people who can encourage and help us; people who will support and lift us up when we fall. There are lots of people who criticise. It's great when we have friends who encourage us.

Games

Game 1

Three-legged Race

PREPARATION	A piece of cord per team.
PLAYERS	Six players per team.
SET-UP	Players line up in relay formation at A in pairs. The legs of the first two people are tied together.
OBJECT	The first pair runs from A to B and back, and then the next pair, etc.
WINNING	The first team complete and sitting down wins.

Game 2

Sack Race

PREPARATION	A potato sack per team.
PLAYERS	Six players per team.
SET-UP	Players line up in relay formation at A.
OBJECT	The first person hops in the sack from A to B and back, and then the next person gets into the sack and sets off.
WINNING	The first team complete and sitting down wins.

Preaching Time

BIBLE LESSON

MATTHEW 28:20

"And surely I will be with you always, to the very end of the age." (Matthew 28:20, New International Version)

This is the last promise Jesus made before he went back to heaven. But it is one of my favourite promises of the whole Bible. It is my guarantee that I will never have to do things alone. Just like you, I sometimes have to do things which are difficult. In fact, sometimes I have to do things which I really find *very* difficult.

The first time I had to speak to children, I felt very afraid. But Jesus promised me, "I am always with you." So when I stand in front of people, I don't feel afraid. Jesus is with me, helping me, looking after me.

Whenever I have to do things which I find difficult (and sometimes God asks me to do things I find difficult), I know that Jesus – now remember, Jesus is God – is with me and helping me. And the most exciting part is this: How long will Jesus be with me? The Bible says he will be with me "always, to the very end of the age". That means Jesus will be there with me forever. If you are a Christian, he's with you as well.

Illustration 1

Lifting The Whole Block

Object needed: *A weightlifting bar.*

We all have problems that we can't solve, things we find very difficult to do. It's like trying to lift a heavy weight all by ourselves – like this one here. *(Try and lift the weight.)*

However, unlike weightlifting bars, which are supposed to be lifted by one person *(try and lift the weight again)*, problems and difficulties are not meant to be sorted out alone. God gave us friends and families. The Bible teaches us that when we become Christians, we not only have our real family, but we also end up with lots of other family. Other Christians become like our brothers and sisters, all there to help us. So there's no need to try and do everything alone. God helps us, and our friends help us.

It's good to be a Christian.

Gauntlet

Object needed: *A picture of an archer.*

A couple of years ago, there
was an arcade game called
"Gauntlet". It was a lot like
games such as "Sonic" in
that the idea was to collect
as many coins and other
bits of treasure as possible.
But, in "Gauntlet" there
were many monsters trying
to stop your progress. You
were given a choice of
characters, such as Elf who

was an excellent archer, Warrior who was strong
with his arms and a Lady character who was an
expert with a sword. I would always play the Elf
character.

The game was the most fun when you played
at the same time as other players. One would be
the Elf, one the Warrior and one the Lady. It
meant that the Lady could fight her way through
certain problems with the sword, then they
would all hide behind the Elf as he used his
arrows to destroy the monsters before they came
too close. Then the Warrior would break through
the walls and allow the players to get to the
treasure. When everyone worked together, the
best results happened. It was then that the
highest scores were achieved.

Christians are not meant to deal with
everything alone. When we learn to work
together and help each other, and also when we
learn to let God help us, then we get the best
results.

It Takes The Whole Village

Needed: *Four girls.*

GIRL 1 is an electrician. *GIRL 2* is a plumber.
GIRL 3 is a carpenter and *GIRL 4* is a bricklayer.

What could *GIRL 1* do if she worked alone? Well,
she could probably wire your house with
electricity, wire a plug, replace fuses. *GIRL 2*
could unblock your toilet, fix your leaking pipes.
GIRL 3 could build you some tables and chairs.
GIRL 4 could put up a nice brick wall. This is
what they could do if they worked alone. But if
they worked together, there is nothing they
could not do. If they worked together, they could
build whole houses, and not only build them,
they could wire them with electricity, put in the
sinks, toilets and central heating, build kitchen
units, and make tables and chairs. When people
work together they can build offices, schools and
factories. While *GIRL 2* is on her own she can
unblock toilets; when she works with others she
can do anything.

In Africa they have a proverb that says: "It
takes a whole village to build a child."

It means that we all have to work together to
help each other. The adults help the children; the
children help the adults; the children help each
other; God helps us all. We need each other. We
need to work together, to help each other and
solve one another's problems. We also need to
know that God is always there to help us, as we
try our best to do what he wants.

● STORY – Mrs Thompson's Class – Clara

It was Thursday evening and Clara was sad. Very
sad! She had watched as her mother read yet
another school report from Mrs Thompson
explaining that Clara was bottom of the class.
Clara was last in mathematics, last in gym, last in
English, last in science, last, last, last. But this
report was worse than the rest. Mrs Thompson
had written a comment on the bottom that read:

"Clara will resit all her tests on Monday
morning. If she fails them again, then I will have
to recommend that Clara restarts this year from
scratch when all her friends go up to the next
school."

Clara's mother didn't know what to say to
her. She knew her daughter tried her best, but
she just didn't find it easy to pass tests. She spent
hours in her bedroom reading the books, but she
just couldn't remember what she had read.

"I am useless!" Clara announced to her
mother.

"No you're not, honey! It'll be all right." Her
mother tried to comfort her.

Clara went to bed and slept as well as she
could. The next morning she set off for school. It
didn't take long before everyone in the

playground knew what was going on. When it came to time for registration, all the children were busy whispering together. It seemed certain that Clara would have to retake the year. Her friends weren't sure what to do. The amazing thing was that even though Clara didn't think she was any good and didn't like herself very much, the rest of her class liked her very much and really wanted to help. They just didn't know what to do, until Harvey had an idea.

Harvey called the class together secretly at lunchtime. Clara saw them all in a corner of the playground chatting; she simply thought that they had decided not to talk to her any more, now that they knew she was going to have to restart the year and not go to the next school with them. She couldn't have been more wrong.

School finished at 3:30 p.m. Clara collected all her things.

"Remember, Clara! The tests are on Monday. Just do your best!" Mrs Thompson urged.

Mrs Thompson asked God to take care of Clara, but even Mrs Thompson felt that no more could be done and Clara was going to have to retake the year.

Clara walked home slowly. She didn't need reminding about the tests. But there was nothing she could do. She had tried her best before and that was that! She tried to eat her dinner, but just didn't feel hungry. She sat in front of the television, but felt guilty about not trying to learn for her tests. She made her way upstairs and tried to read through her books, but they were just too hard. It was then that it started…

At 5 p.m. there was a knock on the door. Clara heard some sort of garbled conversation take place downstairs, and a couple of minutes later Kelly walked into her bedroom.

"Hi, Clara, how's it going? I'm here to help. Get your maths book."

And that was that. For the next two hours Kelly showed Clara how to do every mathematical calculation ever. At just past 7:30 p.m. Kelly left, shouting over her shoulder, "See you on Sunday!"

Clara couldn't remember planning anything for Sunday. She walked back upstairs, her head hurting. Ten minutes later there was another knock on the door, some more garbled conversation, and in walked Jodi.

"Hi, Clara, time for English."

Clara just sat as Jodi explained to her all about capital letters, commas, full stops, exclamation marks, quotation marks… the list went on.

At just after 9 p.m. Jodi left, shouting over her shoulder, "See you tomorrow night! I'd get a good night's sleep now – Harvey will be round at 9 a.m."

Clara was really confused, but she went straight to bed, her head aching with all this studying.

Sure enough, 9 a.m. came and there was a knock on the door. Clara's mum shouted up: "It's Harvey for you, Clara. He says you'll need to wear your tracksuit."

Clara didn't know what was going on; she just did as she was told. And for the next four hours she did sit-ups, press-ups, cartwheels, Arab springs and running with Harvey. She had just got out of the shower at 2 p.m. when Jodi was back.

"OK, Clara, time for a little history lesson," Jodi pronounced.

At 6 p.m. Kelly was back and produced her book on geography. Three hours later Clara went to bed. At 9 a.m. next morning Harvey was back, this time not with a tracksuit, but with all his science books. Straight after lunch, Kelly was back to help Clara with some art work. At 7 p.m. Clara went to bed exhausted. She didn't know who had planned it all, she didn't know if it would work, but she was really glad that she had friends – friends who were there for her.

She woke early on Monday morning. She prayed a prayer asking Jesus to look after her in the tests and set off for school.

Mrs Thompson brought the first test, then the next, then the next. And so the day went on. It ended with gym in the hall, in which Clara had to show Mrs Thompson a short routine.

That night Clara didn't know if she'd passed or failed. All her friends showed up on the doorstep at 7 p.m. They took Clara to McDonalds and told her not to worry. Clara was so glad she had friends. She began to feel better about herself. "If everyone else likes me and will do all this to help me, then maybe I should like myself too," Clara reasoned.

Clara didn't have to wait long for the results. When she got home her mum was waiting.

"I think your friends should hear this too. Call them in," said Mum. Clara's friends all came in.

"I wanted you all to hear this," Clara's mum began, "because I think you all had a big part to play. Mrs Thompson just dropped by with the test results and she is very, very pleased. Clara can stay with the class! Mrs Thompson is delighted with the results!"

They all cheered and then they gathered around the exam paper to look. It read:

Mathematics...	B
History...	A
Science...	B
Geography...	B+
English...	B+

It really was a great report. Clara only got a C for gym, but she wasn't too worried about that. It's good to know that God gives us friends and families who care for us.

Mrs Thompson was pleased as well. But next week she would face the hardest problem of them all: Timothy Winters!

Love Your Neighbour As Yourself

	Programme	Item
Section 1	**Welcome**	
	Rules	
	Prayer	
	Praise	
	Game 1	Backwards Run
	Praise (x2)	
	Fun Item 1	
	Game 2	Kangaroo
	Fun Item 2	
	Bible Text	Luke 10:27
	Announcements	
	Interview	
	Worship (x2)	
Section 2	**Bible Lesson**	The Good Samaritan
Preaching	**Illustration 1**	Feelings
Time	**Illustration 2**	1 Corinthians 13
	Story	Mrs Thompson's Class – Timothy
	Prayer	

Overview Jesus taught us to love our neighbours as we love ourselves. We live in a world where people need to feel loved. It's time to show that love – the love of God.

games

Preaching Time

Game 1

Backwards Run

PREPARATION	None.
PLAYERS	Six players per team.
SET-UP	Players line up in relay formation at A.
OBJECT	The first person goes from A to B and back, running backwards. The next person then goes.
WINNING	The first team complete and sitting down wins.

BIBLE LESSON THE GOOD SAMARITAN (LUKE 10)

"Love your neighbour as yourself." (Luke 10:27, New International Version)

Invite the children to act out the following story.

This is a story Jesus told:

"A man was going down from Jerusalem to Jericho, when he fell into the hands of robbers. They stripped him of his clothes, beat him and went away, leaving him half-dead. A priest happened to be going down the same road, and when he saw the man, he passed by on the other side. So too, a Levite, when he came to the place and saw him, passed by on the other side. But a Samaritan, as he travelled, came where the man was; and when he saw him, he took pity on him. He went to him and bandaged his wounds, pouring on oil and wine. Then he put the man on his own donkey, brought him to an inn and took care of him.

"The next day he took out two silver coins and gave them to the innkeeper. 'Look after him,' he said, 'and when I return, I will reimburse you for any extra expense you may have.'

"Which of these three do you think was a neighbour to the man who fell into the hands of robbers?"

The expert in the law replied, "The one who had mercy on him." Jesus told him, "Go and do likewise."

Game 2

Kangaroo

PREPARATION	None.
PLAYERS	Six players per team.
SET-UP	Players line up in relay formation at A.
OBJECT	The first person hops upright like a kangaroo from A to B and back. The next person then goes.
WINNING	The first team complete and sitting down wins.

Feelings

Object needed: *A whiteboard or a big sheet of white paper to write on.*

We all have feelings. We all have emotions. Different things that happen to us cause us to feel different things. Let's see if we can write down some of those words together.

When people are kind to me and considerate to me, I feel… *(Invite the children to shout out adjectives; write them down as they do so.)*

When they are gentle and nice to me, I feel… *(Keep on writing.)*

But what about when people are cruel and nasty to me? Then I feel… *(Write down this list also.)*

So if people are kind to me, I feel all these positive feelings. If they are unkind to me, I feel all these sorts of negative feelings. The amazing thing is this: people usually treat us the way we treat them. If you want to experience all these negative feelings then make others feel these negatives. If you want to feel all these positive feelings, then help others to experience all these positive feelings.

I know which sort of feelings I want to feel, so I'm going to do my best to treat people in a good way, so that I can feel good too.

1 Corinthians 13

Tell the children that this is a part of 1 Corinthians 13, a portion from the Bible, and that they should listen carefully.

> What if I could speak all languages
> of humans and of angels?
> If I did not love others,
> I would be nothing more than a
> noisy gong or a clanging cymbal.
> What if I could prophesy and understand all
> secrets and all knowledge?

> And what if I had faith that moved
> mountains?
> I would be nothing, unless I loved others.

> Love is kind and patient, never
> jealous, boastful, proud or rude.
> Love isn't selfish or quick tempered.
> It doesn't keep a record of
> wrongs that others do.
> Love rejoices in the truth, but not in evil.
> Love is always supportive, loyal, hopeful
> and trusting. Love never fails!

> For now there are faith, hope and love.
> But of these three, the greatest is love.

● STORY – Mrs Thompson's Class – Timothy

For today's story, you need a file containing sheets of paper.

It was the very first day of the new term and everyone was pushing and shoving to be the first into the new classroom. This was a Year Six class and they thought if they could get in first they could have the best seats. Eventually they were all inside and sitting down. In walked Mrs Thompson. She stood at the front of the class and said: "OK, Year Six. I want you to know something. In my class there will be no favourites. I will treat everyone exactly the same. Is that clear?"

This was quite a tough Year Six class, but they were just a little bit frightened of Mrs Thompson, so they nodded and said, "Yes, Miss".

Well, Mrs Thompson was true to her word: she really did have no favourites. She treated Robin the same as she treated Jacob, and Alex the same as she treated Stephanie. She treated everyone exactly the same.

Well, nearly everyone. You see, there was one little boy, named Timothy, who was the rudest, most obnoxious, most irritating and horrible boy you could ever hope to meet. When Mrs Thompson asked everyone to stand, he would sit. When she asked everyone to stand in line, he would step out; when she asked everyone to be quiet, he would talk; and when she asked everyone to sit down, he would stand on his desk. He really was the most obnoxious, rude, irritating and horrible boy. Mrs Thompson really didn't like him much at all – even though she tried to hide it.

The rest of the class didn't like Timothy much either, not because he was rude, irritating, obnoxious and horrible, but for something they thought was much worse: Timothy was smelly!!! He wasn't just a little bit smelly; he was absolutely gross. You could smell him from 100 metres away.

There was of course a reason why Timothy was smelly. Actually, there were two reasons. The first was simply that he never washed. His hair would stick up in the air, not with gel but with grease. His face and hands were grimy and muddy, his neck was black and he never ever washed under his armpits.

The second reason why Timothy smelled was that he never changed his clothes. His jeans were covered in oil and mud and grass stains and had rips all over. His T-shirt used to be white, but now you could see what Timothy had eaten for the last two months. It had baked beans juice in the corner, tomato ketchup down the front, curry sauce in the middle and Coke splattered everywhere. He never ever changed his socks. Well, he did change them once and they were so bad he could stick them to the wall.

Now, as you can imagine, nobody wanted to be his friend. He spent a lot of time in the playground by himself. Let's face it, would you have been his friend?

Christmas time came around. It was a bit of a tradition that at Christmas everyone would bring in presents for Mrs Thompson. So that's what the children did. There were presents wrapped in gold wrapping paper, presents wrapped in Father Christmas paper, presents wrapped in strawberry red, striped paper. There really were all sorts of presents. And there, lying at the bottom of the pile, was a present wrapped in a brown paper bag. And that present was from…

Allow the children to answer.

Mrs Thompson pushed that present to one side; she was a little bit worried about what she would find inside. She opened the gold-wrapped present – it was a lovely pair of gloves! She opened the striped paper present – a new ruler! She unwrapped a scarf, a new pencil case, a new globe. And then after she had opened all the rest, she came to the final present: the one wrapped in the brown paper bag.

She held the corners of the bag and carefully let the contents fall onto the desk. She looked down and couldn't believe her eyes. There was a bottle of perfume and a bracelet. But, when she looked more closely, she could see that the perfume bottle was nearly empty and the bracelet was beginning to rust.

All the children in the class started to laugh and bang on the desks, chanting, "Timothy's smelly, Timothy's smelly."

Timothy didn't know what to do. He could feel his eyes stinging as he tried to hold back the tears. He had brought in the best presents he had. The class kept chanting, "Timothy's smelly, Timothy's smelly."

Timothy slid down in his chair so that he was nearly under the desk. His eyes couldn't hold back the tears any longer and they ran down his face. Mrs Thompson knew she had to do something, so she grabbed the perfume and sprayed some on. "Isn't that lovely, boys and girls?" she asked.

They all thought, "No, Miss, it's horrible," but they all replied, "Yes, Miss."

Mrs Thompson then put the bracelet on and said, "Isn't that lovely, boys and girls?"

They all thought, "No, Miss, it's horrible," but they all replied, "Yes, Miss."

Mrs Thompson then stood up and announced: "Because you've been so kind and brought me all these presents, you may go home early."

So they all made their way out, until only two people were left in the classroom: Mrs Thompson and…

Let the children guess who.

Timothy walked up to Mrs Thompson and said, "Mrs Thompson, thank you for wearing that bracelet and putting on the perfume. When you did that it reminded me so much of my mother!"

And with that he turned and walked out of the room. Mrs Thompson was now seriously confused. She really didn't know what was going on. She went to the cupboard and pulled out Timothy's reports from when he was in Year Three, and she began to read.

Pull out the file and pretend to read the sheets.

"Year Three: Timothy is a very clever boy. He does well in class. His appearance is always neat and tidy."

Mrs Thompson thought she was reading the wrong report. She checked the file again. It was definitely his. She read on.

"Year Four: Timothy is a very clever boy. He does well in class. His appearance is always neat and tidy."

Then Mrs Thompson noticed some words at the very bottom in a section called "Comments". They read: "Timothy is finding it increasingly hard to concentrate right now, as his mother is really ill." Mrs Thompson continued reading.

"Year Five: Timothy's work has gone from bad to worse. His appearance has gone from bad to worse. His attitude has gone from bad to worse. He's becoming rude and obnoxious. And he's beginning to smell." Then, in brackets at the bottom of the page in the "Comments" section were these words: "Timothy's mother died this year."

And here he was in Year Six. Yes, he was smelly, but that was because his mother had died and his father was so upset that he spent every evening crying and not looking after Timothy. Timothy was so upset that he started being rude and nasty.

If you had known why Timothy was like that, how many of you would have wanted to be his friend?

Expect a lot of hands to go up.

Not everyone whose mum or dad dies becomes like Timothy. Everyone is sad when it happens, but most people learn to cope. Most people don't become rude or irritating or obnoxious or smelly like Timothy, but some do.

You see, the problem is this: people like Timothy are usually too embarrassed or too upset to tell us why they are so upset or why they look dirty. And that's why in a book called the Bible there's a verse which says, "Love one another."

It simply means that we are to look after each other and take care of each other, no matter how the other person looks or acts.

We are responsible very often for making people lonely. But, if we really try, we can be responsible for helping lonely people by being their friend and looking out for them.

Tommy Thomas, Jedi Knight

A Series in Six Parts

Introduction

Title	Themes covered
1 Anakin Skywalker	Our world needs heroes
2 Obi-Wan Kenobi	Discipleship
3 Yoda And The Jedi Council	The need for leaders
4 Qui-Gon Jinn	God wants to use you
5 Queen Amidala	Pretending to be something we're not
6 Darth Maul	We have an enemy

 Series Overview

Star Wars: Episode 1 – The Phantom Menace, the long-awaited prequel to *Star Wars*, was finally released in 1999. This series looks at the characters in the movie one by one and draws from each a biblical principle. This gives you a great opportunity to give away lots of *Star Wars* merchandise. Use it as a mechanism to invite and attract new children to your children's gatherings.

The series looks at the need for heroes, the call to discipleship, the need to be ourselves and the awareness of God's enemy.

① Anakin Skywalker

	Programme	Item
Section 1	**Welcome**	
	Rules	
	Prayer	
	Praise	
	Game 1	Pod Racer
	Praise (x2)	
	Fun Item 1	
	Game 2	Hyperdrive Repairs
	Fun Item 2	
	Bible Text	1 Corinthians 1:27
	Announcements	
	Interview	
	Worship (x2)	
Section 2 Preaching Time	**Bible Lesson**	Peter The Fisherman
	Illustration 1	*Star Wars* (Anakin)
	Illustration 2	Rugby
	Illustration 3	Young Heroes
	Story	Tommy Thomas, Jedi Knight (1)
	Prayer	

Overview Anakin comes from Tatooine, a small planet miles from anywhere. It is interesting that God usually draws his heroes out of obscurity and chooses to make them great. Not many wise people are chosen, not many clever people. God chooses the weak to confound the strong.

Game ①

Pod Racer

PREPARATION	A trike per team or some other children's racing car per team (skateboards in the case of an emergency).
PLAYERS	Six players per team.
SET-UP	The smallest player sits in the car. The others take it in turns (relay formation) to push the car from A to B and back again.
OBJECT	To complete the race first.
WINNING	The first team complete and sitting down wins.

Game ②

Hyperdrive Repairs

PREPARATION	The letters of the word HYPERDRIVE are placed at B on individual cards. One set for each team.
PLAYERS	Four players per team.
SET-UP	Three players stand in relay formation at A. The fourth player is going to assemble the letters at A.
OBJECT	The first person on each team runs from A to B, collects a letter and then returns. The next player then sets off, while the "mechanic" tries to put together the word HYPERDRIVE.
WINNING	The first team back and sitting down with the completed word wins.

PreachingTime

BIBLE LESSON PETER THE FISHERMAN

"But God chose the foolish things of the world to shame the wise." (1 Corinthians 1:27, New International Version)

Peter wasn't special. He wasn't a prime minister. He wasn't a king. He hadn't been to university; he probably hadn't been to school much. He wasn't particularly clever; I don't think he was particularly handsome. He wasn't anything really. Well, that's not strictly true – he was something: he was a fisherman, maybe not a good fisherman (he didn't seem to catch many fish), but nonetheless, a fisherman.

But Peter became one of the disciples, although he was not clever, not cool, not famous, not… the list could go on and on. You see, the God who deliberately chooses people whom nobody else thinks much about, chose Peter.

Over the coming weeks, as part of this *Star Wars* series, we're going to learn about Peter and the amazing things which happened to a very ordinary man.

Illustration 1

Star Wars (Anakin)

Object needed: *A picture of Anakin.*

When we first meet Anakin Skywalker, he is working hard in Watto's shop. He is a young boy, but he is also a slave. Watto owns Anakin and his mother. But although Anakin is a slave, he is still very kind and he is quick to offer shelter to Qui-Gon and Padmé.

Anakin takes his new friends back to his house where his mum, although surprised to see so many people in her tiny home, is nonetheless very hospitable. It is over the dinner table that Qui-Gon discovers that Anakin has Jedi skills. He may have been small, he may have seemed insignificant, he may have been a slave, but he was going to be a hero. He would shortly race in the pod race championship and win his freedom. He would be trained as a Jedi. This insignificant slave from Tatooine would become a hero of great renown.

I think it is incredible that even in a movie like *Star Wars* the hero is a child – someone who doesn't look like they can accomplish anything, someone who doesn't seem to be the typical hero. He doesn't have big muscles, he's not a great athlete, he's not the smartest boy in his school. He has some gifts and talents, but he appears to be a very ordinary little boy. In fact, he is worse off than you and I. He's a slave.

But he's the boy who becomes the hero, who wins the pod race, who goes on to destroy the enemy fighters. One little boy! You too can be a hero – a hero for God.

Rugby

Object needed: *A rugby ball.*

Choose several of the biggest boys to stand at the front and then choose the smallest and youngest boy in the room.

If you were picking a rugby team, who would you pick? You've got these amazing-looking, hunky boys here, and you've got the little guy on the end. Even though he's far cuter and much more handsome than the rest, he doesn't seem to be the strongest of them all. So, who would you choose? The biggest? The strongest? The fastest? The toughest? If God was going to enter a rugby tournament he would choose the youngest and the smallest. Then, he would win the tournament! God does this all the time. He chooses the people who seem weak or foolish or insignificant. Some people would say children are like that – weak, foolish, insignificant – but God uses these people to do great things. He uses them to show others that God is alive and loves them, to help the weak and hurting, to work for those in need.

God's rugby team would be amazing.

Young Heroes

Object needed: *A wine glass.*

The prisoners were as young as twelve years old. All they had to do was take a single sip from the cup to show the watching crowds that they believed the king of Rome was a god and the rightful ruler of the world, and they would be released. Around them were the crosses or the stakes on which many of their parents and relatives would die that day. In the distance they could hear the sounds of hungry animals. Some would end up thrown to the lions that day. All they had to do was drink from the cup and say that the emperor was god.

A single sip. But they would not do it. Yes, they were afraid. They sometimes wept, and they all prayed. But these were Christian young people and they would not deny Christ by saying that the king of Rome was god.

And it is said that for every Christian that died in the jaws of the lions, seven Romans became Christians. This is how the early church grew. They were young, but there is no doubt that they were heroes.

● STORY – Tommy Thomas, Jedi Knight (1)

Play the theme music to Star Wars *when you announce the title at the start and also at the end for a couple of seconds.*

Tommy Thomas was eleven years old. That meant he was in Mr Harris' class. He was "average" – well, that's what all his school reports said:

Games...	Tommy is average
English...	Tommy is average
Maths...	Tommy is average
Science...	Tommy is average

Tommy was average height, he had average-colour mousy hair, he wore average clothes. He wasn't particularly cool. He wasn't the class leader – that job went to Gordon – everyone loved Gordon. He wasn't the class joker – that job went to Jason – Jason was just so funny.

Tommy just sat in the class with the rest and was… well… average. He sat at the same table as Susan, Anna and Chris. Susan and Anna were smart; they were always working very hard. Chris was into dinosaurs; he was always drawing lots of different dinosaurs: T-rexes, pterodactyls and brontosauruses. Tommy would just sit there, and dream….

In his dreams he was a hero dressed in white. He held his lightsaber high and proud. Bullies ran away from him. Everyone loved him and wanted his autograph. He was Tommy Thomas, Jedi Knight, fearless fighter for light and truth, constantly rescuing the beautiful princess who had been captured by the evil Darth Mr Harris. The princess was always Anna. Tommy liked Anna. And so he spent most of his days dreaming. Dreaming of being a hero. Dreaming of being Tommy Thomas, Jedi Knight.

That's what he was doing right now. He was just pushing Darth Mr Harris to the ground with his fluorescent green lightsaber, just about to untie Princess Anna when…

BANG…

Mr Harris' ruler fell hard onto the desk. Tommy almost jumped out of his skin. "Tommy! What is eight times seven?"

Tommy hadn't been paying attention; he was miles away. "Ah, it's, it's, it's… a really big number, sir!" The class giggled. Mr Harris didn't giggle. He walked towards Tommy with his ruler in his hand.

"56," whispered Anna. "The answer's 56."

"56," shouted Tommy. "The answer is 56."

Mr Harris stopped and smiled: "So you were listening." He walked back to the front. Thomas smiled at Anna. She looked away.

Tommy hated Fridays. He liked the fact that it was the last day of school, but that meant field games. In the winter they played hockey, which Tommy hated, but in the summer it was even worse – it was athletics. Tommy hated running, he hated javelin, he hated long jump. He hated the whole lot! He hated the way Jason made fun of him because he was so thin; he hated the way Gordon was so brilliant at absolutely every event; he hated the way Carl picked on him in the changing rooms – Carl was a bully.

Every Friday, the same thing happened. Straight after lunch the children would line up and walk together towards the athletics field. The walk was OK; Tommy didn't mind the walk. It gave him a chance to think and to dream… Now he was Tommy Thomas, Jedi Knight, again. He wasn't walking in line with everyone else now; he was leading his own team of Jedi Knights and he was the leader; his lightsaber was at his side, ready to be drawn at the slightest sign of trouble. He held his head high as he marched, with his battalion following.

Then in the distance he saw Princess Anna. She had strayed out past Darth Mr Harris and there was a death destroyer heading straight towards her! The death destroyer let out a mighty sound…

Wait… this wasn't a dream! Suddenly Tommy was staring at a huge lorry running down the hill, and Anna really had strayed out into the road in front of it. She was going to die! Tommy looked across at Gordon; he was just staring in horror, but he wasn't moving. Mr Harris was shouting, Jason wasn't laughing now, and Anna just stood there, too afraid to move. She seemed tiny in the shadow of this huge lorry. Then Tommy ran – it was almost an instinct. Maybe in his head he was still Tommy Thomas, Jedi Knight, rushing to rescue the princess. Tommy didn't know why – he didn't think about it – he just ran as fast as he could towards Anna. He dived and pushed Anna out of the way.

Anna rolled out of the path of the lorry, and found herself on the pavement, dazed and just a little bruised.

The weak, insignificant daydreamer was a hero. God likes to take his heroes from obscurity and make them great.

Tommy looked up – and saw the enormous lorry rushing towards him! Three metres away, two metres… The driver slammed on the brakes but there was no way the lorry would stop in time. The brakes screeched.

The whole class stared at the scene, and Tommy was…

(Find out what happens next when we move to part 2 of "Tommy Thomas, Jedi Knight".)

② Obi-Wan Kenobi

	Programme	Item
Section 1	**Welcome**	
	Rules	
	Prayer	
	Praise	
	Game 1	Copy
	Praise (x2)	
	Fun Item 1	
	Game 2	Followers
	Fun Item 2	
	Bible Text	Ephesians 5:1
	Announcements	
	Interview	
	Worship (x2)	
Section 2	**Bible Lesson**	Peter (Follow Me)
Preaching	**Illustration 1**	Obi-Wan Kenobi
Time	**Illustration 2**	Promises
	Illustration 3	The Teacher
	Story	Tommy Thomas, Jedi Knight (2)
	Prayer	

 **verview** Obi-Wan was a disciple. Qui-Gon Jinn was a Jedi Knight and he had taken it upon himself to train Obi-Wan. Obi-Wan became a disciple. He had to learn to be teachable. He had to learn from another.

games

Game 1

Copy

PREPARATION	You will need a fairly fast piece of music.
PLAYERS	Everyone.
SET-UP	The leader stands at the front and the music is played.
OBJECT	The leader works through an aerobic workout. The children try and copy what he/she does.
WINNING	The team that copies best wins.

Game 2

Followers

PREPARATION	A blindfold per team.
PLAYERS	Four players per team.
SET-UP	Three players stand in relay formation. The first is blindfolded.
OBJECT	The fourth player must guide the blindfolded player from A to B and back again without touching him/her. When he/she returns to A the blindfold is placed on the second player and so it continues.
WINNING	The first team back and sitting down wins.

Preaching Time

BIBLE LESSON ## PETER (FOLLOW ME)

"Be imitators of God."
(Ephesians 5:1, New International Version)

Peter wasn't special. We established that last week. But he did do something very special. One day Jesus came to him and said, "Peter, follow me and I will make you a fisher of men."

Peter instantly left his nets and followed Jesus. He wanted to spend his life being a follower of Jesus. He wanted to be a disciple. He wanted to learn everything he could from the Son of God. Peter watched everything Jesus did. He listened to the words he spoke. Sometimes Jesus would tell him that he'd done something wrong; sometimes Jesus would tell him he'd done something right. Peter wanted to learn. And so he became a disciple.

Illustration 1

Star Wars (Obi-Wan Kenobi)

Object needed: *A picture of Obi-Wan Kenobi.*

When we first meet Obi-Wan he has just arrived on the planet of Naboo with his master Qui-Gon Jinn. He has come with his master to bring a peaceful end to a trade dispute there. It isn't long before they end up in a fight with enemy robots.

Obi-Wan is a disciple. He has chosen to be a disciple (that word "chosen" is important – nobody has forced him to become Qui-Gon's disciple). Obi-Wan wants to be a Jedi Knight and has chosen to learn the best way there is. He has chosen to let someone who already is a Jedi Knight teach him and help him. The Jedi would guide him, tell him when he was doing things right, and tell him when he was doing things wrong.

People are disciples in all sorts of things. If you want to be the best Jedi Knight you can, you train under a Jedi Knight. If you want to be the best basketball player, you train with a good basketball coach. If you want to be the best ballet dancer, you train with the best ballet teacher.

And if you want to be the best Christian, you must find a good Christian leader and learn from them. That's why we want you to come here, to learn from people who are good Christian leaders. You can learn from them how to become disciples for Jesus.

By the end of the movie, Obi-Wan has become a fully qualified Jedi Knight. He has learned his lessons well. And now he has become the master and he has a disciple of his own. The disciple's name is Anakin Skywalker.

Promises

Objects needed: *None.*

Who has ever had a friend make them a promise? Who has ever had a friend make them a promise that they didn't keep? Maybe you have heard promises like these:

"I'll be your best friend forever, I promise!"

"I'll keep the secret, I promise!"

"We won't go to the park without you, I promise!"

Lots of people make promises. Lots of people make promises they don't keep. How do you feel when someone makes a promise to you and doesn't keep it? You feel sad, hurt, upset, angry...

Can you imagine how bad Qui-Gon would feel if, after six months, Obi-Wan decided that he didn't want to be his disciple any more and instead became a starship engineer? I think Qui-Gon would be very saddened and just a little angry.

I wonder how many people have said to Jesus, "I promise to follow you forever" – and then haven't. I wonder if Jesus feels sad and hurt? I think he probably does. If we say we will follow Jesus, then that's what we need to be doing. We need to be promise-keepers and not promise-breakers.

The Teacher

Object needed: *A picture of a teacher.*

How many people like school?

Some people like school; some people don't. Do you know something interesting? Some teachers like school and some teachers don't! It must be quite difficult to try and teach children sometimes because you can't make people learn if they don't want to.

It's very similar for us. We can't make people become Christians. We can teach them what  Jesus said, but we can't make them learn. We can tell them that the only way to become a Christian is to ask God to forgive the wrong things they've done and promise to follow him, but we can't make them do it.

Some people choose to be Christians; some people choose not to. Some people choose to be followers of Jesus; some choose not to. Some become Christians (that is, Jesus disciples); some choose not to.

We can tell you that only Christians go to heaven, but that will not make you become Christians. You see, you have to choose to become a disciple. You can't be forced.

Later on, we'll let you choose.

● STORY – Tommy Thomas, Jedi Knight (2)

Play the theme music to Star Wars *when you announce the title at the start and also at the end for a couple of seconds.*

Anna rolled out of the path of the lorry, and found herself on the pavement, dazed and just a little bruised.

Tommy looked up – and saw the enormous lorry rushing towards him! Three metres away, two metres... The driver slammed on the brakes but there was no way the lorry would stop in time. The brakes screeched.

The whole class stared at the scene, and Tommy ducked and curled himself up into the tiniest ball you've ever seen. The lorry rolled over the top of him without even touching him, and when the lorry had passed, Tommy was totally unharmed. He stood up! The whole class went wild! Tommy was a hero. He had saved Anna.

As I told you last week, God is in the habit of taking those who aren't that special and making them absolute heroes.

The fuss lasted some weeks; the newspapers printed stories and took lots of pictures; then everything went back to normal. Tommy was still quite ordinary in real life, and in his dreams he was still Tommy Thomas: Jedi Knight.

Tommy was average at absolutely everything, except one thing – computers. When it came to computers Tommy was incredible. He could programme in many different computer languages, he could design and construct incredible arcade-style games, and he had developed scores of Internet websites. He was really good, so good that Mr Harris decided that Tommy should be the one to show Gordon how to use the computer. Gordon was the class leader, but he was absolutely useless at computers. Every time he tried to use the computer, things went wrong. The screen went blank; the computer crashed. It was not a pretty sight.

So Tommy was to teach him. Tommy was excited about the opportunity. In his mind Tommy became Tommy Thomas, Jedi Knight, and Gordon became his disciple. Tommy Thomas, Jedi Knight, would teach Gordon the secrets of defeating the Dark Lords. He would show him the secrets of Jedi mind control. In reality he would just show him how to start the computer up, and how to install new programs. It was fairly basic really.

But Gordon didn't think of it as exciting at all. He found the whole thing very embarrassing. Tommy may have been a hero, he may have

saved Anna a couple of weeks ago, but Gordon didn't see him as anything other than the most uncool person in the whole school, who was totally obsessed with *Star Wars*.

Tommy tried to show Gordon how to start up the computer, but Gordon was far too busy trying to look cool. He didn't want people to see him with Tommy. He wanted to look cool all the time. When Tommy tried to show him how to install software, Gordon just walked up and down the classroom trying to impress the girls.

Several weeks went past and then it came time for the end-of-term test in using the computer. Tommy got his usual A, but Gordon got an F. He didn't know how to start up the computer; he didn't even know what software was, let alone how to install it.

Mr Harris called Tommy and Gordon into his office when everyone had gone, to find out what had gone wrong. Tommy explained that he really had tried his best to teach Gordon. Gordon had to admit that Tommy had tried really hard. Gordon just hadn't tried to learn. He was too worried about other people to be a proper disciple.

How about you? Are you too concerned with what others think of you to be a proper disciple for Jesus, or are you able to make a commitment today to become a follower of Jesus? This is a promise you mustn't go back on. It is a promise to be a Christian, a follower of the King of all kings.

It's decision time. So, do you want to be a disciple – someone who learns about God? Remember, *you* must choose; nobody can force you.

(Next week: part 3 of "Tommy Thomas, Jedi Knight".)

Yoda And The Jedi Council

3

	Programme	Item
Section 1	Welcome	
	Rules	
	Prayer	
	Praise	
	Game 1	Good And Bad Directions
	Praise (x2)	
	Fun Item 1	
	Game 2	Find The Leader
	Fun Item 2	
	Bible Text	Deuteronomy 28:13
	Announcements	
	Interview	
	Worship (x2)	
Section 2 **Preaching** **Time**	Bible Lesson	Peter (Sent Out)
	Illustration 1	*Star Wars* (Yoda)
	Illustration 2	Sheep
	Illustration 3	Different Leaders
	Story	Tommy Thomas, Jedi Knight (3)
	Prayer	

Overview — We all need leaders. Leaders are people who tell us, and more importantly show us, which way to go. We all need leaders, but some of us actually need to become leaders.

games

Preaching Time

Good And Bad Directions

PREPARATION	Two treasure maps per team. One of the treasure maps contains clues to finding five chocolate bars that you have hidden; the other provides directions to nowhere in particular.
PLAYERS	Five per team.
SET-UP	Each of the teams is given two maps.
OBJECT	To discover which map is the real map and then use it to recover the chocolate bars.
WINNING	The team that finds the chocolate and identifies the real map wins.

Game 2

Find The Leader

PREPARATION	Five labels, each showing the title of a leader, at A, for example, queen, prime minister, pope, etc. Five pictures of those leaders at B.
PLAYERS	Five players per team.
SET-UP	Five players stand in relay formation.
OBJECT	The first player runs from A to B and collects a photograph. On returning to A, the correct title is attached to the photograph and the next person sets off.
WINNING	The first team back and sitting down with the correct labelling wins.

BIBLE LESSON PETER (SENT OUT)

"The Lord will make you the head, not the tail."
(Deuteronomy 28:13, New International Version)

Peter may not have appeared to be a leader. He didn't seem to have the qualifications of a leader, but God had chosen him to be a leader. One day Jesus asked Peter a very important question. He asked Peter, "Peter, who do people say that I am?"

He answered, "Some say Elijah, and others John the Baptist; some say that you are one of the prophets."

And then Jesus asked Peter, "But who do *you* say that I am?"

Peter thought for a moment and then he gave this answer: "You are the Christ, the Son of the living God."

Peter was going to be a great leader because he knew Jesus. He knew that Jesus was the Son of God. And great leaders need to be great followers. If you want to be a great leader, you must learn how to follow Jesus.

Illustration 1

Star Wars (Yoda)

Object needed: *A picture of Yoda.*

Yoda is part of the Jedi Council. He is one of the most important leaders you could ever become. He makes very important decisions; he is very wise; he never rushes or is hasty in his words. Yoda really is a great leader.

Yet, even before Master Yoda could be that leader, he too had to have been a follower, for that is the Jedi way. Each Jedi, as we learned last week, is first of all a disciple. Then, when they become a Jedi themselves, they are allowed to teach others, to become a leader. The system is very simple: before we can be a leader, we first must be a follower.

182 **Tommy Thomas, Jedi Knight**

God works on a very similar system. Before we can be a leader with God, we must first learn to serve others, to help others, to follow strong Christian leaders. If you want to be a leader (and some of you will become leaders), learn to be a good follower.

Sheep

Objects needed: *A toy sheep or a video clip from One Man and His Dog.*

Who has ever watched sheepdog trials? They really are the most amazing things. The dogs run around listening to the commands of the farmer. One sort of whistle has one meaning; another whistle means something different. It's quite interesting to watch.

But the best dogs know something about the way sheep behave. The dogs know, for example, that sheep always follow the other sheep. They know it's very difficult to stop the sheep doing that. When it comes to splitting some sheep off from the others, it becomes quite difficult because sheep just want to follow each other.

Sometimes on farms, sheep fall down holes. Now because sheep like to stay together, when one falls down a hole, sometimes the other sheep just follow them down!

People can be as stupid as sheep, as well. People sometimes decide to do things just because others are doing them. They smoke because others do it! That's stupid. They steal things because others do! That's stupid. Don't be like a sheep. Be a leader. Don't just do what others do – that's stupid. Be a leader! Do what's right.

Different Leaders

Objects needed: *The pictures from the earlier game, "Find The Leader", with the inclusion of a picture of Jesus. A bowl of water and a towel.*

There are many different leaders in the world. Many of them do different jobs. I'll hold a couple of pictures up, and you can tell me what these people do.

Hold up each of the pictures in turn* and let the children comment on the role of each person. Finally, hold up a picture of Jesus and await comments. Then begin...

Jesus is the Son of God and the best leader of them all. He was there at the creation of the world. The Bible tells us that he holds all things together by the power of his word. He can do anything; he can be anywhere; he knows everything. But Jesus, the greatest leader of them all, did something incredible. One day, he knelt down in front of his followers and washed their feet. He wanted them to know something. He wanted them to know that even though he was the greatest leader of them all, he was prepared to serve and help.

If we want to be great leaders (and God wants you to be great leaders), we must also learn to follow and to serve others.

*Update as necessary.

● STORY – Tommy Thomas, Jedi Knight (3)

Play the theme music to Star Wars when you announce the title at the start and also at the end for a couple of seconds.

It was that time of year again – time to choose the school president. Tommy hated the way that the people who were nominated spent the next week trying to get as many people as possible to vote for them.

But this year it would be very different.

Everyone knew that Gordon would win. Gordon was the most popular person in the whole school. Every girl in the school liked Gordon – even Anna. And all the boys looked up to him. He was the best football player, best rugby player, best at everything. Gordon was sure to win.

Everyone was so sure that Gordon would win that no one else bothered putting his or her name forward. But Mr Harris wasn't happy with this. He liked it when lots of different people were nominated to be school president. He liked the way that they tried hard to get chosen – he called this "campaigning". And he liked the fact that everyone got to vote – he called this "democracy". He was very unhappy with the fact that no one else was standing for school president. And right now Mr Harris was letting everyone in assembly know exactly how unhappy he was.

"Come on, there must be someone out there who's going to be brave enough to stand against Gordon. There must be one. Come on, we only need one person to stand up and we can do this properly," Mr Harris bellowed.

Nothing would have happened – everything would have gone without incident – except that Tommy Thomas was dreaming again. Tommy Thomas, Jedi Knight, had just rescued Princess Anna from Darth Mr Harris yet again. And now he was fighting his way past the robots; he had just reached the final stage and had to jump out of one spaceship into another. But he got so carried away with his dream that he really did jump, and in doing so, he was left standing. There in front of hundreds of other children sitting in assembly, Tommy Thomas was standing.

Mr Harris just stared. There were some sniggers and there was some laughter. Then Mr Harris started to clap his hands slowly together.

"Well, well! Tommy Thomas, you really are a surprising person. It'll be great to have you in the contest. So there it is, everyone! In one week's time we will have to decide who will be the school president: Gordon or Tommy."

Tommy really didn't know what he had done until Anna explained it to him. When he realised what he had done he was horrified. It was going to be very embarrassing. Gordon would get all the votes and he would get none, and then everyone would laugh at him – even Anna.

So Monday morning came and the campaigning, as Mr Harris called it, began. Gordon was all set. He'd had badges made, saying:

He was sticking them everywhere. He was walking all around the school trying to look cool, waving to people and smiling a lot. The vote would be on Friday. Tommy didn't do anything. He didn't think he had any chance, so he was just himself. And so the week progressed:

Monday:
- Gordon gave out hundreds and hundreds of his badges.
- Tommy helped Suzy to the school nurse after she fell and cut her leg. After all, she was only seven.

Tuesday:
- Gordon put up loads of posters with his name on them.
- Tommy did nothing at all except get totally confused during maths – Anna had to help him.

Wednesday:
- Gordon gave out free chocolate bars to everyone who said they would vote for him.
- Tommy bought dinner for one of the younger children after a bully tripped the child up and made him drop his lunch tray.

Thursday:
- Gordon arrived in school wearing a T-shirt saying "Gordon For School President".
- Tommy helped some of the ten-year-olds with their computer homework. He'd totally given up on winning the context. He never thought he had a chance anyway.

Friday:
- Gordon arrived early, wearing a T-shirt saying "The Winner".
- Tommy came late – he'd been dreaming on the way.

Throughout the morning everyone had the chance to go to the dining room and vote for the person they wanted as school president. Tommy went and voted as well. He was so sure that Gordon would win that he voted for Gordon himself. Tommy just waited patiently for the voting to finish and for the result to be announced.

He was a bit surprised when Anna came up to him during the morning, smiled at him and whispered, "I voted for you, Tommy! I hate big-heads like Gordon."

He was even more surprised when one of the older lads came to him and said, "Me and my mates have voted for you, Tommy. Thanks for helping my sister when she fell on Monday."

And so it went on. At break time the guy whom Tommy had bought dinner for came up to him and said, "I'm voting for you, mate! And so is my whole class. I told them what you did for me and they think it was a cool thing to do."

During lunch – Tommy spent most of his lunchtimes in the computer room – he received lots and lots of e-mails from people telling him that he would get their vote.

And sure enough, at the end of the day when the votes were counted, the result was amazing:

Gordon	1 vote
Tommy	400 votes

Tommy couldn't believe it. Gordon couldn't believe it either. Tommy was the new school president.

And that's what happens. People want leaders, people need leaders and God is raising up leaders. But they must be a certain type of leader. These leaders must be like Jesus, not big-heads, or pushy people.

So Tommy was school president and that was great. But Gordon was very angry and very embarrassed and he said he'd get his own back...

(Next week: part 4 of "Tommy Thomas, Jedi Knight".)

Qui-Gon Jinn

	Programme	Item
Section 1	Welcome	
	Rules	
	Prayer	
	Praise	
	Game 1	Risk Takers
	Praise (x2)	
	Fun Item 1	
	Game 2	Risk Takers In Reverse
	Fun Item 2	
	Bible Text	2 Timothy 1:7
	Announcements	
	Interview	
	Worship (x2)	
Section 2	Bible Lesson	Peter
Preaching	Illustration 1	Qui-Gon Jinn
Time	Illustration 2	The Train
	Illustration 3	The Cripple
	Story	Tommy Thomas, Jedi Knight (4)
	Prayer	

**verview** Qui-Gon Jinn was a Jedi Knight and was committed to the other Jedis. But Qui-Gon was also prepared to take risks. Sometimes, serving Jesus involves doing things which are a bit risky.

games

Game 1

Risk Takers

PREPARATION	Using chairs, tables, ropes, and anything else you can lay your hands on, construct an obstacle course.
PLAYERS	Five per team.
SET-UP	The teams stand in relay formation at A.
OBJECT	One by one the teams go through the obstacle course and back.
WINNING	The team that completes first and sits down wins.

Game 2

Risk Takers In Reverse

PREPARATION	As above.
PLAYERS	Five players per team.
SET-UP	As above.
OBJECT	The players again work their way through the obstacle course in relay formation, but this time they do it facing backwards.
WINNING	The first team back and sitting down wins.

Preaching Time

BIBLE LESSON **PETER**

"God did not give us a spirit of timidity." (2 Timothy 1:7, New International Version)

Peter had spent much time with Jesus, but nothing had prepared him for the sight he would see on this particular night.

Peter was lying in the boat in the middle of the Sea of Galilee. It had been a long day. Jesus had done some amazing things and then when it was time to leave, he had insisted on staying behind. Peter was exhausted and had fallen asleep very quickly. He was dreaming of being in a warm comfortable bed when he heard, "Ghost! Gggggghost! Look! It's a ghost! Peter, wake up!"

Peter had thought this was part of his dream, but as the shouts got louder he realised that he was mistaken. He sat up and looked around. The scene in the boat was chaotic; the other disciples were running around shouting, "Ghost!" Peter looked in the direction of their pointing fingers. Then Peter too was afraid. For sure enough, walking towards them across the misty waters, was a figure. It must be a ghost – for one thing, the figure was walking on top of the water. Peter stared.

Then a voice came from the ghostly figure: "Don't be afraid! It's me – Jesus!"

Peter almost couldn't believe it. He shouted back, "Jesus, if that is really you, call me to walk to you across the water."

Jesus said, "Come."

Peter was afraid, but not of the figure. He was afraid of the waves that were hitting the sides of the boat. Nevertheless, Jesus had told him to come, so Peter stepped out of the boat and began to walk towards Jesus. He was definitely afraid, but he was actually walking on water. He had taken a big chance getting out of the boat, but now he was walking – on water!

Peter took a few more steps, but then he became so afraid that he began to sink. Jesus reached over and took his hand. The two of them walked back to the boat.

Peter had taken a chance, and even though he began to sink towards the end, still he had walked on water.

Peter was glad he took a chance.

Star Wars (Qui-Gon Jinn)

Object needed: *The following.*

> A LONG TIME AGO
> IN A GALAXY
> FAR, FAR AWAY...
>
> The Galactic Republic was in turmoil. The greedy trade Federation wanted control of all trade routes and had unlawfully surrounded the peaceful planet of Naboo with hundreds of giant warships.
>
> Two Jedi Knights – Qui-Gon Jinn and his young apprentice, Obi-Wan Kenobi – were sent by the Republic's Supreme Chancellor, Valorum, to settle the dispute. As the guardians of peace and justice in the galaxy Jedi were the perfect choice to handle the difficult situation – before it led to war...

This is the start sequence from *Star Wars – The Phantom Menace*. It speaks of a man called Qui-Gon Jinn. Some on the Jedi council saw him as a rebel, someone who didn't always do the things they wanted him to do. Qui-Gon took chances. But this was the man the council had sent to sort out one of the most potentially explosive events in the galaxy. Sometimes it is important to take risks; it is important to take chances. Sometimes even God is looking for people who are prepared to take chances, people who are prepared to take risks.

The Train

Object needed: *A picture of a train.*

It is difficult to know when to take risks and when not to take risks.

Some people do very foolish things with their lives. They take chances that are very silly. I once watched a gang of boys stand beside a

railway track. They would wait until the trains – Intercity 125s – were less than 100 metres away and then they would run across the track. They reached the other side and lay on the grass, laughing about how clever they had been.

Some of the risks that we take are quite frightening, but they are not foolish; some of the risks that we take are both frightening and foolish. We have to choose which risks we take.

These boys played the game too many times, and on one occasion one of them got trapped on the track. The train came and ran the boy over. He died.

Don't take foolish risks!

The Cripple

Object needed: *None.*

This story could be presented as a small drama sketch.

When Peter got older, after Jesus had died and risen from the grave, he took a risk...

Every day, a man was carried to the temple gate and placed there. He was placed at the temple gate because he couldn't walk. He had been a cripple since his birth. He just lay there every day begging for money from people. He would sit and wait for people to come and give him money. He would sit there from sun up, to sun down. It wasn't much of a life.

Then one day Peter and John were on their way to the temple to pray. They saw the man beside the gate and Peter decided to take a risk. It really was a risk; Peter trusted God, but he was still a bit nervous.

He walked up to the man. The man lifted his head and asked for money as he usually did. Peter smiled, then said, "Silver and gold we don't have, but what we have we give to you. In the name of Jesus Christ whom we serve, stand up and walk!"

Then Peter reached out his hand and began

to help the cripple up. The cripple had never walked. He couldn't walk. But now the servant of God – Peter – had taken a risk. He had dared to command the man to stand up and walk in the name of Jesus.

The cripple began to walk, to jump, to run… God did a miracle, and he did it through Peter. Now that is the sort of risk that we all need to take: an exciting risk.

● STORY – Tommy Thomas, Jedi Knight (4)

Play the theme music to Star Wars *when you announce the title at the start and also at the end for a couple seconds.*

So Tommy was school president. He hadn't wanted to be school president. He'd only volunteered by accident, he didn't think he'd get chosen, and then to Gordon's disgust, Tommy had won the election. Tommy Thomas was the school president. He still found it very difficult to believe. But, believe it or not, Tommy was it! Now what exactly was the school president supposed to do?

Tommy's mind began to wander. He was Tommy Thomas, Jedi Knight, once again. He marched through the space station. People stood aside as he passed. But what was this? Dark Lords were taking space credits off some of the smaller aliens. He marched towards them. He drew his lightsaber. A green fluorescent light shone into the air. The Dark Lords turned to face the Jedi Knight…

Then Tommy realised where he was. He had wandered around the back of the school, into an area he had never been in before. Standing there was a gang of lads, older than him. In fact, they were much too old to be in the school; they were at least 16 years old. They sneered at Tommy. "What do you want, Mr School President?"

Tommy noticed that some of the Year One children were coming around and handing money to the lads, then walking away. "What are they doing?" Tommy asked.

"Nothing to do with you. Now get lost!" came the rather aggressive response.

Tommy walked back around the side of the school and caught up with one of the boys whom he had seen giving his money away. "Excuse me, mate! Why did you just give your money to those boys?" he asked.

"Nothing to do with you, Tommy. Now leave me alone." But Tommy was not giving in and eventually the boy told Tommy, "They grabbed me a couple of weeks back by the school gates. They told me that every Monday I am to walk around the back of the building and give them £1 or they will come looking for me and beat me up. They've done it to lots of us, and we're too frightened not to pay."

Tommy was amazed. He didn't think this sort of behaviour happened in his school. But he was pretty sure that he, Tommy Thomas, Jedi Knight, would put a stop to it. After all, he was the school president now. But how was he going to change things? He could go the headmaster, but he wouldn't be able to stop them.

Solving this problem would mean taking a risk. He put up some posters advertising a special meeting: "Come and hear Tommy Thomas, Jedi Knight!"

"That will pull a crowd," thought Tommy. "They'll come just to laugh at me."

Sure enough, that lunchtime hundreds of people poured into the hall to listen to Tommy Thomas, Jedi Knight. Tommy began: "I got you all here because you thought you were coming to hear me talk about my favourite movie, *Star Wars*. I'd love to talk to you about that – I know you'd laugh lots – but today I've got something a bit more important I need to talk to you about: bullies behind the old school building."

Some of the children lowered their heads to look at the ground. Tommy realised that lots of people already knew about this. Tommy continued: "We've got to put a stop to it. Who's with me?"

There was absolute silence. Nobody moved, nobody spoke, and certainly nobody put his or her hand up. Tommy thought for a moment and then he took the risk. "Tomorrow at lunchtime I will be walking around the back of the old building and telling the bullies to leave our school for good. If you are not there, I'm doing this by myself."

Eleven-year-old Tommy Thomas was going to face the bullies, alone if necessary. He really was taking a risk.

Sometimes it's important to take risks, particularly when we know that we're doing the right thing. When we take risks to do the right thing, God will always help us.

Tommy didn't sleep well that night. He couldn't help thinking that he was going to end up being pummelled the following day. He woke up early. He didn't even have time for daydreaming on the way to school. He walked slowly and steadily. He sat through his morning lessons, but really wasn't listening to Mr Harris.

Lunchtime came. Tommy went around to the

back of the old school building and walked towards the waiting bullies. He was quite frightened now, but he was going to take the risk. He marched up to them and announced: "OK, lads! Get out of my school. Get out now!"

They stared at him. They couldn't really believe what he was doing. After all there were ten of them and only one of him.

"You have got to be joking!" the tallest of the lads exclaimed. "You had better turn around and walk away while you're still able to walk."

Now Tommy was very afraid. But still he walked closer to the lads and repeated: "Get out of my school!"

The lads had run out of patience and started walking towards Tommy. It was like a scene from a movie. As Tommy approached the gang, some people from his class appeared around the side of the building and walked up and stood with Tommy.

The leader of the bullies laughed and said, "So what? A handful of you are going to take on my mates and me? I don't think so." But before he could finish his sentence, more children had walked around the side of the building. Now there were over 20. Soon there were over 50. And then over 100... The bullies didn't look so brave now.

"Get out of our school," Tommy commanded, his voice now sounding confident. There were 200 children gathered there now, then 300. The bullies began to walk backwards. Tommy walked towards them. 300 children walked towards them. "Get out, get out," the children chanted. Now the bullies were running, pursued by hundreds of children.

Tommy took a risk, but it worked. Tommy was a hero.

Sometimes, doing the things God wants means taking a risk. Maybe God will ask us to go and pray for a sick person. Sometimes just being a Christian or becoming a Christian involves taking a risk – how will my friends react? Will they laugh? But these are good risks to take.

5 Queen Amidala

	Programme	Item
Section 1	Welcome	
	Rules	
	Prayer	
	Praise	
	Game 1	Animal Relay
	Praise (x2)	
	Fun Item 1	
	Game 2	Face-building
	Fun Item 2	
	Bible Text	Isaiah 29:13
	Announcements	
	Interview	
	Worship (x2)	
Section 2 Preaching Time	Bible Lesson	Peter's Denial
	Illustration 1	Queen Amidala
	Illustration 2	Masks
	Illustration 3	Chameleon
	Story	Tommy Thomas, Jedi Knight (5)
	Prayer	

 **Overview** Many of us pretend to be things we're not. Queen Amidala does just that on her visit to Tatooine. There are many reasons for pretending to be things we're not, but God knows exactly what we're like.

games

Game 1

Animal Relay

PREPARATION	None.
PLAYERS	Five per team.
SET-UP	The players stand in relay formation at A. Each of the players is given an animal that they must pretend to be as they run around the relay course.
OBJECT	The team members run in relay formation from A to B, making the sound and walking in the style of their animal.
WINNING	The first team to complete the relay wins. However, any player considered not to be doing the sounds etc., will be disqualified along with his or her team.

Game 2

Face–building

PREPARATION	A picture of Queen Amidala per team. The picture must be cut up to form a jigsaw placed at B.
PLAYERS	Four players per team.
SET-UP	Three players stand in relay formation.
OBJECT	The first player runs from A to B, collects a piece of the queen and returns to A. The next player then sets out. The fourth player spends all his or her time constructing the jigsaw.
WINNING	The first team to complete the jigsaw wins.

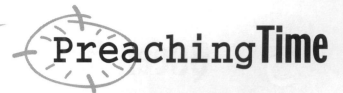

PreachingTime

BIBLE LESSON PETER'S DENIAL

"These people come near to me with their mouth... but their hearts are far from me." (Isaiah 29:13, New International Version)

Sometimes even Peter wasn't what he pretended to be. During the Last Supper, Jesus announced to the disciples that they would soon flee away and forsake him. Peter boldly pronounced, "Jesus, I will never forsake you."

Jesus replied very gently, "Peter, before the cockerel crows tomorrow you will deny me three times."

Peter refused to believe it. He told Jesus that he would never leave. He told Jesus that he would rather die than leave him.

But when the guards came to arrest Jesus, Peter followed them from a distance. A girl asked him if he was one of Jesus' disciples and he denied it. Later, as Peter warmed his hands by the fire, someone else asked him if he was a servant of Jesus. He denied it again. And finally just before sunrise one of the high priest's servants asked him if he was a follower of Jesus. He denied it a third time. The cockerel crowed, just as Jesus had promised. Peter ran into the night, disgusted with himself. He had told Jesus he would never deny him. But that's exactly what he did!

Illustration 1

Star Wars (Queen Amidala)

Object needed: *A picture of Queen Amidala.*

Queen Amidala has travelled with the Jedi from her home planet of Naboo to the desert planet of Tatooine. There the queen stays on board the starship while her handmaiden Padmé accompanies Qui-Gon onto the planet.

At least, this is what we are led to believe. Later on in the movie we discover something very interesting: Padmé is not a handmaiden at all, but the queen herself. One of the handmaidens was pretending to be the queen.

Queen Amidala was pretending to be someone she was not for good reasons: to keep herself protected and also so that she would be allowed to travel with Qui-Gon. Some people pretend to be something they are not for completely different reasons.

Masks

Objects needed: *A set of masks: a clown, a happy face, a sad face. Make them with paper plates if you don't have ready-made masks.*

Who has ever worn a mask like one of these? We wear masks for birthday parties sometimes, or for special fancy dress parties, or maybe even for the school play. I like dressing up; I like to wear different clothes and different masks. Let's see what some of you look like in some of these masks. *(Allow some of the children to try on the masks.)*

Masks really can be a lot of fun. But some people wear masks all the time. They wear masks to try and be something they're not.

(Place the clown mask on someone.) Some people play the clown. They pretend to be funny and tell lots of jokes when really they don't feel very funny at all. Some people who joke around all the time are really quite sad inside.

(Place the happy face on someone.) Some people pretend to be happy all the time. They keep smiling no matter what and always tell you that they're fine when you ask them how they are. But often they are actually quite sad. They wear their smiley mask to hide how they really feel.

(Place the sad face on someone.) Some people who pretend to be sad all the time may not actually be sad at all. Some people pretend to be sad just to get attention.

However, even if we pretend to be something we're not on the outside, God knows exactly what we're like. He looks way past our faces and looks into our hearts. He knows how we really feel, and what we're really like. And even when he knows exactly what we're like, God still loves us.

The Chameleon

Objects needed: *Pictures of lizards including a chameleon.*

Does anyone know what a chameleon is? It's a lizard that can do something amazing: it can change the colour of its skin. This is very good for camouflage. The chameleon can merge into its surroundings so that no one knows it's there.

Some of you do something very similar to that. When you are here with us you sing all the songs, you pretend to be a Christian and you do lots of Christian things. When you go to school on Monday you don't tell anyone you're a Christian; you just behave like everyone else. They swear, so you swear. You just blend in to your surroundings. They tell lies, so you tell lies. You just blend on in. They get into fights, so you get into fights.

Are you like a chameleon too? God knows if you are a real Christian or not. You cannot fool God!

● STORY – Tommy Thomas, Jedi Knight (5)

Play the theme music to Star Wars *when you announce the title at the start and also at the end for a couple of seconds.*

Anna had liked Tommy for quite some time. She couldn't help admiring the person who had saved her life. But what was all this Tommy Thomas, Jedi Knight, stuff? One day Anna walked up behind Tommy as he was on his way to school. She noticed that he began striding and looking from side to side. She knew he was daydreaming again. She did so like him, but she wasn't going to spend time with a boy who spent most of his life in a fantasy world.

Sure enough, Tommy was in his fantasy world. He was marching along with his head in the air. He wasn't Tommy any longer. He was Tommy Thomas, Jedi Knight. His lightsaber sliced through the air in front of him; Dark Lords dived for cover as he passed...

"Hello, Tommy!"

Tommy snapped out of his daydream and spun around. "Ah! Hello, Anna. I didn't hear you coming."

"That's because you were dreaming again, isn't it?" Anna enquired. Tommy thought about denying it. But he knew that she wouldn't believe him if he did. Anna knew the truth anyway. She announced: "Right! This is it, Tommy. Either you stop daydreaming all the time, or I stop being your friend."

With that, Anna marched off into the distance. Now Tommy was upset. He had often thought about the way he spent all his time daydreaming. He knew why he did it. He remembered the very first time he'd become Tommy Thomas, Jedi Knight. It was that night his dad had been shouting at his mum and eventually told Tommy that he was leaving. Tommy remembered how he had felt, how he had spent the whole night crying, and then in the morning he had to go to school. He didn't know if he could face all his friends. He was only six – and a very upset six-year-old at that.

That's when it happened. He became Tommy Thomas, Jedi Knight. He had seen *Star Wars* a couple of weeks before and he thought if he could be a Jedi Knight he would be able to handle anything – even his mum and dad's divorce. So he'd become Tommy Thomas, Jedi Knight, and gone to school. His friends had found the whole thing quite a lot of fun. They wanted to be Jedis as well. After all, they were all only six years old.

But now, five years later, his friends weren't playing Jedi games any more. But Tommy was. Whenever he thought about his parents' divorce and the fact that he hadn't seen his dad since that night, he began to cry; to stop the tears he became the Jedi Knight. The problem now was that Anna wouldn't be his friend unless he stopped doing it, and if he stopped doing it, he didn't think he would be able to cope.

He knew he should stop pretending to be something he was not, but it would be very difficult. Lots of people pretend to be something they're not. It's not always easy to be ourselves. Sometimes we cover up all sorts of pain and hurt. We need to learn that Jesus came to bind up the broken-hearted. He wants to heal our hurts; he wants to set us free. He wants us to be ourselves.

Tommy was very quiet for the rest of the day. He sat opposite Anna and said very little the whole time. His brain was working so quickly. Should he tell her? Should he just ignore her and carry on anyway? Should he just carry on being Tommy Thomas, Jedi Knight? But what would happen when he changed schools? What would happen when he left school? He couldn't be a Jedi Knight forever. On the way home from school Anna caught up with Tommy and asked, "So what's it going to be? Me or Jedi Knights?"

But Anna wasn't ready for the response. She was expecting a "yes" or "no". Instead Tommy burst into tears and ran off. Anna was more than a little surprised. After her dinner she walked over to Tommy's house to see what was going on. She knocked on the door.

"Hi, Mrs Thomas. Is Tommy in?"

"Um! Yes, Anna. He's sitting in the garden. He's very quiet. Is there something I should know?" Anna shrugged. She explained what she had said to Tommy that morning and how she just wanted him to stop pretending all the time. Mrs Thomas nodded; she understood now. Mrs Thomas knew that Tommy had invented Tommy Thomas, Jedi Knight, because his dad had left, and so she explained this to Anna. Anna listened and then she understood. She walked out to the garden to talk to Tommy. Tommy took one look at Anna and burst into tears again. "You don't understand!" he sobbed.

But Anna did understand. She put her hand on Tommy's shoulder and waited until he stopped crying. "Tommy!" she said. "You don't have to pretend to be something you're not. I like you just as you are. And Tommy, it's OK to cry."

Tommy cried, but he felt much better now. Tomorrow would be a brand new day. But he would be himself. He would face it as Tommy. He would be just fine. And of course, Anna was going to be his special friend.

It's important to be ourselves. We don't have to pretend to be something we're not. God loves us just the way we are.

6 Darth Maul

	Programme	Item
Section 1	**Welcome**	
	Rules	
	Prayer	
	Praise	
	Game 1	Destroyer
	Praise (x2)	
	Fun Item 1	
	Game 2	Duel
	Fun Item 2	
	Bible Text	John 10:10
	Announcements	
	Interview	
	Worship (x2)	
Section 2	**Bible Lesson**	Peter
Preaching	**Illustration 1**	Darth Maul
Time	**Illustration 2**	Weapons Of War
	Illustration 3	The Orange
	Story	Tommy Thomas, Jedi Knight (6)
	Prayer	

Overview

Darth Sidious hated the interfering Jedi. He sent his apprentice Darth Maul to put a stop to them. The Jedi had a very real enemy, intent on hurting them. We too have an enemy; the Bible says that the devil prowls around like a roaring lion, seeking whoever he can devour. If we don't know it, it doesn't change it. We do have an enemy.

games

Game 1

Destroyer

PREPARATION	If the leader in this game can dress in a Darth Maul costume it would become even more fun.
PLAYERS	Five from each team plus one impartial leader who is very fit.
SET-UP	The leader stands at B. The team players stand in relay formation at A.
OBJECT	When the game begins the players run from A to B and back again. On their return the next player goes. The leader runs from B to A and back again. If the leader catches up with any player (note: he must catch up with them; he cannot tag them if he is running past them), he must tag them on the back. They are then out of the game. The game continues until only one team has players left.
WINNING	The team that has players left wins.

Game 2

Duel

PREPARATION	None.
PLAYERS	Four players per team.
SET-UP	The teams line up in relay formation.
OBJECT	When the game begins the players run from A to B and back. The first player back stays in the game. The rest go to their seats, and the next heat happens. This continues until only one team has players left.
WINNING	The team with players left at the end wins.

PreachingTime

BIBLE LESSON PETER

"The thief comes only to steal and kill and destroy." (John 10:10, New International Version)

Jesus said some very interesting things to Peter. On one occasion, before Jesus was crucified, he said to him, "Peter, the devil desires to sift you like wheat, but I have prayed for you and when you recover encourage the others."

You see, when you become a Christian your problems don't just disappear. Some things actually become a whole lot worse. For one thing, you get an enemy, quite a nasty enemy. Your enemy has many names: he is called Lucifer, Beelzebub, Satan and, most usually, the devil. The devil really doesn't like you if you serve Jesus. Jesus is the devil's ultimate enemy. Jesus stands for everything that is right and honest and pure and clean; the devil stands for everything that is wrong and dishonest and impure and dirty. The battle lines are drawn. The devil has his followers, and Jesus has his. The battle has started.

Illustration 1

Star Wars (Darth Maul)

Object needed: *A picture of Darth Maul (or have someone dress up as him).*

Darth Maul is a man with a purpose (if he is a man at all). He is intent on destroying the Jedi Knights. He will stop at nothing to stop them doing what they have been told to do. The devil too will stop at nothing to prevent us from doing what God has called us to do. God has called us to live right, to be kind to others and to do our best to tell others about Jesus. The devil will do everything he can to stop us doing that.

The Jedi don't know that they are in a battle. They have no idea that the evil Darth Sidious has sent his apprentice Darth Maul to stop them. They don't know, but it is still true.

Peter didn't know too much about the battle,

but he was in it. He probably didn't even know that he had an enemy called the devil, but he did. This enemy wanted to destroy Peter. The Bible tells us that the devil wants to steal from us everything which is good and that he wants to destroy our lives.

The upside is this: the same Jesus who was protecting Peter is protecting us. Not only can the devil not hurt Christians – he is actually afraid of Christians. We have Jesus with us, and Jesus is stronger than the devil, so the devil tries other ways to hurt us.

Weapons of War

Objects needed: *Pictures of weapons.*

Have someone dress up in a devil suit or dark clothes, looking sinister.

The devil knows that he can't defeat us by simply appearing before us and going "Boo!" So instead, he comes up with other weapons to fight with. He doesn't use weapons such as guns or knives; he uses a much more subtle weapon. The devil has another name in the Bible… *(As you talk about the things below, the devil character skulks around the children, whispering, telling lies, gossiping, etc.)* He is called "The Father of Lies". The devil does his best to mess up your life by telling lies. **He tells lies to you** such as:

"You are not very good."
"You can't do anything!"
"The devil is stronger than Jesus!"

These are all lies. But sometimes we believe those lies. Sometimes the devil tells us we can't do anything, and we believe this. Then we end up fed up and sad. Don't believe the lies.

He also tells lies about people, such as:
"Your friends don't like you."
"He's horrible."
"She stole your money."
"They're talking about you."

Don't believe the devil's lies. He does it to try and turn friends against each other. He hates Christians getting on well with each other.

The Orange

Object needed: *An orange.*

The devil comes to steal, kill and destroy. If the devil could get hold of this orange he would drain every last bit of juice out of it and leave it dry and rotting. He tries to do exactly the same with our lives; he tries to drain the life out of us. He tries to give us a rough time. His plan is simple:

• He wants to STEAL all the good things in our lives.
• He wants to KILL our bodies.
• He wants to DESTROY our spirits – that part of us that can talk to God.

He really hates us. But remember, God is stronger than the devil. Jesus loves us. Even though the devil tries to give us a rough time, we need to tell him to let us alone in the name of Jesus who is stronger than he is. The devil hates the name of Jesus and will always run away when he hears that name.

We are in a battle, but we are the ones who win. The devil has no chance if you're a Christian.

● STORY – Tommy Thomas, Jedi Knight (6)

Play the theme music to Star Wars *when you announce the title at the start and also at the end for a couple of seconds.*

It was Sunday evening. The rain beat down on Tommy's bedroom window. The last couple of weeks had been quite hectic. He had made a lot of friends. He had become school president. He had learned to be himself and in doing so had become Anna's special friend. Tommy was happy and things were looking good.

But not everyone was in bed. Tommy had also made some enemies. He had embarrassed Gordon in the school elections and he had chased the bullies out of the school. And now

Gordon was in a dark back alley and he was talking with those same bullies. The only thing they had in common was that they had all come to hate Tommy. And now as the rain trickled off their noses they were preparing to get even.

Let me leave you in no doubt at the end of our *Star Wars* series. The devil hates you. If you are a Christian and you love Jesus, he hates you.

If anyone were close enough to hear, they would have heard Gordon explaining Tommy's every move: his route to school, the shops he visited, the names of his friends...

Tommy slept. He knew nothing of all this. But he had an enemy. And this enemy really hated him.

The following morning Tommy walked to school quickly. He was excited about a project that he had in mind. He wanted the school to be involved in planting a garden. It would be the most amazing place, with flowers of many colours, a small fish pond and a bench where people could sit. His idea was to involve the whole school in planting the garden and then charge parents 50p a time to come and see it. All the money would go to Children In Need.

All that day the children in the oldest classes dug up the garden area. The older boys had the job of putting a fence around it and a gate for the entrance. They really did work hard. The other children had each brought a potted plant or flower to put into the garden.

The project was going very well. Only one unusual thing happened. Tommy had left his new trainers at the entrance to his garden project while he wore his wellington boots for digging; when he finished digging he discovered his trainers had gone. He really had liked those trainers – they had his name written into the grips on the soles. Somebody said they had seen Gordon near them, but Gordon denied it. Tommy's mother wasn't very happy and Tommy had to wear his shoes for the rest of the week.

Planting went on through Tuesday and Wednesday. By the end of Wednesday the garden looked amazing. It had the most beautiful flowers all over it. On Thursday morning the younger children put the fish in. They had been down to the pet shop and chosen some beautiful fish. The garden looked extraordinary. There wasn't a colour you could think of that wasn't there. And the smell was wonderful.

On Thursday night, invitations went out to all the parents to come and see this most amazing sight. Tommy slept soundly that night, pleased with how the garden project had gone.

But that Thursday night, the garden project had some early visitors. They jumped over the fence, trod on the flowers and pulled them out of the ground, drained all the water out of the fish pond and trampled over everything else.

The devil likes to damage the things that we do, the things which are good and right.

Tommy set off for school on Friday morning. He was pleased when he saw the queues of parents all lined up. But he couldn't understand why the police were there. Then Anna walked past him with tears in her eyes and said, "Why did you do it, Tommy? It was your idea. Why did you do it?"

Tommy was confused. Some of the younger children took one look at him and burst into tears. As he got closer to the garden project, everyone went quiet and stared at him. He didn't understand. He turned the corner and looked at the mess in the garden. He didn't know what to say. He looked at the faces, the staring eyes all focused on him. He muttered, "I'm sad too. You don't think I had anything to do with this, do you?"

Then everyone moved aside so he could see the garden more clearly. There were footprints all over the garden and they had made very distinctive marks. All the footprints had the same pattern. And the pattern formed the word:

TOMMY! TOMMY! TOMMY! TOMMY! TOMMY! TOMMY! TOMMY!

Tommy stared. He shouted, "My trainers were stolen! They were stolen!"

This is how the devil works – he tells lies to you and about you. He tries to destroy you. He whispers into the ears of others and tries to turn them against you. We need friends who will not listen to lies and will be our friends, no matter what.

The police came and took Tommy to the police station. They kept asking him, "So why did you do it, Tommy?"

Tommy kept saying, "It wasn't me. Why don't you believe me?" Tommy was in real trouble...

Anna felt bad. How could she be so wrong about Tommy? Why would he come up with this great project idea, only to destroy it? And why did Gordon look so smug? He'd been grinning like a Cheshire cat all day.

Anna walked around to the garden project. She looked at the messed-up flowers. She looked at the dead fish. She couldn't believe Tommy could do this.

You see, the devil does try and destroy us, but we must learn to trust each other and to stick together.

It was beginning to look even worse for Tommy. The police had just found his muddy trainers – in his own dustbin. They were convinced it was him. He was in a lot of trouble.

Anna was walking away from the garden project when she happened to look up. She saw the sun in the blue sky, she saw a bird fly past and perch on the CCTV camera, and she saw the caretaker fixing a broken window…

Then she thought again. What had she seen? A CCTV camera. The school had had them fitted recently to catch the people who were breaking the windows. Maybe, just maybe… Anna called up to Mr Noble, the caretaker: "Mr Noble, Mr Noble! I need to see the CCTV video."

Mr Noble was very helpful and got the videos out for Anna. She looked through them one at a time until she found the bit she wanted. Then she declared: "I knew it, I knew it!"

"Knew what, Anna?" shouted Mr Noble from next door.

"It doesn't matter – I've got to get to the police station!"

Anna ran all the way. But it was worth it. When the police sergeant watched the video, he was left in no doubt that Tommy was innocent. The video showed Gordon and a lot of older boys jumping all over the garden project – and Gordon was wearing Tommy's trainers.

Tommy was free. He was innocent. But Gordon and his new friends were in serious trouble. Gordon was suspended from school for a month and the older boys were put in prison for six months.

Eventually the devil always loses. He always has, and he always will. God is bigger and stronger than the devil. Good always wins over evil.

The following week Tommy and his friends set to work rebuilding the garden project. By the end of the week it looked even better than before. Many parents did come to see it, and Children In Need received an amazing £2,500 from Tommy's school.

Kimberly's Quest
Restoring The Treasure

A Series in Five Parts

Introduction

Lesson	Title	Themes covered
1 Topaz	Everyone Has A Purpose	Destiny
2 Emerald	Sort It Out	Forgiving others
3 Amethyst	No Room For Baggage	Letting go of past hurts
4 Ruby	It Gets Tough Sometimes	It isn't always easy being a Christian
5 Sapphire	The Treasure Of Greatest Worth	God's greatest treasure is you

Series Overview

Over the next five weeks (five days for holiday clubs, etc.), we will be looking at the life of Jeremiah and working through the story of three friends and their adventure. Each part of the story will involve a precious stone.

The adventure will see the friends recognising their importance and ultimately their value. As the three friends come to understand their self-worth and how valuable they really are, it is my prayer that the children who hear this lesson will also come to understand what it means to be loved and given a destiny by the Creator of the universe.

Construct a table as follows:

Topaz

Emerald

Amethyst

Ruby

Sapphire

It is not a coincidence that the first letters of these words spell "tears" when read downwards. The first letter of each word must be deliberately large to emphasise this.

Also, on one of your side walls you will need to display this poem (after Lesson 1 is finished):

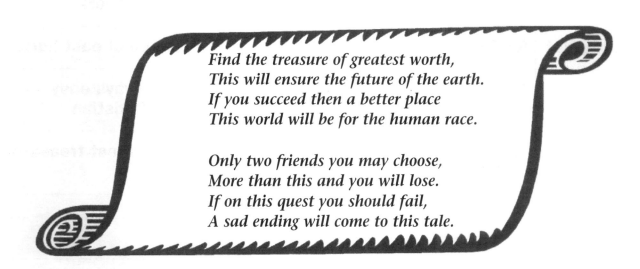

Find the treasure of greatest worth,
This will ensure the future of the earth.
If you succeed then a better place
This world will be for the human race.

Only two friends you may choose,
More than this and you will lose.
If on this quest you should fail,
A sad ending will come to this tale.

TOPAZ
Everyone Has A Purpose

Programme	Item
Section 1	
Welcome	
Rules	
Prayer	
Praise	
Game 1	Island Hopping
Praise (x2)	
Fun Item 1	
Game 2	Treasure Hunters
Fun Item 2	
Bible Text	Jeremiah 29:11
Announcements	
Interview	
Worship (x2)	
Section 2 Preaching Time	
Bible Lesson	Jeremiah 1
Illustration 1	Spectacles
Illustration 2	Drinking Glasses
Illustration 3	People
Story	Kimberly's Quest (1)
Prayer	

 **verview** We all have a purpose and a destiny. Not everyone knows that. Jeremiah was chosen before he was born, but there was still some preparation to be done. We too need God to prepare us for the great purpose he has for our lives.

games

Game 1

Island Hopping

PREPARATION	Four pieces of cardboard (cut out to look like islands) per team.
PLAYERS	Six players per team.
SET-UP	Players line up in relay formation at A, with the front member of the team holding the pieces of cardboard.
OBJECT	The whole team together must journey from A to B and back, without stepping on anything other than the islands.
WINNING	The first team to complete the relay and sit down wins.

Game 2

Treasure Hunters

PREPARATION	A black bag full of rubbish and containing five yellow stones* per team is placed at B.
PLAYERS	Five per team.
SET-UP	Five players line up in relay formation at point A.
OBJECT	The first person runs from A to B, searches for a yellow stone and returns to A with it. On returning to A, they tag the next player who then repeats the process.
WINNING	The first team back and sitting down wins.

* The precious stones that we are using each week will help us remember the lesson. They can be obtained from most craft shops. You don't need actual topaz, rubies, sapphires, etc. Any stones of matching colour will do.

Preaching Time

BIBLE LESSON | **JEREMIAH 1**

"I will bless you with a future filled with hope – a future of success." (Jeremiah 29:11)

For the next five weeks we will be talking about a man called Jeremiah. He had a few adventures that are very interesting and sometimes very unpleasant.

He was born in a place called Anathoth in Israel. Anathoth was a tiny village in the middle of nowhere. Jeremiah's parents had never done anything really special. He grew up in a place which wasn't particularly special. But Jeremiah was very special. God said to Jeremiah, "Jeremiah, I am your Creator, and before you were born, I chose you to speak for me to the nations."

I think that is absolutely amazing. Before Jeremiah was even born God had a special job for him to do – a special job which only Jeremiah could do. He was to speak for God. We have a special word for people who speak for God; the word we use is "prophet". A prophet is someone who hears what God is saying and tells others. Jeremiah was a prophet. Even before he was born God had chosen him to be a prophet.

Amazing though it may seem, God also has a special job for us to do. He's chosen us to do something very special for him as well. Some of you may be prophets like Jeremiah; some of you may go to other countries and tell people about Jesus; for others, God may want you to become school teachers, doctors or car mechanics.

We must find out what God wants us to be and do. God has something he wants each and every one of us to do for him.

Illustration 1

Spectacles

Object needed: *A pair of spectacles.*

Spectacles are very important to some people. Without them they wouldn't be able to see and they would keep walking into walls and lamp-posts.

Every pair of spectacles is made for a specific purpose. Some people use spectacles to read with – these reading spectacles are made in a special way. Some people use their spectacles to see things that are far away – these people need spectacles that are made for that purpose. Others use spectacles to see things close up – these people need a different type of spectacle. It depends what the people need. In the same way that every pair of spectacles is different, every person is different. But every person also has a special purpose, something God wants them to do.

Glasses

Object needed: *A drinking glass and an egg cup (both containing juice).*

A person comes running onto the stage looking and sounding very tired out. They take hold of the egg cup and try to drink the juice.

Egg cups are not very good for drinking juice out of, are they? One sip and they're empty. It hardly quenches your thirst. It's probably because egg cups are for holding eggs and not for drinking juice out of.

The person then takes the glass and drinks some juice.

That's much better! Glasses are designed for drinking out of. That's their purpose. Everything has a purpose. Spectacles, glasses, even people – they all have a purpose. We all have something God wants us to do.

People

Object needed: *The drinking glass with juice from the previous illustration.*

A person walks onto the stage and tries to drink the juice from the glass used in the previous illustration – except that they try to lift the glass with their nose, then their ear, then their foot…

I can't do this. I want to drink some juice and I can't get it to my mouth. What is the problem? I've tried my nose, my ear, my foot! Why can't I get it to my mouth?

Wait until someone says, "You need to use your hand." Then lift it to your ear and pour!

What's going wrong? I'm using my hand like you said, but it's all running down my neck!

Wait until someone says, "It goes into your mouth."

That's amazing! I can actually drink it very well if I lift it with my hand and drink it with my mouth. I guess the job of my hands is to lift things, and the job of my mouth is to drink things – and my ear? Well, that's probably for hearing things. When my nose tries to do my hand's job, or my ear tries to do my mouth's job, what a mess!

Every person who is a Christian has been given a special job that God wants them to do. It's important that we try and find out what that job is, or else we might try and do someone else's job and make a mess of it. Let's find out what God wants us to do, and do it.

● STORY – Kimberly's Quest (1)

Asil is pronounced "a-seal".

Kimberly's life had never been very exciting. She had read long stories of the intrepid men who had made their way through the freezing cold and eventually reached the North Pole. She had read with jealousy the stories of the people who were the first to climb Mount Everest, and with even more jealousy of those who later canoed down that mighty mountain. She longed to be like one of the missionaries she heard of in church who made their way through dense dark jungles in search of people to tell about Jesus. In short, she longed for an adventure.

Kim's life was far from an adventure. Her parents had divorced several years ago. She lived with her mum. She was ten years old. This morning, a Saturday, she had woken up looking for something to do. But, since she had fallen out with her friend Melanie, she had no one to go and play with. Jamie from next door came around to play sometimes, but Kim knew that he had been sleeping at his friend's house and hadn't come back yet. If only Melanie hadn't been so mean to her yesterday and taken her pen without asking. But she had, so Kim definitely wasn't talking to her.

"My life really is very uninteresting," Kim moaned to her mum.

"Cheer up, honey!" her mum replied. "I've got a special job for you to do this afternoon. I want you to go up into the attic and sort out all the old rubbish up there."

"But Mum!" Kim protested. That's not an adventure. That's a nightmare."

But sure enough, that afternoon Kim found herself up in the dusty old attic trying to sort out what seemed like a million different things. She stacked all the board games. She pushed the old furniture to the side. She collected her old dolls and put them into cardboard boxes. Finally, she took hold of the old wooden chest and began to pull it across to the rest of the furniture. It was very heavy!

"What could possibly be in here?" Kim wondered.

She undid the lock and lifted the lid. There inside was an old painting. It looked like a picture of an island – a desert island. And there in the middle of the island stood an angel. She rubbed some of the dust off the picture and stared at it. For a split second she was sure she could hear the waves; she was sure she could hear the angel speaking; she was sure she heard him say, "So, young Kimberly. It's an adventure you're looking for, is it?"

Kim just stared at the picture: "I must be imagining things," she thought to herself.

She looked at the picture once again – she was sure the angel's wings were moving. The angel actually looked as if it was getting closer... And then, the angel was there, in the attic! An incredible brightness shone into every corner – Kimberly could hardly look at him.

"My name is Asil," came the booming voice of the angel. "You wanted an adventure, Kim. Well, I have one for you. I have a quest for you to fulfil. A quest from the Creator. Do you accept the quest?"

Kim thought very quickly. She was almost too afraid to answer. But she also felt very excited. After all, it wasn't every day that an angel came to visit.

"Will it be dangerous?"

"Oh yes!" Asil replied.

Kim didn't know what to do. But eventually she said, "I accept the quest!"

With that, Asil was gone and all that was left where he had stood was a scroll. A rolled-up scroll. Kim picked it up, opened it and began to read:

Find the treasure of greatest worth,
This will ensure the future of the earth.
If you succeed then a better place
This world will be for the human race.

Only two friends you may choose,
More than this and you will lose.
If on this quest you should fail,
A sad ending will come to this tale.

Then, just when she was sure it was a dream, the voice came once more: "Kimberly, you have four days to complete your quest. Sleep well tonight. You may not sleep so well after that."

Kimberly finished clearing up the attic at record speed. After she had finished she went to the bathroom and cleaned herself up. But her mind was working overtime. She went to her room and read the scroll again. She placed it on her dressing table next to her favourite stone. Kim had a piece of topaz – a yellow stone that she liked to play with sometimes. She picked it up and held it in her hand.

"You never know," she thought. "This may just be the treasure of greatest worth."

Then she went to bed. She thought about her quest. Now she had a purpose. She was on an adventure.

God has a quest for all of us – a purpose which God has chosen us for. Probably we won't be told what it is by an angel, but that doesn't mean that God doesn't want to speak to us. Maybe right here, right now, God will whisper to us and tell us that he wants us to tell our friends about him. Maybe he'll whisper to us and tell us that one day we'll be missionaries in other countries, telling people about Jesus. We need to begin to listen to God.

Kim closed her eyes. "What will be the treasure of greatest worth?" she thought to herself. "And will I really be able to find it in just four days?"

(To be continued...)

EMERALD
Sort It Out

	Programme	Item
Section 1	Welcome	
	Rules	
	Prayer	
	Praise	
	Game 1	Treasure Chest
	Praise (x2)	
	Fun Item 1	
	Game 2	Restoring The Treasure
	Fun Item 2	
	Bible Text	Matthew 18:35
	Announcements	
	Interview	
	Worship (x2)	
Section 2	Bible Lesson	Jeremiah
Preaching	Illustration 1	Dirty Spectacles
Time	Illustration 2	Dirty Drinking Glasses
	Illustration 3	People
	Story	Kimberly's Quest (2)
	Prayer	

Overview We have all been given a unique and special purpose by God, but before we can fulfil that purpose, we must "get ready". There is a work of preparation that must be done before God can use anyone – this starts with making sure our relationship with God is right, and also our relationship with others.

games

Game 1

Treasure Chest

PREPARATION	A cardboard box per team.
PLAYERS	Two players.
SET-UP	Players sit at A with their "treasure chest" (the box).
OBJECT	The leader calls out all sorts of items that the two people must gather and place in their box. The first team back each time wins a point. Items should include shoes, socks, combs, jumpers, hair bands, etc.
WINNING	The team with the most points after ten or so rounds wins.

Make sure that a leader in each team has an emerald*, and then call this out as one of the items to go into the box. Don't give the items back yet. That will form the basis of Game 2.

Game 2

Restoring The Treasure

PREPARATION	The cardboard "treasure chest" from game 1.
PLAYERS	Five per team.
SET-UP	Five players in relay formation at point A.
OBJECT	The first person collects an item from the box and runs from A to B. On their way back to A they must return the treasure to its rightful place. On returning to A they tag the next player who then repeats the process.
WINNING	The first team to "restore the treasure" wins.

* The precious stones that we are using each week will help us remember the lesson. They can be obtained from most craft shops. You don't need actual topaz, rubies, sapphires, etc. Any stones of matching colour will do.

Preaching Time

BIBLE LESSON · **JEREMIAH**

"If we cannot forgive those who sin against us, God will not forgive us." (Matthew 18:35, paraphrased)

Jeremiah was an amazing man. He had been chosen by God even before he was born. But before he began to serve God, God said something to him. God said, "Jeremiah, get ready!"

Even though God had chosen Jeremiah before he was born, Jeremiah still had to "get ready". As I said to you last time, God has chosen us as well. He has a special job that only we can do. But God is also saying to us: "Get ready!"

There are some things which we have to do *before* God can let us serve him properly.

Illustration 1

Spectacles

Object needed: *A dirty pair of spectacles.*

We are going to look at the three objects we looked at in Lesson 1 once again. Firstly, the spectacles.

We said that spectacles are very important to some people. Without them they wouldn't be able to see and they would keep walking into walls and lamp-posts.

But sometimes, even when the spectacles are prepared for a particular need, even though they are the right spectacles for the right person, they're not very good, because they're not clean. They may have bits of dirt on the front. Maybe they've got covered in dust.

Before these spectacles can be of any use, something has to happen to them. Can you guess what? *(You're looking for the answer: "They must be cleaned.")*

Likewise, before God uses us, we too need to be clean. The Bible says: "All of us have sinned and fallen short of God's glory."

Glasses

Objects needed: *A drinking glass that is obviously dirty; a carton of juice; a bowl containing water and washing-up liquid.*

A person comes running onto the stage looking and sounding very tired out. He or she begins to pour some juice into the glass then, seeing the state of the glass, stops.

Glasses are designed for drinking out of. That's their purpose. Everything has a purpose – spectacles, glasses, even people. But I'm not drinking out of this glass. It's too dirty for me. I'll have to clean it before I can have any juice.

As the person washes the glass, he or she continues to speak.

We have a purpose, something God wants us to do. But God can't use us while there are things wrong in our lives. He can't use us while we are dirty, while we still have sin – sin is the junk, garbage and rubbish in our lives. While that is still there, God can't use us. But the Bible says, "If we confess our sins to God, he can always be trusted to forgive us and take our sins away."

People

God really does want to use us. But we have to get ready. We have to make sure that there is nothing wrong between us and God. We must make sure that we have asked God to forgive all the wrong things we've done. But also, before God can use us, we must make sure there is not a problem between us and other people. The Bible says, "If we cannot forgive those who sin against us, God can't forgive us."

So, if you've got a quarrel with a friend, or someone you know, God can't use you until you sort it out. God wants us to do amazing things for him. He has a great purpose for us, but we must make sure that everything is right between us and God, and also between us and other people.

When these things are sorted out, there is nothing God can't do through us.

● STORY – Kimberly's Quest (2)

Kim closed her eyes. "What will be the treasure of greatest worth?" she thought to herself. "And will I really be able to find it in just four days?" It took her a while to eventually drop off to sleep, and even when she did, she had the strangest feeling she was moving.

Kimberly woke early in the morning with the sun shining through her curtains. But something was not right. She was sure that she still had that strange rocking feeling that she had felt last night. And another thing: she was fairly sure that these curtains didn't look like her own curtains, and this room looked nothing like her bedroom! Where was she?

She got out of bed and walked across the wooden floor to the window. She pulled back the curtains and couldn't believe what she was seeing. Yesterday morning she'd pulled back her curtains and there was her street and the old familiar trees and the lamp-posts and the boys from across the road, playing on their bikes. Today she could see nothing but water – water stretching for kilometres and kilometres.

Kimberly walked over to the door and opened it. Yesterday there had been a set of stairs going down to the hallway. Today there was instead a set of wooden steps going up. She climbed up the stairs and opened another door. She stepped out, and the wind and the spray from the water hit her in the face.

She looked around! She was on a ship, a very old sailing ship. The sails were flapping in the wind. The sun was beating down. The waves were splashing against the sides, and the ship was moving forward at quite a pace.

She read once again the scroll in her hand:

Find the treasure of greatest worth,
This will ensure the future of the earth.
If you succeed then a better place
This world will be for the human race.

Only two friends you may choose,
More than this and you will lose.
If on this quest you should fail,
A sad ending will come to this tale.

Then Kimberly sat down to try and let her mind work out what was going on! "What now?" she thought. "What do I do now?"

She began to shout as loud as she could: "Asil! Where are you? I need some help here!" Suddenly, the wind became calm! The sails stopped moving and a huge angel began to materialise in front of her.

"Hello, Kimberly! I hope you're making yourself comfortable," said Asil when he had fully appeared. This time he didn't look so bright. He looked like an ordinary person, except, of course, he was seven feet tall.

"Where am I?" Kimberly demanded. "What have you done with my bedroom?"

Asil smiled. "Nothing, Kim. You're on your quest, remember? You're heading for that island there."

Kim could just about make out the island in the distance. "But what do I do there?" she asked.

"Oh! It's quite straightforward really! You solve the problems and collect the treasures. If you solve all the problems you will have all the treasures. Then, you must tell me which is the treasure of greatest worth."

Kim thought it all sounded straightforward enough.

"But be warned. If you fail, then your world will suffer. And Kimberly, I must warn you that I can't always come when you call. I'm one of God's warrior angels. I have other jobs to do as well as looking after little girls on quests. One more thing! Read the second part of the scroll again. You can't do this alone!"

And with that, Asil had disappeared. The wind had returned and the ship was moving again. Kim looked at the second part of the scroll:

Only two friends you may choose,
More than this and you will lose.

"But who will I choose?" she wondered. She began to think.

"I know I should choose Melanie," she thought. "But she really has been nasty to me. She took my pen without asking."

She thought some more and then decided. She shouted: "I want Jamie to help me!"

For a moment, nothing seemed to happen and then a voice came from behind: "Kimberly! Where am I?"

Kim turned around to see a rather confused-looking Jamie. Rather calmly, Kim said, "Hello, Jamie! You've come to help me make the world better."

Then, after spending a couple of minutes telling Jamie what was going on, and all the time seeing the island coming closer, and after answering what seemed like 3 million of Jamie's

questions, most of which involved warrior angels, Kim was ready to choose her next helper.

"You have to choose Mel," Jamie stated. "You know she'll be excellent at this. She's very clever and she's supposed to be your best friend."

"Well, best friends don't steal each other's pens," Kim replied. And all the time, the island was getting closer. She knew she had to decide before they arrived. Finally Kim gave in. She raised her voice and declared: "I want Mel!"

With that, Melanie appeared, looking even more confused than Jamie – if that was possible. But before asking where she was, Mel looked straight at Kim and said, "I didn't steal your pen. I just borrowed it."

Kim shouted back, "No you did not!"

Mel shouted, "Yes I did!"

And if Jamie hadn't jumped in quickly they probably would have ended up hitting each other. Jamie stood between them and said, "Mel! Kim! Stop shouting at each other. We've got a quest to sort out."

Then for the first time Mel looked around. "Where am I?" she began.

Kim looked a bit embarrassed and said, "I've called you here to help me with my quest to make the world a better place."

Mel smiled and then said, "You chose me? So you are still my friend." And with that, and after a lot of explaining, Kim and Melanie hugged and they were the best of friends again.

"Come on, then," Kim shouted. "We'd better get to this island. We have some treasure to find."

But Melanie opened her hand and said, "Maybe this will help." In her hand was an enormous green emerald. Also out of her pocket she pulled a map – a treasure map. (Place the world Emerald under the word Topaz.) Then Kim realised. If she hadn't chosen Mel, she never would have got the second treasure.

And we too will never be able to do what God wants us to do unless we have asked God to forgive the wrong things we've done to him and also asked other people to forgive the wrong we've done to them. Maybe we can take a few minutes to pray about those things now.

Finally the ship came close to land and Kimberly, Jamie and Melanie were able to walk onto the sandy shores. The sun had gone down, the moon was rising and it was time to sleep. That night the three friends slept on the beach, not knowing that someone was watching them. They had three days left to complete their search for the treasure of greatest worth.

(To be continued…)

3 AMETHYST
No Room For Baggage

	Programme	Item
Section 1	Welcome	
	Rules	
	Prayer	
	Praise	
	Game 1	Treasure Makers
	Praise (x2)	
	Fun Item 1	
	Game 2	Treasure Seeker
	Fun Item 2	
	Bible Text	1 Peter 5:7
	Announcements	
	Interview	
	Worship (x2)	
Section 2	Bible Lesson	Jeremiah
Preaching	Illustration 1	Carrying Alone
Time	Illustration 2	What's In The Bag?
	Illustration 3	Running The Race
	Story	Kimberly's Quest (3)
	Prayer	

 **Overview**   To complete God's quest we need to learn to travel light. We must drop all the baggage of unforgiveness, hurt, bitterness and resentment and run the race God has mapped out for us with diligence.

games

Preaching Time

Game 1

Treasure Maker

PREPARATION	Cut out the individual letters of the word AMETHYST for each team and place them at B.
PLAYERS	Four per team.
SET-UP	Players line up at point A.
OBJECT	The players run from A in relay formation, collect a letter at B and return to A. This repeats until all the letters are back.
WINNING	The first team to construct the word AMETHYST and sit down wins.
	On completion, show the children an amethyst.

Game 2

Treasure Seekers

PREPARATION	While the children watch (but the players don't), several purple stones are hidden in the room.
PLAYERS	Three from each team.
SET-UP	Three players in relay formation stand at point A.
OBJECT	The first person runs from A, finds a purple stone (helped by a shouting team) and returns to point B.
WINNING	The team to collect five amethysts first wins.

* The precious stones that we are using each week will help us remember the lesson. They can be obtained from most craft shops. You don't need actual topaz, rubies, sapphires, etc. Any stones of matching colour will do.

BIBLE LESSON **JEREMIAH**

"God cares for you, so turn all your worries over to him."
(1 Peter 5:7)

Jeremiah didn't have an easy job. What God had told him to say to the people was not the nicest message to have to bring.

Jeremiah had to tell the people that because they had done wrong things (things the Bible calls sin), God was going to punish them by allowing a foreign army to come and take them all away as prisoners.

God didn't do this because the people had sinned. He did this because even though he'd told the people again and again to live right and to do right things, they'd kept ignoring God's warnings. And so even though God loves people very much, he can't allow sin to carry on forever.

The people didn't want to hear what Jeremiah had to say. They didn't like to be told that they would be taken away and become slaves in a different land. They hated Jeremiah. Many of them were very cruel to him. But Jeremiah kept speaking the message God had told him to. He was very brave indeed. Even though the people kept saying bad things to Jeremiah and they were cruel to him, Jeremiah kept telling them what God wanted them to hear. He didn't keep the hurts and pains in his heart. He kept giving them to God.

Jeremiah knew that he would end up with lots of hurts, but he knew that he would always be wise to give all his hurts to God.

It isn't wrong to get hurt. Everyone gets hurt at some point in their lives. But we should never keep those hurts, or hold on to them; they will stop us completing our quest. We must give our hurts to God.

Carrying Alone

Object needed: *A sports bag.*

You will need either to load the bag with heavy objects, or pretend it is heavy.

PERSON 1: *(Dragging the bag)* This is so heavy.
PERSON 2: That looks heavy.
PERSON 1: *(Still dragging)* It *is* very heavy.
PERSON 2: How far do you have to go?
PERSON 1: To the other side of the stage.
PERSON 2: That far? That's quite a long way. Do you want some help?
PERSON 1: *(Still dragging)* Oh no! I like to carry my own baggage, thank you.
PERSON 2: Why?
PERSON 1: I think it's good for me to carry this bag myself.
PERSON 2: Why?
PERSON 1: Stop asking me these silly questions.

Eventually Person 1 falls down and shouts.

PERSON 1: OK! Help me then.
PERSON 2: *(Dragging together now)* See, it's easier with two.

The two people remain for the next illustration.

What's In The Bag?

Objects needed: *The words "hurts", "revenge" and "unforgiveness" must be in the bag, written on flash paper*.*

PERSON 3: What are you two doing?
PERSON 1+2: We're carrying this bag.
PERSON 1: It's easier with two.
PERSON 3: Are you sure you should be carrying it?
PERSON 1: Of course! It's my bag.
PERSON 3: But what's in it?

PERSON 1: Just things.
PERSON 3: What things?
PERSON 1: Oh, just things!
PERSON 3: Show me.

Person 1 opens the bag and takes out the first piece of paper.

PERSON 3: It says "unforgiveness".
PERSON 1: Yes! I got it when Ashley broke my bike and I promised I'd never forgive him.
PERSON 2: I didn't know you had that stuff in there. This is nothing to do with me – I'm out of here.

Person 2 walks off. Person 1 takes out the next item.

PERSON 3: It says "hurts".
PERSON 1: Yes! I got it when Tina next door was really horrible to me.
PERSON 3: When was that?
PERSON 1: Oh, about five years ago.

Person 1 takes out the final item.

PERSON 3: It says "revenge".
PERSON 1: Yes! Mr Harold across the road burst my ball when it went over his fence for the fiftieth time last year. So when I'm a bit bigger I'm going to smash all his windows.
PERSON 3: But that's terrible!
PERSON 1: I know! That ball cost me £1.99.
PERSON 3: No, not that! You wanting to smash his windows. In fact, you shouldn't be carrying any of these things. You're supposed to give them all to God. You have to forgive people and let things go. You have to give all your hurts to God.
PERSON 1: I know! But it's really hard to let go.
PERSON 3: But you have to. Let me show you why!

They both stand still as our runner friend from Lesson 1 and 2 walks on. If you're short of people, Person 2 needs to have dashed off and returned in a tracksuit.

* Flash paper is available from www.tricksfortruth.com

Running The Race

Objects needed: *None.*

A runner (from Lesson 1 and 2) takes up his position, looking as if he's about to start a race.

PERSON 2: Look, he's ready to start his race. On your marks, get set, go!

The runner begins to run frantically – on the spot of course. Person 2 commentates.

PERSON 2: *(In commentator voice)* And our runner is off to an amazing start, leaving everyone else miles behind. He is clearly the fastest and the best. No one can catch him, surely he will win...

(To Person 1) But watch this.

Person 2 picks up the bag and hands it to the runner.

PERSON 2: Just hold this for me please, mate!

The runner takes the bag and collapses under its weight.

PERSON 2: *(In commentator voice again)* Oh dear. It's all gone terribly wrong. Everyone is overtaking him. He'll never finish the race now.

The runner remains on the ground.

PERSON 2: You see! With all those bad things, he could never finish the race. We too have a race to run – not an actual race, more something we have to do in our lives for God. But if we keep holding on to all these bad things we'll never do anything for God.

PERSON 1: So how do I get rid of all this stuff?
PERSON 2: You pray and ask God to take it away.
PERSON 1: *(Praying)* God, there's a lot of bad things here. Will you take them away please? I forgive Ashley for breaking my bike.

Person 2 sets fire to flash paper with the word "unforgiveness".

PERSON 1: And I forgive Tina for being horrible to me.

Person 2 sets fire to flash paper with the word "hurts".

PERSON 1: *(Stops praying)* Do I have to forgive Mr Harold too?!
PERSON 2: Yes!
PERSON 1: Oh well! *(Prays)* And I forgive Mr Harold and I won't smash his windows.

Person 2 sets fire to flash paper with the word "revenge".

PERSON 2: Feels better, doesn't it?
PERSON 1: Yes, I guess it does.

● STORY – Kimberly's Quest (3)

Finally the ship came close to land and Kimberly, Jamie and Melanie were able to walk onto the sandy shores. The sun had gone down, the moon was rising and it was time to sleep. That night the three friends slept on the beach, not knowing that someone was watching them. They had three days left to complete their search for the treasure of greatest worth.

The three friends awoke early the next morning. The sky above them was blue; the sun was shining brightly. But Kimberly, Melanie and Jamie weren't in the sun at all. They were surrounded by a large group of people. The friends couldn't clearly see the faces of those that surrounded them, because they were silhouetted by the sun. But these people were clearly very tall and extremely thin. For some time they just stood and stared at the three friends. Then the tallest person spoke. It was a deep resonating voice. It said: "You are carrying a lot of baggage. You will never finish your quest with all that!"

Kimberly was surprised. She looked at her friends. None of them had any baggage, not even a carrier bag. She knew she wasn't carrying anything, so she was naturally confused.

The person looked at them again for some time and then said, "Your hearts are carrying a lot of baggage. And now you will see what you are carrying."

The person mumbled some words, and then all the people were gone. Everything seemed as it did before. The sky was very blue; the sun shone brightly; the sea lightly broke onto the sand. Jamie was the first to speak: "Well! I have no idea what that was about, but if we're going to complete this quest in the next three days we had better get on with it."

The three friends got to their feet and looked at the map. It had an "x" marking a place called "greatest treasure". They set off towards a path which led them into the trees. But as they walked they suddenly felt something on their backs. All three friends were now carrying rucksacks, and try as they might, they couldn't shift them. They seemed almost glued on. They felt quite heavy, but certainly not too heavy to walk with.

They made their way into the woods and along a path that led gently up the side of a hill. The trees crowded in on both sides, but there was plenty of room to walk. The sun was blazing, the sky was blue and a gentle breeze blew in from the sea. Jamie, who was at the back, shouted, "It's very nice, this quest, isn't it?"

"More like a holiday in Spain," Melanie responded. But Kimberly said nothing. She was sure that there would be more to it than this, and she didn't want to become too comfortable.

When they started out, the rucksacks they carried seemed very light. Now the sun was beginning to set, the top of the hill still looked some distance away and the rucksacks were starting to feel heavy. As they walked, Jamie was sure he heard a loud crashing sound in the trees. Then they all heard it: "Bang! Crash! Stamp!"

Kimberly walked over to the edge of the trees and stared into the woods. Then she screamed.

"Run! It's a rhinoceros! It's coming this way!"

The three friends rushed further into the woods as fast as they could. The rhinoceros must have picked up their scent and changed course to charge after them. They ran through some branches that scratched their faces, through brambles that ripped their clothes and through mud that soaked their feet. But all that was better than a rhinoceros hitting you with his huge horn. They ran and ran deeper into the woods with the animal getting closer and closer. He was now only a half-metre away from Melanie when Kimberly shouted, "Jump!" The three friends jumped sideways into what they thought was a pile of mud. The rhinoceros was too big and too heavy to stop. It kept on running into the distance.

"Phew! That was a close one," shouted Jamie.

"I thought we were going to get squashed," responded Kim.

"I don't think we're in the clear yet!" came Melanie's shaking voice. As Jamie and Kim looked around they could see that Melanie was up to her waist in the mud and sinking fast. But before they had a chance to help her, they too began to sink. Before long, they were up to their chests in mud. Kim began shouting frantically, "Asil! Asil! Where are you? Help us!"

Kim prayed: "God, we desperately need your help! Send Asil your angel to help us." Nothing happened, but Kim was sure she heard a voice in her head whispering: "This time you must help yourself, Kim."

She looked at her friends. They were all up to their necks now. "Get the rucksacks off!" she hollered. But try as they might the rucksacks wouldn't come off their backs.

"I've got it!" shouted Jamie. "The rucksacks won't come off because they are a part of us. The strange people took the things which were in our hearts and put them on our backs. What does mine say?"

Kim stretched around and read the word. "BULLIES! Yours says BULLIES!" she exlaimed.

Jamie's mind flashed back to the playground. He was seven years old and surrounded by a circle of big boys who were four or five years older than him. They were pushing him from one part of the circle to the other and all the time calling him names. They had already taken his dinner money. Then one of them punched him in the nose. He felt the blood beginning to pour. He slumped to his knees crying. Jamie knew what was going on. He had never forgiven those bullies. He hated what they had done to him, he hated the way that they had humiliated him, and he hated having to miss his lunch. He began to sink lower. "OK! OK!" he shouted. "I forgive them. They did upset me a lot, but I forgive them."

Then an amazing thing happened. Instead of sinking, he started being pushed up, until he was standing on dry ground again. His rucksack had gone. He looked down at Kimberly and Melanie, and explained quickly: "All the stuff that's hurt you and that you haven't forgiven people for, is in your heart. You have to forgive to drop the rucksack, or you will sink. Mel, turn around! Let me see yours."

The word DEATH was written there.

"What does that mean?" asked Jamie. But Melanie knew. She never talked about it with anyone. She hid it deep in her heart. "I used to have a little sister," she sobbed, "but some stupid man knocked her down with his car." Melanie knew that it hadn't been the driver's fault, but she couldn't forgive him anyway. She had hated the driver. She'd even had dreams of growing up and buying a car just so she could knock him down. But Melanie knew that her hate and her desire for revenge was wrong. She knew she would have to forgive. "I forgive him," she sobbed. "I forgive him."

Sure enough, the rucksack disappeared and she was pushed back to solid ground.

"Now what's on yours?" Jamie asked Kimberly, who was disappearing fast.

The word DIVORCE was written on Kimberly's rucksack. "It's your parents' divorce, Kim," Jamie said. "What happened?"

Kim's mind flashed back to the nights of constant shouting in her house – nights when her dad came home late and hollered at her mum, nights when Kim came in from playing and found her mum crying. She hated her dad.

"Kim, you have to forgive him," Jamie and Mel urged. Kim was sinking fast. She had to decide. She didn't like what her dad had done, but she knew what she had to do.

"I forgive him!" she shouted.

And just like Jamie and Mel before her, she was back on solid ground.

We too may have hurts in our hearts that will weigh us down and stop us completing the quest God has for us. Let's take a couple of minutes to pray and ask God to help us forgive those who've hurt us.

The friends were covered in mud. But they felt much better. Their hearts didn't carry any more of that nasty baggage. They saw a waterfall in the distance and headed towards it to get cleaned up. The gushing water soon swept away the mud. Then Melanie looked across and asked, "Jamie, what have you got in your hair?"

It looked like a ball of mud. But when Mel took it and washed it in the waterfall it glistened brightly, a lovely purple colour. It was an amethyst – the third jewel. *(Place the word Amethyst under the word Emerald.)*

The sun finally went down and Kim, Melanie and Jamie lay down for the night, knowing that they only had two days to go. And they still didn't know where to find the treasure of greatest worth.

Tomorrow they would arrive at a very special place.

(To be continued…)

RUBY
It Gets Tough Sometimes

	Programme	Item
Section 1	**Welcome**	
	Rules	
	Prayer	
	Praise	
	Game 1	Treasure Map
	Praise (x2)	
	Fun Item 1	
	Game 2	Fill The Treasure Chest
	Fun Item 2	
	Bible Text	Jeremiah 6:16
	Announcements	
	Interview	
	Worship (x2)	
Section 2	**Bible Lesson**	Jeremiah
Preaching	**Illustration 1**	Two Paths
Time	**Illustration 2**	Testimony
	Illustration 3	Rubies
	Story	Kimberly's Quest (4)
	Prayer	

 Not everything is easy when you're a Christian. Not everything falls conveniently into place. Sometimes things are difficult; sometimes things are hard. But true Christians keep on going.

games

Game 1

Treasure Map

PREPARATION	Make three copies of a map of the room in which you hold your activities. Mark on the map the locations of ten rubies (red stones)* which you have pre-placed. Also copy a fourth map onto acetate and display it on the OHP so that all the children can see the locations of the stones.
PLAYERS	Four per team.
SET-UP	All players stand at A with a map per team.
OBJECT	The teams go out together or split up. They have to collect the rubies (red stones).
WINNING	The team with the most rubies (red stones) after two minutes wins.

Game 2

Fill The Treasure Chest

PREPARATION	Lots of coloured stones* in a box at A. An empty box per team at B.
PLAYERS	Three from each team.
SET-UP	Three players line up in relay formation at point A.
OBJECT	The first person runs from A to a point about two metres before B (mark the point with a masking tape line), carrying a coloured stone. He or she then throws the stone into the box, returns to A and the next person goes.
WINNING	The team with the most stones in its box wins.

* The precious stones that we are using each week will help us remember the lesson. They can be obtained from most craft shops. You don't need actual topaz, rubies, sapphires, etc. Any stones of matching colour will do.

PreachingTime

 **BIBLE LESSON** **JEREMIAH**

"When you stood at the crossroads, I [God] told you, 'Follow the road your ancestors took, and you will find peace.'" (Jeremiah 6:16)

Doing the things God wants us to do isn't always easy. Jeremiah learned that himself. He knew that telling people what God wanted them to know wouldn't make him popular.

Doing the things God wants us to do will mean doing things we don't always like doing. Jeremiah told the people of Israel that God was saying to them, "Follow the road your ancestors took and you will find peace."

He was asking them to walk an old path, a path that not many people walked. It would be a difficult path, but if they walked it, they would find peace. He was telling the people of Israel to do what God wanted, and even though it might seem hard at times, it was the best way.

Jeremiah himself is a good example of a person who serves God and doesn't always find it easy. Just because he told the people what God was saying, he was put in prison, he was thrown down a well and he was mocked by many people. But when God eventually sent in the Assyrian army to take the people of Israel away, God kept Jeremiah safe, just as he had promised.

Walking the way God wants isn't always easy. But God really does protect us and keep us safe.

Two Paths

Objects needed: *Six cans of Coke.*

You will need a volunteer for this illustration. Choose a "sensible" volunteer who won't give you "silly" answers. Explain this to the volunteers.

Here are two paths. You can't see them, but I will describe them to you.

The first path is a very easy-looking path. It is nice and straight. There are no trees or bushes on the sides, so no one will be able to jump out and attack you. The sun shines nicely on this path. It's the ideal path, with no jagged stones or nasty holes. It's a great path really.

The second path is altogether different. It isn't so straight; it has some quite severe bends. There are lots of brambles on the sides and some of them are growing onto the path. In fact I'd say it's a path that not many people used. There are places near it where bad people could hide, and then jump out and attack you. The sun shines on it, but it also rains here, and sometimes there are hailstones. It's not the nicest path I'd ever want to go for a walk on.

If you had to choose which path you'd like to walk down, which would you choose? *(Wait for a response.)* Of course, you would choose the easiest path. Most sensible people would.

But suppose I said to you, "If you walk down that harder path for one mile, you'll get these cans of Coke. And if you walk down that first great path for one mile you'll get nothing at all." Which path would you choose then? *(Wait for a response.)* Fair enough! If you choose the harder path, you get a reward. That seems to be a good reason for walking the harder path.

If you live your life as a Christian, it might be harder – it might not – but at the end of it you are guaranteed to go to heaven and live forever with God. If you don't live your life as a Christian, you don't live forever with God.

Now, suppose I said to you, "If you walk down the harder path, it might be more difficult, but it'll be much more exciting than the nice path. Dangers may come, but God will always look after you. Things may sometimes go wrong, but God will always keep you safe. If you walk down the other path, it might be easier – it might not – but there will be nobody protecting you, nobody keeping you safe. There'll be no excitement." Which path would you choose?

You see, if you choose to live as a Christian, it won't always be easy, but God will always protect you. It might get tough sometimes, but it'll be very exciting.

Which path will you choose? Will you be a Christian, or not?

Testimony

Invite a capable child or a leader to come and talk about what it means to be a Christian. It is important, in order to flow with the theme, that they point out that there have been times when it has been difficult, but God always looks after them.

Rubies

Object needed: *A ruby or a red stone.*

Rubies look very nice, but they also have all sorts of exciting uses. Did you know that rubies are used to focus the beam of a laser? Does anyone know how to make rubies? *(Take some responses.)*

It's not dissimilar to the way that diamonds are made. Certain chemicals are trapped very, very deep underground. And then, the ground pushes them from all directions. They are put under immense pressure. It would squash a person to nothing. But the pressure over many years eventually produces this lovely ruby.

A similar process happens with people. Some of the loveliest people I know have had to cope with some very bad things. For example, some people's parents split up, some never even knew their parents, some were orphans, some are disabled and have had to cope with many difficulties. But because of those things these people have learned to ask God to help. They have learned to trust God. And they are some of the nicest people I know.

Sometimes pressure on us makes us much better than we were before. Sometimes God allows bad things to happen to us because he knows it will make us better people.

● STORY – Kimberly's Quest (4)

The sun finally went down and Kim, Melanie and Jamie lay down for the night, knowing that they only had two days to go. And they still didn't know where to find the treasure of greatest worth.

Kimberly awoke early the next morning and looked at the map that Asil had given her.

"Come on, everyone!" she said. "Time to get moving! This is our last but one day, remember, and if this map is right, we have a long way to go today if we are to get to the other side of the island by tomorrow."

Melanie and Jamie woke slowly. Their tummies were informing them that they hadn't eaten properly for some time, and this adventure didn't seem so exciting on an empty stomach. They drank some water from the waterfall. They ate some coconut which Jamie had dragged down from one of the trees. And then they set off.

The sun seemed hotter than ever. The breeze from the sea had disappeared and the three friends felt very tired. It took them several hours to walk up the hill beside the waterfall, and even when they reached the top, the path was far from pleasant. Brambles were tangled with nettles and they found that walking was hard work. Jamie, who was normally very positive, began to complain about the long journey. Melanie had a blister on the heel of her foot which was becoming unbearable, and even Kimberly, who had longed so much for an exciting adventure, was beginning to feel sad.

Eventually they came to a point where the path split in two. One path moved further up the hill and the other stretched downwards. They could now see the beach beneath them and longed to be on it. They would have loved to go splashing in the cold, refreshing sea.

Kimberly opened the map and the three friends stared at it. It was clear to everyone that the map was pointing them to go up the hill.

"But the path's going to come out on the beach eventually," Jamie protested. "Why should we go up and down a stupid hill just to end up in the same place? Let's just go straight down this path here to the beach now."

Kimberly was tired as well, but she knew that she should follow the map. They argued for some time. Finally they decided to take a vote.

"All those in favour of going straight to the beach…" Jamie said, "…hands up now!" Jamie put his hand up. "All those in favour of going over this stupid hill…" Jamie continued, "…hands up now!" Kimberly put her hand up. "Well, that's one vote for each. I guess it's down to you, Mel."

Melanie was really under pressure. She didn't want to hurt Kim's feelings and she didn't want to upset Jamie. She really was finding it difficult

to choose. Just then something unusual happened. About 50 metres down the path towards the beach the strange people appeared again. The tallest of the group, the one who had talked to them before, spoke to the three friends, his deep voice carrying easily through the silence.

"Well done, children! You have earned your reward. Come this way; we have prepared this feast for you." Then the strange people moved aside to reveal a banquet. There were sandwiches and cakes; there was pop, ice cream, trifle and biscuits.

"But Asil told me to follow the path," Kimberly shouted. The strangers said nothing. Melanie looked at the food. She was so hungry. Her tummy had been rumbling for a long time.

"That's it," she declared. "I'm going down this path."

"Hurrah!" shouted Jamie, and took off after her. Kimberly just stood and watched. Her friends rushed to the food and began to eat. But as they bit into the food, it turned to sand! Jamie spat it out quickly. "What's this?" he demanded.

"This is a test – that's what this is!" the tallest stranger responded. And with that, to Kimberly's horror, a cage suddenly appeared around her two friends. The man went on: "Bring us all the treasures by tomorrow, Kim, or your friends will die."

The people suddenly vanished, along with her friends. Kimberly stood transfixed. What was she to do now? She couldn't complete this quest on her own.

Sometimes God's way may seem harder, but God will always look after us if we walk the way he wants us to. If we are determined to do what God wants us to do, he will keep us safe.

"It's time to eat, Kim." It was the soothing voice of Asil.

Kimberly spun around: "Where are my friends, Asil?"

"They were told to follow the map. The hill may look harder, but it is safer," Asil responded. "Now eat." Asil handed Kim some food. Then he handed her something to drink. Kimberly felt something gritty in her mouth. She put her finger in to pull out what was there. As her fingers came out, there in her fingers was a ruby. It was a bright red precious stone. Kimberly stared at the stone. She would have loved to be feeling excited, but she just felt sad. She had lost her friends. *(Place the word Ruby on the list underneath Amethyst.)*

"Now sleep, Kimberly," said Asil. "You must still bring me the treasure of greatest worth."

Kimberly felt her eyelids begin to droop. She was so tired. She was so sad. She was on her own. She began to fall asleep, hoping that somehow tomorrow would be better. How was she to bring the treasures to the strangers *and* bring the treasure of greatest worth to Asil? What was she going to do?

(To be continued...)

SAPPHIRE
The Treasure Of Greatest Worth

	Programme	Item
Section 1	Welcome	
	Rules	
	Prayer	
	Praise	
	Game 1	Treasure Map
	Praise (x2)	
	Fun Item 1	
	Game 2	Fill The Treasure Chest
	Fun Item 2	
	Bible Text	John 11:35
	Announcements	
	Interview	
	Worship (x2)	
Section 2	Bible Lesson	Jeremiah
Preaching	Illustration 1	Value
Time	Illustration 2	My Mum!
	Illustration 3	Mother Teresa
	Story	Kimberly's Quest (5)
	Prayer	

Overview There is nothing more valuable in all of creation than humankind. God sent his only Son to die for humankind. Jesus wept over humankind. The Bible even tells us that God loves us in exactly the same way that he loves Jesus. We are the treasure of greatest worth.

Game 1

We are going to repeat the game from Lesson 4. This time, however, the various kinds of different-coloured stones are hidden and are all worth different points:

> topaz – 5, emeralds – 6, amethysts – 7, rubies – 8, sapphires – 10

Don't tell the children the values of the stones. Simply point out that there is a precious stone which we haven't talked about, yet it is worth the most points. At the end of the game, award ten bonus points to the team that can guess the name of the stone of greatest worth.

Treasure Map

PREPARATION	Make three copies of a map of the room in which you hold your activities. Mark on the map the locations of ten rubies (red stones)* which you have pre-placed. Also copy a fourth map onto acetate and display it on the OHP so that all the children can see the locations of the stones.
PLAYERS	Four per team.
SET-UP	All players stand at A with a map per team.
OBJECT	The teams go out together or split up. They have to collect the rubies (red stones).
WINNING	The team with the most rubies (red stones) after two minutes wins.

Game 2

Fill the Treasure Chest

PREPARATION	Lots of coloured stones* in a box at A. An empty box per team at B.
PLAYERS	Three from each team.
SET-UP	Three players line up in relay formation at point A.
OBJECT	The first person runs from A to a point about two metres before B (mark the point with a masking tape line), carrying a coloured stone. He or she then throws the stone into the box, returns to A and the next person goes.
WINNING	The team with the stones of most accumulated value wins.

* The precious stones that we are using each week will help us remember the lesson. They can be obtained from most craft shops. You don't need actual topaz, rubies, sapphires, etc. Any stones of matching colour will do.

PreachingTime

BIBLE LESSON **JEREMIAH**

"Jesus wept." (John 11:35, New International Version)

Jeremiah is often called "the weeping prophet" because he wept openly about the wrong things that the people of Israel did. He would also cry because nobody would listen to him.

Jeremiah did not cry because he was weak. And it wasn't because of a nasty and gloomy personality that he told the people about the bad things that would happen to them if they didn't stop doing bad things. He cried because he loved his people and he loved God.

Jeremiah was very sensitive and wept because the people wouldn't turn back to God. Jeremiah loved the people so much that he wept.

Over 500 years later another man could be seen crying, and crying for the same reason as Jeremiah. This man was crying because he didn't want to see the people he loved not going to heaven. He was crying because he loved people more than anything else in all of creation.

His name was Jesus. He was the Son of God.

Value

Objects needed: *A video clip of the Crucifixion (there are many to choose from), a chocolate bar, a can of pop, a games console.*

The more something is worth, the more you are willing to pay for it.

This is a chocolate bar. It's worth about 30p, so you'd be willing to pay 30p for it.

This is a can of pop. It's worth about 50p, so you'd be willing to pay 50p for it.

This is a computer. It's worth about £150, so you'd be willing to pay £150 for it.

Some things are harder to put prices on. There's a story in the part of the Bible called the Old Testament about a man who worked for fourteen years so that he could marry the woman he loved.

How much do you think a person might be worth? Now Jesus was prepared to do this… *(Show the video clip.)*

The Bible says, "With his blood Jesus purchased people for God." You were worth so much that Jesus was willing to die for you.

My Mum!

As with all allusions to personal situations, you should replace the story listed with a similar one from your own experience – in this case, your own childhood experiences.

How many of you have ever had chicken pox?

When I was much younger I had this horrible disease called "chicken pox". Some of you may have had chicken pox. It isn't very pleasant, is it?

It was a very bad case – I couldn't go to school for three weeks. Some of you may think that was good. But I hated it. I had nothing to do all day because all my friends were at school, and

I couldn't sleep at night because the chicken pox made me itch so much. I was covered in this horrible pink cream – I looked like Mr Blobby – but it didn't stop me itching.

One night it was so bad, I lay in my bed crying. My mum came in to see if I was all right. She saw how upset I was and she said something incredible. She said, "If I could have chicken pox instead of you, I would!"

Now my mum didn't really want chicken pox. Nobody does. But because she loved me so much she would rather have had chicken pox than see me suffer. She said it just because she loved me.

Jesus loves me too. He loved me so much that he wanted to take a terrible disease away from me – not chicken pox, but sin. He loved me so much that he took all my sin onto himself and died on a cross so that one day I would have the chance to go to heaven.

I must be very special for Jesus to do that for me. He also died on that cross for you. He loves you very much as well.

Mother Teresa

Object needed: *A picture of Mother Teresa.*

Mother Teresa was born in Albania in 1910. She spent most of her life in India taking care of the poor. She died in 1997, but in her lifetime she founded many orphanages and took care of the poor.

India is not the easiest place for a missionary to live. Recently many Christians were murdered there just for telling others about God. During her time in India several wars broke out, and many missionaries fled the country. But Mother Teresa stayed. She refused to leave. Despite the great dangers, Mother Teresa lived in India, helping the poor and looking after orphans until she died there in 1997.

Mother Teresa didn't stay in India through all the trouble and problems because she was forced to. She stayed there helping the poor because she loved the people. She knew how much God loved them and she wanted to make sure that she showed that love to the people of India.

● STORY – Kimberly's Quest (5)

Kimberly felt her eyelids begin to droop. She was so tired. She was so sad. She was on her own. She began to fall asleep, hoping that somehow tomorrow would be better. How was she to bring the treasures to the strangers *and* bring the treasure of greatest worth to Asil? What was she going to do?

The rest of Kimberly's quest didn't seem exciting at all. She continued her journey to the top of the hill. Ahead of her, lying on what looked like a sundial, was the final precious stone. It was a dark blue stone – a large sapphire. Kimberly picked it up and placed it in her pocket. *(Add Sapphire to the list under Ruby.)*

She had them all! Five days had passed since the quest began and now in her hand she held the five precious stones: the yellow topaz, the green emerald, the purple amethyst, the red ruby, and now the blue sapphire. She wondered which one was the "treasure of greatest worth". She remembered the poem:

> **Find the treasure of greatest worth,**
> **This will ensure the future of the earth.**
> **If you succeed then a better place**
> **This world will be for the human race.**
>
> **Only two friends you may choose,**
> **More than this and you will lose.**
> **If on this quest you should fail,**
> **A sad ending will come to this tale.**

This should have been an exciting moment. But Kimberly didn't feel excited at all. The poem made her think of her friends. She was lonely. She wanted to know where her friends had gone.

Kimberly didn't have to wonder for long. As she approached the edge of the hill, which descended rapidly back down towards the beach, she could see her friends there. They were still in the cage. The strangers were standing perfectly still watching Jamie and Mel in the cage. They made no movement at all; they looked as if they were waiting for something. Then Kimberly realised at last: they were waiting for her. She made her way down the steep hill, taking care not to fall.

She walked towards the waiting strangers. They looked almost like statues. When Kimberly was only 50 metres away, they turned and looked at her. Kimberly walked closer. She could see Melanie and Jamie sitting on the floor of the cage. She approached more slowly now, more cautiously. But the strangers did nothing. They simply waited until Kimberly was standing right in front of them and then the leader spoke:

"Welcome, Kimberly. We have been waiting and watching. We saw you collect the final precious stone from the ground. Now you have all five stones."

Kim simply stood and listened. She was very afraid, but she was far more concerned with her friends' safety. The leader continued: "Do you want your friends back, Kimberly? Do you really want them back?"

"Of course I want them back!" Kimberly retorted, surprising herself with how much force she put into the reply. "Give my friends back now!"

"By all means!" the leader responded. "But it will cost you. If you want your friends back, you will have to give me the precious stones."

"But", Kim started, "I must take these to Asil. That is my quest. I am to bring Asil the treasure of greatest worth. If I don't, the world will get worse!"

The leader said nothing. He stood and waited. Kimberly was stuck. She had to give up the treasure or she would never see her friends again. She looked at the five precious stones: topaz, emerald, amethyst, ruby, sapphire. She didn't have to think long. She walked over to the stranger and placed them in his hand.

"Take them. My friends are worth much more than these stones."

The stranger took the stones and immediately the cage opened. Melanie and Jamie rushed out. They all hugged each other.

"Well," said Kim, "we might as well go back to the ship. There's no way we can find any more treasure, and our time is up." The three friends walked towards the ship, unaware that behind them an angel had appeared and was busily talking to a tall stranger.

"What do you think?" Asil asked the tall stranger.

"I think you have chosen well, Asil. She is a very good choice indeed. Still, she has yet to tell you what the treasure of greatest worth is."

"I think she'll know," Asil replied. With that, the cage and the strangers and Asil disappeared.

Kimberly and her friends made their way to the ship. Once on board they found some food and drink and sat down to eat. As they sat, Asil appeared before them; he shone brighter than the sun. "Kimberly, what is the treasure of greatest worth?" His voice seemed to boom louder than the water from the waterfall.

"I don't have it!" Kimberly said. "The strangers took it."

"Kimberly! What is the treasure of greatest worth?" Asil repeated.

Kimberly was shaking. She had lost the stones – surely Asil knew this? Then all at once she knew the answer. What had been more important to her than the precious stones? What had been worth giving up those precious gems for?

"My friends!" Kimberly shouted. "They are the treasure of greatest worth! And all the boys and girls of the world – they are the treasures of greatest worth. It's not the stones, it's the people. The boys and girls of the world are the treasure of greatest worth!"

Asil stopped glowing. His voice became calm and sombre: "You have answered rightly, Kimberly. Well done. The precious stones were just a clue. If you take the "t" from topaz, and the "e" from emerald, and the "a" from amethyst, and the "r" from ruby, and the "s" from sapphire, you form the word "tears". And 2,000 years ago my Lord and Master Jesus wept tears of sorrow because he loved you so much, you and the children of the world. Tell them all, Kimberly – tell them all that Jesus loves them."

Kimberly just stared. She knew God loved people, but until now she didn't realise how much.

"Now, Kimberly! You have done well. You have completed the quest. But this is not the end, Kimberly. God only tests those he wants to use. King Jesus has many things that he wants you to do, Kimberly. We will meet again."

With that, Asil was gone. The island also disappeared. The three friends continued eating their meals. But that night as they made their way below deck, they knew that they would wake in their own beds the following morning. The quest was over. Well, at least for now.

The Jackie Pullinger Story

A Series in Seven Parts

Introduction

Title	Themes covered
1 The Arrival	God gives us the desires of our heart
2 The Adventure	Serving Jesus can be very exciting
3 Only Jesus	Jesus is the only answer to sin
4 Favour With God And Men	It's not wrong to be liked
5 Sometimes You Just Have To Keep Going	Tenacity
6 Telling Others	Evangelism
7 Thinking Big	Visionaries

 Series Overview

The biographies of great men and women of God and the lives of modern-day missionaries should be presented to the children as often as possible. If we can sow the seeds of destiny into these young lives, then they will stay true to Christ. The biggest deterrent to sin was never, and will never be, religious rules and regulations. It is catching a sense of God's purpose for our lives.

This series looks at a modern heroine – Jackie Pullinger. The stories are based on her book *Chasing the Dragon* (Hodder & Stoughton), which is compulsory reading for presenting this series well. For our Bible lessons we turn to the parables of Jesus.

This is the last series in the book and the last lesson is of great importance. Present it with passion. It can change lives.

1 The Arrival

	Programme	Item
Section 1	**Welcome**	
	Rules	
	Prayer	
	Praise	
	Game 1	Hong Kong Hats
	Praise (x2)	
	Fun Item 1	
	Game 2	Hong Kong
	Fun Item 2	
	Bible Text	Psalm 37:4
	Announcements	
	Interview	
	Worship (x2)	
Section 2	**Bible Lesson**	Lilies And Ravens
Preaching	**Illustration 1**	Go!
Time	**Illustration 2**	What Are You Good At?
	Illustration 3	Hong Kong
	Story	Jackie Pullinger (1)
	Prayer	

Overview

Somehow we have the idea that God will only get us to do the things we don't like: if I hate the cold, God will make me a missionary to Eskimos, etc. However, God is not like this. He actually wants to give us the desires of our hearts.

games

Preaching Time

Game 1

Hong Kong Hats

PREPARATION	You will need a pointed, Chinese-style hat (or an upside-down, unbreakable fruit bowl) per team.
PLAYERS	Four per team.
SET-UP	The players are lined up in relay formation at A. The first person wears the hat.
OBJECT	To run from A to B wearing the hat. The hat must not be held, and if it falls off, the player must restart.
WINNING	The team that finishes first wins.

Game 2

Hong Kong

PREPARATION	On separate pieces of card write the letters of the words HONG KONG.
PLAYERS	Four per team.
SET-UP	The letters are placed at B. The teams line up in relay formation at A.
OBJECT	To run from A to B, collect a letter and return. This continues until all the letters have been collected. The team then constructs the words HONG KONG from the letters.
WINNING	The first team that completes the words wins.

BIBLE LESSON **LILIES AND RAVENS**

"And he will give you the desires of your heart." (Psalm 37:4, New International Version)

Jesus often told stories. These were very special stories that had a meaning. They are called parables. One such story he told went like this:

Look at the birds. They do not farm fields; they don't have a storeroom to keep their food in, yet God feeds them. Look at the flowers – look how beautiful they are! They don't worry about their clothes, because God clothes them.

God loves you more than the birds or the flowers; he cares for you more than anything else in all of his wonderful creation. Then Jesus said an amazing thing; he said, "Don't worry, little flock. Your Father has been pleased to give you the kingdom."

The kingdom is that place where Jesus is. God's intention is to give us good things, things that make us happy. Why do we spend so much time thinking God wants to give us things we will not like?

Illustration 1

Go!

You will need two people, one to play the part of God, one to play the part of Joe Ordinary Person. Alternatively, the ordinary person could be a puppet.

JOE: My word, it's cold today. I hate the cold.

GOD: Hey! Joe Ordinary Person! I want you to go and tell the Eskimos about me.

JOE: But God, I hate the cold!

GOD: I know – that's why I'm sending you there.

JOE: Well, in that case: I love snow! I hate the sun.

GOD: Oh! Well, go to the Sahara desert. Go and tell the people there about me.

JOE: But it's too hot; I don't want to go there!

GOD: That's why I'm sending you there.

You know, we actually think that God is like this. We think God wants to give us things we don't like and send us to places we don't want to go. God is not like this.

What Are You Good At?

Objects needed: *A sheet of paper or a whiteboard, and a pen.*

So, who wants to tell me what they like doing? *(Write down the answers on the board.)*

And who would like to tell me what they would like to do when they grow up? *(Write down the answers on the board.)*

Some of you actually think that if you give your life to Jesus, he will stop you doing what you like doing. And you think he won't let you do what you want when you grow up. But I know a little secret. Some of the things that you like to do – you like doing them because God has helped you to like them! God may have made you good at them. And some of you need to know a secret about the things that you want to do when you grow up: God may actually have planted those dreams in your heart.

We sometimes forget that God made us. He put us together. He knows what he put inside us. He knows what dreams, what hopes, what desires we have.

So you want to be a fighter pilot. Well, God needs fighter pilots. Otherwise, how will the other fighter pilots find out about Jesus? So you want to be a teacher. Well, just maybe, God will allow you to go to other countries to teach people there about him. So you like learning new languages. Well, maybe you can tell people who don't speak English about the God who loves them.

God allows us to do the things that we want to do.

Hong Kong

Object needed: *A map of Hong Kong.*

Display acetate of map.

Geography time! Who can tell me what this place is? It's called Hong Kong. It's an interesting place. Here are four amazing facts about this city. Hong Kong has:

1. more cars per head of population than anywhere in the world.
2. 500,000 Christians.
3. a huge divide between rich and poor.
4. streets controlled by triad gangs, who are major criminals.

Hong Kong is going to be important to us over the next couple of weeks as we talk about a woman God sent there.

● STORY – Jackie Pullinger (1)

Jackie was eight years old when she first went to church to listen to a missionary speak. This missionary had been in Africa, telling people about Jesus. Jackie thought that she seemed very strict and was dressed a little strangely. But by the time the woman asked the boys and girls if any of them thought that they would like to be a missionary one day, Jackie had decided that she would like to be a missionary very much.

Jackie told some of her friends that she was going to be a missionary, but telling them wasn't the best idea in the whole world – from that time on, whenever she did anything wrong her friends would say, "And you want to be a missionary!" And then they would all laugh.

So Jackie stopped telling people. Then she actually forgot that she wanted to be a missionary. But God didn't forget.

It was many years later before Jackie eventually gave her life to Jesus and once again began praying about her future. It was then that God gave her a very strange dream. As she dreamt, she saw the continent of Africa but there in the middle of Africa was another place. That place was Hong Kong.

Jackie was unsure what this meant. She

continued to pray. She was a graduate of the Royal Academy of Music, but she knew her future would involve something more than music. She prayed some more. And then she went to ask a Christian minister, whom she knew well, if he could help.

Sometimes it's a good idea to ask other Christians for help. They often have some very good advice. And sometimes it's just possible that God will tell them what to tell you. Jackie went to see Richard Thompson, a friend who was also the minister in a nearby church. They talked for some time and then Richard gave this advice: "Jackie, I think you should go and buy a ticket for the longest journey on a ship that you can find. And when God tells you to get off, then get off and be a missionary. Start telling the people there about God."

Jackie was amazed at the advice. She was most surprised because it was something she would certainly enjoy doing. She loved to travel, so the idea of going around the world on a ship really appealed to her. She wondered if it was really an idea from God. She wasn't sure that God told us to do things that we really like doing. She didn't understand the Bible text that says this about God: "He will give you the desires of your heart." Like many other people, Jackie thought God only gave us difficult things to do. But she decided to take Richard's advice.

Her parents thought it was utter madness but agreed to support their daughter's decision. So Jackie got onto a ship and set off on her round-the-world trip. At each port, she walked to the exit and looked at the harbour in the new country. She asked God if this was the place. If she felt nothing, she turned around and went back onto the ship.

She visited many places and then eventually arrived in Hong Kong harbour. It was a wild, bustling place with much activity. And then she remembered the dream of Hong Kong; she felt God say, "This is the place, Jackie. Time to get off."

She did as God asked and left the ship. She marched up to the customs officials, expecting to be let straight into Hong Kong. But instead, she was commanded to answer many questions.

"Where are you going to live?" asked the customs officer.

"I don't know," came Jackie's very honest reply.

"Where are your friends?"

"I don't have any."

"Where will you work?"

"I don't know."

"Where's your return ticket?"

"I don't have one!" (God had told Jackie to go; she hadn't thought about getting back.)

The man was not happy with the answers. Then he asked one more question: "How much money do you have?"

Jackie counted quickly. "About £6," she replied.

"It's not enough!" he roared. "That will not last long at all. You must get back on the boat."

Surely she hadn't come all this way to be sent home! Had Jackie not heard from God at all? What would happen now?

(To be continued…)

② The Adventure

	Programme	Item
Section 1	Welcome	
	Rules	
	Prayer	
	Praise	
	Game 1	Walled City
	Praise (x2)	
	Fun Item 1	
	Game 2	Chopsticks (girls)
	Fun Item 2	
	Bible Text	Joshua 1:6
	Announcements	
	Interview	
	Worship (x2)	
Section 2 Preaching Time	Bible Lesson	Gold
	Illustration 1	*Hook*
	Illustration 2	Hymns
	Illustration 3	Adventurers
	Story	Jackie Pullinger (2)
	Prayer	

Overview Jackie was in an unknown place, far from anyone she knew. She could have felt a whole array of feelings, but she felt excited. God had placed within Jackie the spirit of an adventurer.

Game 1

Walled City

PREPARATION	A pile of building blocks per team.
PLAYERS	Four per team.
SET-UP	The blocks are placed at B. The teams line up in relay formation at A.
OBJECT	The first person runs from A to B, collects a block from B and returns to A. The next person then goes. This repeats until all the blocks are collected. The team then constructs a building.
WINNING	The team that builds the highest building wins.

Game 2

Chopsticks (girls)

PREPARATION	A bowl of rice and a pair of chopsticks per team.
PLAYERS	Four per team.
SET-UP	The rice is placed at B along with the chopsticks. The teams line up in relay formation at A.
OBJECT	To run from A to B, eat as much rice as possible using the chopsticks, and return to A.
WINNING	The team that eats the most rice wins.

Preaching Time

BIBLE LESSON GOLD (Matthew 25)

"Be bold and very courageous." (Joshua 1:6)

This story along with many of the other parables in this series will be worth acting out using the children as the central characters – it will make the stories more fun and ultimately more memorable.

Once a man called together his servants and said, "I am going on a trip. I am going to give each of you some money to invest for me."

He gave five bags of gold to one, two bags of gold to another, and one bag of gold to the last – dividing it in proportion to their abilities – and then left on his trip.

The servant who received the five bags of gold began immediately to invest the money and soon doubled it. The servant with two bags of gold also went right to work and doubled the money. But the servant who received the one bag of gold dug a hole in the ground and hid the master's money for safekeeping.

After a long time the master returned from his trip and called all the servants together. The servant to whom he had entrusted the five bags of gold said: "Sir, you gave me five bags of gold to invest, and I have doubled the amount."

The master was very pleased: "Well done, my good and faithful servant. You have been faithful in handling this small amount, so now I will give you many more responsibilities. Let's celebrate together!"

Next came the servant who had received the two bags of gold, with the report: "Sir, you gave me two bags of gold to invest, and I have doubled the amount."

The master said: "Well done, my good and faithful servant. You have been faithful in handling this small amount, so now I will give you many more responsibilities. Let's celebrate together!"

Then the servant with the one bag of gold came and said: "Sir, I know you are a hard man, harvesting crops you didn't plant and gathering crops you didn't cultivate, so I was afraid I would lose your money; I hid it in the earth and here it is."

But the master was not very happy and replied: "You wicked and lazy servant! You think I'm a hard man, do you, harvesting crops I didn't plant and gathering crops I didn't cultivate? Well, you should at least have put my money into the bank so I could have some interest. Take the money from this servant and give it to the one with the ten bags of gold."

The men who had been adventurous, even though they had to take a chance to do it, were rewarded. Sometimes it pays to be adventurous.

Hook

Object needed: *A video clip of the movie* Hook.

This is one of my all-time favourite movies. It's the story of Peter Pan when he's grown up. He goes back to Neverland and finally defeats Captain Hook and saves his children. There's a great bit towards the end of the movie and it happens like this.

Hook has been defeated. Peter stands opposite Tinker Bell and Tinker Bell says to him, "So Peter, I guess your adventures are over now."

Peter looks at Tinker Bell and says these words: "Tink, to live is an adventure."

Those people who will give their lives to Jesus and allow God to do whatever he wants with them will discover that living for Jesus really is an adventure.

Hymns

Object needed: *A hymn book.*

As with all the drama-style presentations, this could be done with people or with puppets.

A person walks onto the stage and stands there looking as miserable as possible. He remains for some 30 seconds, looking at his hymn book and then looking miserable again.

NARRATOR: What are you doing?
PERSON: I'm being a Christian.
NARRATOR: Sorry! I don't understand.

PERSON: I'm being a Christian. You know, one of those miserable people that goes to church each week and sings sad songs.
NARRATOR: Are you sure that's what a Christian is?
PERSON: Oh yes. A sad-looking person who sings songs.
NARRATOR: How do you know this?
PERSON: I've seen them.
NARRATOR: Oh!

NARRATOR: Sometimes Christians do appear to be like this. I need you to know that this is not how God intended it to be. Christians are supposed to have a spirit of adventure, to be brave and bold and even happy. That's what Christians in the Bible were like.

Adventurers

Objects needed: *If possible, pictures of the characters mentioned below.*

I like exciting people. I like Indiana Jones in his movies. I like the way he takes on amazing enemies and is brave and adventurous. I like the way Peter Pan fights Captain Hook in the movie *Hook* and wins through. I like movies about heroes, about adventurers – people like the Three Musketeers or the Scarlet Pimpernel, or Robin Hood.

And I like some real adventurers – people like George Washington and Davy Crockett who fought to establish the United States of America. There are famous people scattered throughout history who did amazing things for their countries and their friends.

The Bible is full of such people: Moses, who led millions of people out of a foreign land where they were slaves; Joshua, who led the same nation to take over a new country; Samson, who wiped out whole armies single-handedly.

And nearer our own time we have all these amazing missionaries: David Livingstone who went to Africa; Amy Carmichael who went to India; Gladys Aylward and Hudson Taylor who went to China. These were amazing men and women who did amazing things for God.

God doesn't want people who only want to sit in churches. He wants adventurers.

● STORY – Jackie Pullinger (2)

"How much money do you have?"

Jackie counted quickly. "About £6," she replied.

"It's not enough!" he roared. "That will not last long at all. You must get back on the boat."

Surely she hadn't come all this way to be sent home! Then suddenly Jackie remembered something. She remembered that her mum had a godchild here in Hong Kong; he was a policeman.

"Wait!" shouted Jackie. "I do know somebody here. He's a policeman."

Suddenly the customs officer's eyes went wide and he looked afraid. In Hong Kong at that time policemen were not only respected – they were also feared. They could lock people up for no reason. The man stood aside and began to apologise.

So Jackie had arrived. She was in the country God had wanted her to go to. She soon found another Christian there, a woman called Mrs Donnithorne who ran a primary school and was soon encouraging Jackie to come and teach there. But Jackie had no idea where Mrs Donnithorne's school was or what she had let herself in for. She had no idea that the school was in an area of Hong Kong where she was going to spend many years. Mrs Donnithorne's school was in the Walled City.

Jackie's first visit was not what she had expected. She and Mrs Donnithorne had walked through what appeared to be a fairly nice area and then they had turned a corner and pushed through an entrance and now everything looked very different. The walls were high; the buildings were piled on top of each other. There were no building regulations here. The buildings leaned and looked as if they would fall. The towering blocks of flats had exposed electricity cables hanging down; people could easily be electrocuted. There were 32,000 people here and two holes in the ground that were used for toilets. There were no drains or sewers. People would throw their dirty water and sometimes empty their bedpans over the side of the balconies.

As Jackie walked through this dark place she felt her feet squelching on all sorts of nasty things. She didn't dare look down to see what she was walking on, for she knew that if she did, she would probably be sick.

She passed drug addicts who were lying on the ground; she passed men and women who were too drunk to walk and who just staggered from side to side. She passed small children who were dirty and uncared for. Many of them had no parents to look after them. She eventually came to the school she would teach in. It was in the very heart of the Walled City.

You might think that Jackie would be sad. You might think that Jackie would want to go back to the green hills and bright skies of the England that she had left behind. But this was not the case. Like scores of missionaries before her, she had found herself in the worst possible conditions – and yet she felt happy. She felt genuine joy. She was where God wanted her to be. This was her adventure. She was an adventurer.

Next time I'll tell you how Jackie's adventures really got going. But for now it's enough to know that God doesn't want us to serve him so that we can have boring, unfulfilled lives. God is looking for adventurers! Do you think you could be one?

(To be continued…)

3 Only Jesus

	Programme	Item
Section 1	**Welcome**	
	Rules	
	Prayer	
	Praise	
	Game 1	Chopsticks (boys)
	Praise (x2)	
	Fun Item 1	
	Game 2	Pearl Finders
	Fun Item 2	
	Bible Text	Mark 16:16
	Announcements	
	Interview	
	Worship (x2)	
Section 2	**Bible Lesson**	The Pearl Of Greatest Worth
Preaching	**Illustration 1**	Only Way To Heaven
Time	**Illustration 2**	Only Way To Healing
	Illustration 3	Only Way To Forgiveness Of Sins
	Story	Jackie Pullinger (3)
	Prayer	

 **Overview** Jackie was in a strange place. The Walled City was a place of drug addicts, alcoholics and wild gangs. Yet this English woman had with her the only cure.

games

PreachingTime

Game 1

Chopsticks (boys)

PREPARATION	A bowl of rice and a pair of chopsticks per team.
PLAYERS	Four per team.
SET-UP	The rice is placed at B along with the chopsticks. The teams line up in relay formation at A.
OBJECT	To run from A to B, eat as much rice as possible using the chopsticks, and return to A.
WINNING	The team that eats the most rice wins.

BIBLE LESSON **THE PEARL OF GREATEST WORTH**

"Anyone who believes me and is baptised will be saved. But anyone who refuses to believe me will be condemned." (Mark 16:16)

To help us understand what the kingdom of heaven is like, Jesus told a story about a shop owner who was looking for fine pearls. The shop owner looked everywhere for a particularly beautiful pearl. He searched far and wide. He scoured the world. If he had been alive today he would have been surfing the Net looking for pearls.

Eventually, after finding a very valuable one, the owner went and sold everything he owned, in order to buy that one pearl.

Jesus is like this pearl. It's worth everything to find Jesus. There are many things which may be worth selling everything for – maybe. But Jesus is the greatest treasure of them all. Only Jesus!

Game 2

Pearl Finders

PREPARATION	A bag of rubbish per team. Each bag also contains four white stones or marbles.
PLAYERS	Four per team.
SET-UP	The bags are placed at B. The teams line up in relay formation at A.
OBJECT	To run from A to B, find a marble or white stone and return.
WINNING	The team that completes the game first wins.

Illustration 1

Only Way To Heaven

Object needed: *A Bible.*

There are a lot of different ideas about how to get to heaven. Some people think that you can get to heaven by going to church, by praying to statues, by doing good things, by helping old people across the road. There are lots of strange ideas about how to get to heaven. But the Bible makes it very clear. The only way to get to heaven is through Jesus. In fact the Bible actually says, "Anyone who believes me and is baptised will be saved. But anyone who refuses to believe me will be condemned."

Only Way To Healing

Object needed: *A Bible.*

The Bible tells us that Jesus came to bind up the broken-hearted. This means that Jesus actually can heal the hurts on the inside as well as the hurts on the outside. For example, Jesus can heal hurts caused by people being unkind, people being nasty – all sorts of things. Also, people who have been hurt in accidents or who are unwell can be healed by Jesus.

Jesus can heal our bodies and our hearts. Only Jesus has the power to do this. Only Jesus!

Only Way To Forgiveness Of Sins

Object needed: *A Bible.*

The Bible tells us that we have all done wrong things. The Bible calls these things "sins". These sins build up in our hearts. They stop us being God's friends and stop us going to heaven when we die. But Jesus came and died on a cross to take the punishment for our sins. And now, if we ask him, Jesus has the power to take away our sins.

Only Jesus! Only Jesus has the power to take away the wrong things we have done. Only Jesus!

● STORY – Jackie Pullinger (3)

The Walled City, where Jackie now worked, was a terrible place to be. There were shops that sold everything. Next to a shop that sold secondhand furniture there was a shop that sold food, and next to the shop that sold food there was a shop that sold children. Boys and girls were sold because their parents couldn't afford to keep them any longer.

Most of the children who lived in the Walled City never finished school. They dropped out. Many of them became criminals; many of them

started selling drugs; many of them began taking drugs.

Jackie knew that God cared for these people very much, but she didn't really know what to do. She decided to rent her own shop and run it as a youth club. She organised table tennis and games and afterwards she would tell the young people about God. But even though she had good ideas and really wanted to help, it didn't seem to work. Lots of young people came to the youth club and enjoyed the games and the table tennis but none of them seemed interested in learning about God.

For a whole year Jackie kept opening the youth club and for a whole year lots of young people came and had fun. But none of them wanted to listen about God. This was difficult for Jackie. She knew that they desperately needed Jesus. They needed to learn about a God who loved them. Their lives were full of junk and garbage, the stuff the Bible calls sin. Without God they would never go to heaven. Without God they would never have all that junk taken away from their lives.

Jackie kept running the youth club every week. Then, after a year, Jackie realised something very important. She realised she would never be able to help these people; she would never be able to get them to heaven; she would never be able to take all their sins away. This was God's job. Only Jesus, who is God, could take away this sin. Only Jesus.

So Jackie began to pray that Jesus would do just that. She asked Jesus to help the young people find out about him. Jackie prayed every morning.

Then one day, as Jackie came to the youth club, she found a young man leaning against the wall outside. He had a special sweatband on his head; it showed everyone that he belonged to a triad gang called the 14K. The triad gangs ruled the Walled City. They sold drugs and murdered people and were always fighting with other gangs. He had been in a fight with another gang, a gang called the Jin Yu. Jackie helped the young man, whose name was Christopher. She protected him until he was better. Then she allowed Christopher to leave.

She wasn't sure that Christopher would ever return but she kept remembering that only Jesus could help Christopher. She kept praying. Only Jesus!

Then one day Christopher returned to the youth club. He had come to ask Jackie the question: "Jackie, why do you bother to do what you do?"

Jackie smiled and simply answered, "Because Jesus bothered."

She took Christopher to a quiet area and began to explain why only Jesus could help him. She asked Christopher if he remembered the way his T-shirt looked on the nights he got beaten up. Christopher nodded. He remembered how his T-shirts sometimes got stained with blood. Then Jackie asked him what he did with his dirty T-shirt. Christopher remembered that he took off the blood-stained T-shirt and put on a clean T-shirt.

Jackie said, "Christopher, that is what Jesus wants to do with your heart. He wants to take your stained, dirty heart, your heart that is stained by the wrong things you have done, and replace it with a clean heart, a pure heart."

Christopher gave his life to Jesus and before long, many other young people followed. Only Jesus was able to change Christopher's heart. Only Jesus was able to help all those people in the Walled City.

(To be continued...)

Favour With God And Men

	Programme	Item
Section 1	**Welcome**	
	Rules	
	Prayer	
	Praise	
	Game 1	Favourites (boys)
	Praise (x2)	
	Fun Item 1	
	Game 2	Favourites (girls)
	Fun Item 2	
	Bible Text	Luke 2:52
	Announcements	
	Interview	
	Worship (x2)	
Section 2	**Bible Lesson**	The Two Men
Preaching	**Illustration 1**	Teacher's Pet
Time	**Illustration 2**	Favour With Men
	Illustration 3	The Balance
	Story	Jackie Pullinger (4)
	Prayer	

verview Jackie began to win favour with the people of the Walled City. We don't need to be people's favourites but we do need to have favour with people.

games

Game 1

Favourites (boys)

PREPARATION	None.
PLAYERS	One boy to begin with.
SET-UP	The first player stands at A.
OBJECT	The boy runs from A, collects a friend and they then run to B, holding hands. When they return to A they collect another friend and set off for B. This continues until there are seven players in the chain.
WINNING	The first team back at A with seven people wins.

Game 2

Favourites (girls)

PREPARATION	None.
PLAYERS	One girl to begin with.
SET-UP	The first player stands at A.
OBJECT	The girl runs from A, collects a friend and they then run to B, holding hands. When they return to A they collect another friend and set off for B. This continues until there are seven players in the chain.
WINNING	The first team back at A with seven people wins.

Preaching Time

BIBLE LESSON — THE TWO MEN

"Jesus became wise, and he grew strong. God was pleased with him and so were the people." (Luke 2:52)

Jesus told a story to some people who thought they were better than others and who looked down on everyone else.

Two men went into the temple to pray. One was a leader in the church and the other collected taxes. The church leader stood over by himself and prayed, "God, I thank you that I am not greedy, dishonest, and don't do anything wrong like other people do. And I am really glad that I am not like that tax collector over there."

The tax collector stood off at a distance and did not think he was good enough even to look up toward heaven. He was so sorry for what he had done that he stood and cried: "God, have pity on me! I am such a sinner."

Then Jesus said, "When the two men went home it was the tax collector who was pleasing to God."

Some people make the mistake of trying to get people to like them by doing things that God doesn't like. We need to be friends of people, but if it means that we will no longer be God's friends then we must choose God first.

Illustration 1

Teacher's Pet

Object needed: *A picture of a teacher.*

When I was in school we used to call children who were always the teacher's favourite "the teacher's pet". It wasn't because the teacher kept them in a cage at the back of the class; it was because the teacher always seemed to like them more than anyone else.

Now I know some of you hate the idea of being the teacher's pet, but some children go to the other extreme and actually go out of their way to upset the teacher. They deliberately misbehave in class and cause the teacher all sorts of problems.

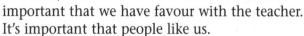

We don't need to be teacher's pet; we don't need to be the teacher's favourite; but it *is* important that we have favour with the teacher. It's important that people like us.

Favour With Men

Object needed: *A multicoloured coat or jacket.*

In the Bible there was a boy who had a multicoloured coat a bit like this one. God gave him a dream that he would be a great leader. His brothers sold him as a slave and sent him to Egypt, but even there, God's chosen person had favour with men – he ended up in charge of an important man's household. He was later thrown into a dungeon but even there, God's chosen person had favour with the jailer, who looked after him. Finally he became the second-in-charge governor of the whole of Egypt. When God chooses a person, they get favour with people as well.

Daniel lived several hundred years after Joseph but he too was God's chosen person who had favour with people. He became second-in-charge governor of all of Babylon.

The Bible says that Jesus also had favour with God and with men.

The Balance

Object needed: *A seesaw.*

There is of course a balance here. Some people spend all their time trying to be liked by people.

Some people try so hard to win favour with others that they will do anything just to keep in with their friends, no matter what happens. They put all their weight on this side of the seesaw. But this is not balanced. Paul, a famous Bible person, said this: "If I was trying to please people, I wouldn't have become a servant of Jesus."

We must do our best to be liked by people, but always remember that being liked by God is far more important.

● STORY – Jackie Pullinger (4)

Jackie was making good progress. Many people had given their lives to Jesus and she felt she was gaining respect in the Walled City. Then one evening her opinion changed.

She was woken early one morning by a constant ringing. She reached for the telephone.

"Hello!" she croaked.

"Miss Poon [this is what Jackie was called in Hong Kong], you must come quickly – someone has broken into the youth club and there's a terrible mess." The voice was that of Ah Ping, a triad member who had given his life to Jesus.

Jackie dressed quickly and since it was too early to get a taxi she ran all the way to the Walled City. She was expecting to see a mess, but nothing prepared her for the sight that greeted her when she entered the youth club. All the equipment had been smashed up, the table tennis bats had been broken, the skateboards snapped, the tables overturned. But worse than that, someone had smeared mud and grime from outside onto the floors and windows. Her nice clean youth club had been dirtied from outside.

Jackie was distraught. She thought that the young men of the area had come to respect her, and now she felt that they were just using her. She was very upset. She knew that Jesus taught that we should always keep going when things go wrong; she knew that when people are horrible to you, Jesus teaches that we should still be kind in return, but this was going to be difficult. Jackie was angry and upset and wasn't feeling very charitable.

She spent the rest of the day cleaning up the mess. She swept and fixed and cleaned and mended, to try and have the youth club ready for the evening. But all the time she was sweeping, she kept thinking about how it would be easier for her to be in Kensington High Street in London with her friends, going to Bible studies and dinner parties. She didn't mind pouring her life out for these people, but she wasn't going to be treated like this. She kept cleaning, wondering what would become of her.

Finally the job was complete, and she opened the youth club as usual. She was surprised to see so many young people still coming, and even more surprised by how well they behaved. She was further surprised by the presence of the new young man who stood outside. All the people who were coming to the youth club were showing him great respect as they walked by. Eventually Jackie walked out to speak to the man and ask, "Who are you?"

He responded slowly, "Have you got any trouble?" Jackie shook her head. The man continued: "If you have trouble you must tell me; I will deal with the trouble."

Jackie was unsure who this man was or where he came from. She asked again, "Who are you?"

"Who I am is unimportant. My name is Winson, but what is important is that Goko sent me!"

Now Jackie really was surprised. She knew who Goko was, although his name was rarely mentioned. Goko was the leader of most of the gangs in Hong Kong; he was the boss of the bosses. Jackie had sent many messages to Goko to say that Jesus loved him, but she didn't know if they had got through. She had never met him.

Clearly those messages must have been getting through, for Goko was on Jackie's side. She later found out that Goko had dealt seriously with those who had damaged the youth club and had commanded the young people to go back. He had also ordered Winson to stand guard every night outside the youth club to make sure no trouble came. Jackie was to discover that Winson was a high-ranking triad member.

But Jackie was to make an even greater breakthrough: several weeks later, Winson, this high-ranking triad boss, gave his life to Jesus.

Jackie truly had favour with people.

(To be continued...)

Sometimes You Just Have To Keep Going

	Programme	Item
Section 1	Welcome	
	Rules	
	Prayer	
	Praise	
	Game 1	Noodles 1
	Praise (x2)	
	Fun Item 1	
	Game 2	Noodles 2
	Fun Item 2	
	Bible Text	John 6:68
	Announcements	
	Interview	
	Worship (x2)	
Section 2	Bible Lesson	The Sower
Preaching	Illustration 1	The Farmer
Time	Illustration 2	Bill Wilson
	Illustration 3	The Marathon Runner
	Story	Jackie Pullinger (5)
	Prayer	

Overview Jackie was working hard; she was giving everything she could to help the people. She was determined. But suddenly everything had gone wrong. Everyone called of God faces this situation at least once – the temptation to give up.

games

Game 1

Noodles 1
(A welcome return to Chinese food!)

PREPARATION	A bowl of noodles and a pair of chopsticks per team.
PLAYERS	Four per team.
SET-UP	The noodles are placed at B along with the chopsticks. The teams line up in relay formation at A.
OBJECT	To run from A to B, eat as many noodles as possible within two minutes using the chopsticks, and return to A.
WINNING	The team that eats the most noodles wins.

Game 2

Noodles 2
(When a game tastes this good it would be a crime to only do it once.)

PREPARATION	A bowl of noodles and a pair of chopsticks per team.
PLAYERS	Four per team.
SET-UP	The noodles are placed at B along with the chopsticks. The teams line up in relay formation at A.
OBJECT	To run from A to B, eat as many noodles as possible within two minutes using the chopsticks, and return to A.
WINNING	The team that eats the most noodles wins.

Preaching Time

BIBLE LESSON **THE SOWER**

"Simon Peter answered, 'Lord, there is no one else that we can go to! Your words give eternal life.'" (John 6:68)

A farmer got up to sow
And began to throw the seed across the field
But some seed fell on the footpath
Where feet would crush
And birds rush to eat each last shred.
Later, the teacher said:
The seeds that spread and fed the birds instead
Are the ones who only hear the words in their
    head
And the evil one comes, and numbs their heart
And keeps them dead.

But other seed fell
And when what's sown, lands on stone,
Yes, it might have grown for a while
But the farmer's smile has gone.
For no seed can grow with no soil below.
For no seed is freed from the need for food.

And the teacher said
His words may bed in the hearts of some for a
    while
They begin to believe, they receive with joy
Until the day when troubles come
And trials wile their ruthless way
To their rootless prey
And their faith wanes away.

But who is it that warns
The seed that was thrown among thorns?
They grow up together, side by side,
And thorns hide their beguiling smile
And bide their time, until the day
When the field feels a little too small
For them all.
But it's not the thorns that fall.

And the teacher said:
These seeds are the ones who hear
And get so near.
But fear and find
Their mind will wind around

And worries hound, till they're gagged and
    bound and choked, by worries and wealth
they'll be found wanting.

But other seed fell well
And time was to tell how high the crop would
    swell
To thirtyfold, or sixtyfold, or a hundredfold.
And the teacher told
That souls would grow when the seed found the
    ground
Where no thorns would bind; no rock, block;
Or birds flock to pick or peck.
And he knew
That good soil would oil the oath,
Would grace the growth,
Of the ones who heard the word and understood.

Those that have ears to hear, let them hear.
Those that have eyes to see, let them see.
Those that have a heart to heal, let them feel.
But those that will not see, let them be.

(This poem is by Rob Lacey. Used by permission.)

The Farmer

Object needed: *A picture of a farmer.*

Farmers have to be
very disciplined. They
know that there are
certain times of year
to plant their crops,
and that there are
certain times of year
to harvest their crops.
    But can you
imagine if farmers
weren't so disciplined?
Can you imagine what would happen if the
farmer decided to give up? He would have
planted many crops in the ground. He would
have them growing all around him – and then he
would walk away and leave them.
    If anyone saw him doing this, they would
think him very foolish indeed. Some people quit
just before the exciting stuff happens.

Bill Wilson

Object needed: *The book* Streets of Pain –
    published by Word (UK).

Bill Wilson lives and works in New York City. He
started a children's club that is similar to ours,
but his club has 20,000 children in it every week.
It's an amazing set-up. Bill has been there for
many years, but it has been far from easy.
    On one occasion Bill was walking through
the streets of Brooklyn when some teenagers
rushed up behind him and knocked him out with
a house brick. They then proceeded to kick him
while he was on the ground. He had some
broken ribs and was hurt pretty badly. But worse
was to follow. He found out that a part of his eye
had been damaged and he would have to have an
operation. He would have to fly to a city called
Dallas where the doctor would perform the
operation.
    Bill was afraid of the operation. It involved
taking his eye out, repairing the damage and
replacing his eye. He was very afraid. He wanted
to run away.
    But Bill stuck in there just long enough. On
the morning the operation was to take place Bill
Wilson woke up and could see perfectly out of
both eyes. God had performed a miracle. Bill was
healed.
    Some people quit just before the exciting
stuff happens.

The Marathon Man

Object needed: *None.*

A man dressed in a jogging suit enters, running.

NARRATOR: Here we are, ladies and gentlemen, at
    the end of the New York marathon.
    Here, approaching the finish line, is

what will surely be the new world champion. He's looking very good after running 26 miles. This is going to be one of the fastest marathons ever run. Here he comes; he's only ten metres from the finishing line. He's nearly there. *(The runner stops.)*

What's going on? He's stopped. Why has he done this?

This would be absolute madness, wouldn't it? To get so close and then give up. But some people give up just a little too early. We need to learn to keep going, even if it's hard sometimes.

Some people give up just before the exciting stuff happens.

● STORY – Jackie Pullinger (5)

Like the Walled City boys, Jackie now slept by day and got up at night, at least in theory. In fact, since she had language lessons, court appearances, prison visits and other matters concerned with sorting out problems for them, it meant that she was also up by day.

Every day on waking, the only way she could get out of bed was by promising herself that she could come back and sleep later in the day.

"I will. I really will," she would mutter as she struggled into consciousness, but she never did. Instead she learned how to catnap, sleeping on buses.

One night, Jackie took a group of Walled City boys to the hills for a barbecue. It was the Autumn Moon Festival and the boys had strung up paper lanterns all over the hillside. In the clear moonlight she saw a large, rough-looking young man sitting amongst the others stuffing himself with pork chops, beef steaks and chicken wings. As she had bought all these herself and reckoned on sufficient for our entire coach load she was quite mad at him. But while she watched, the other boys gave him their food too and seemed mesmerised by his every word.

Ah Ping whispered that this was his own *daih lo*, the leader of his particular gang and of most of those present. He was actually the real brother of Goko [whom we heard about last time], and was the number two in the Walled City. As more and more of his "brothers" had been attending

the youth club, Sal Di, curious and maybe a little jealous, had decided to come to this function himself. If he chose to, he had the power to run all the boys and the club himself, so there was a distinct possibility that this was a take-over bid.

"Would you mind coming for a talk?" Jackie asked him and indicated a small patch of scrub just over the crest. He was amused at this request from a mere girl and made a great show of rising from his haunches and lumbering towards me amidst many comments and whistles. But when they were out of earshot he dropped the macho image and began to listen to Jackie. Jackie explained why the club existed; she explained that she was telling the boys about the love of God.

His reply was very interesting; he said: "We've been watching you. Many missionaries come to Hong Kong to help us poor people. They put us in sociological boxes and analyse us. They take our pictures to shock the Westerners by our living conditions. They get famous because they've been here. But inside the Walled City we usually get rid of them within six months."

He spoke perfect English: "We find ways to discourage them until they have no heart to continue. If you had been a man we would have had you beaten long ago."

He added, "We couldn't care less if you have big buildings or small ones. You can be offering free food, free schools, judo classes, or needlework to us. It doesn't matter if you have a daily programme or hymn singing once a week. These things don't touch us because the people who run them have nothing to do with us. What we want to know is if you are concerned with us. Now you have been here for four years we have decided that maybe you mean what you say."

Jackie didn't shout out for joy in front of this man, but she wanted to. Now that the people who only came for what they could get had left the club, Jackie found that those who remained were the ones who wanted to be friends and who eventually would become interested in spiritual things. Jackie never gave up, she never gave in and she was determined not to leave these people.

(To be continued...)

6 Telling Others

	Programme	Item
Section 1	Welcome	
	Rules	
	Prayer	
	Praise	
	Game 1	Table Tennis 1
	Praise (x2)	
	Fun Item 1	
	Game 2	Table Tennis 2
	Fun Item 2	
	Bible Text	Matthew 18:14
	Announcements	
	Interview	
	Worship (x2)	
Section 2 **Preaching** **Time**	Bible Lesson	The Lost Sheep
	Illustration 1	Whoops! I Forgot!
	Illustration 2	The Vaccine
	Illustration 3	Good News
	Story	Jackie Pullinger (6)
	Prayer	

Overview Jackie shared the good news of a God who loved people wherever she went. But even she was surprised how easily some people decided to become Christians. Sometimes people are eager and ready to become Christians, but nobody is telling them about Jesus.

games

PreachingTime

Game 1

Table Tennis 1

PREPARATION	A table tennis bat and a table tennis ball per team.
PLAYERS	Four per team.
SET-UP	The teams line up in relay formation at A with the front person holding the bat and ball.
OBJECT	To run from A to B while bouncing the ball on the bat and return to A. The bat and ball is then swapped and the next player sets off.
WINNING	The team that returns first wins.

Game 2

Table Tennis 2

PREPARATION	A table tennis bat and a balloon per team.
PLAYERS	Four per team.
SET-UP	The teams line up in relay formation at A with the front person holding the bat and balloon.
OBJECT	To run from A to B while bouncing the balloon on the bat and return to A. The bat and ball is then swapped and the next player sets off.
WINNING	The team that returns first wins. If a team bursts its balloon the players are disqualified.

BIBLE LESSON THE LOST SHEEP (Matthew 18)

"He doesn't want any of these little ones to be lost." (Matthew 18:14)

Jesus told this story:

If any of you has a hundred sheep, and one of them gets lost, what will you do? Won't you leave the ninety-nine in the field and go look for the lost sheep until you find it? And when you find it, you will be so glad that you will put it on your shoulder and carry it home. Then you will call in your friends and neighbors and say, "Let's celebrate! I've found my lost sheep."

Jesus said, "In the same way there is more happiness in heaven because of one sinner who turns to God than over ninety-nine good people who don't need to."

Illustration 1

Whoops! I Forgot!

Object needed: *None.*

I forget things a lot. If somebody tells me something, I have to be sure to write it down or I will not remember it ten minutes from now. If I go to the shop to buy bread and milk, I either forget the bread or I forget the milk.

The good thing is that if I forget a loaf of bread it's quite sad (no toast for my beans on toast), but it isn't the end of the world. I can always eat something else.

But just suppose I was the man who had the job of stopping people going up a certain road, because at the top of the road the bridge wasn't finished and there was a big drop into the river. If I forgot to stop the people, that might be much more serious. People could die. Or

if I was a signalman beside a railway track and I forgot to change the signals, that could be very serious.

Some things we forget just aren't important. Some things we forget are incredibly important.

If I forget to tell people how much God loves them, then it is just possible that when they die they will not be able to go to heaven because they don't know God. We need to tell people about God. It's very serious.

The Vaccine

Object needed: *A first-aid box with a green cross on the side.*

Imagine I have just arrived in a foreign country and this is my medical box. In this medical box I have all sorts of amazing medicines – medicines that can cure all sorts of terrible diseases. The people in this country are dying of a particularly nasty illness and I have the cure right here in my box. But it's my box and I can do what I want with it. So I decide to keep the box closed and watch the people die.

What do you think? Am I a good person or a bad person? Am I being kind or not?

Now sin is a much worse disease. It is the junk and garbage in our lives that stop us

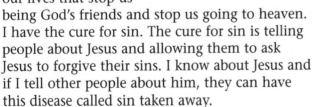

being God's friends and stop us going to heaven. I have the cure for sin. The cure for sin is telling people about Jesus and allowing them to ask Jesus to forgive their sins. I know about Jesus and if I tell other people about him, they can have this disease called sin taken away.

How about you? You know about Jesus too. Will you keep it to yourself or will you tell others?

Good News

Object needed: *A lottery or raffle ticket. (You may miss this illustration if it causes a moral dilemma!)*

If I had just won the lottery and was the winner of millions of pounds, firstly it would be a miracle because I've never bought a lottery ticket, but secondly it would be amazingly good news. I think I would tell everyone about it. I would be running up and down the street shouting at the top of my voice that I had just won the lottery. I would be so happy.

That would be good news. It would be great to tell everyone. In the Bible, the true story of Jesus being born, living a perfect life and dying on a cross for us is described as good news. It means that we can go to heaven when we die and get the chance to have all the things we've done wrong forgiven right now. It is very exciting. It is good news. And remember, it is good to share good news.

● STORY – Jackie Pullinger (6)

Jackie had spent much time with David. David had been taking drugs since he was ten and he was very messed up and constantly in and out of jail. Eventually, after much time, David announced to Jackie that he had had enough of being in and out of jail and he wanted to become a Christian. Jackie was delighted but also very keen that David inform his gang leader. She wanted David to cut all his connections with crime and stop being a villain.

Jackie asked David to allow her to talk to his gang leader. She wanted to convince the gang leader to allow David to go. Also she wanted a chance to tell the gang leader about Jesus. Jackie asked David who his leader was. She was slightly shocked to find out that the gang leader went by the name of Jesus, but she thought that might even make it easier to tell him about the real Jesus.

David wasn't sure that "Jesus" the gang leader would talk to Jackie but Jackie simply said,

"Why don't you ask him? If you're going to be a Christian you can't follow two different leaders called Jesus. You must decide which one you will follow."

"OK," said David. "I'll try to find him."

At last David came back, looking surprised. "He'll see you," he told Jackie. "You are to go to Block 20 of Chaiwan Settlement estate at midnight tonight and find the noodle stall. Someone will meet you there and take you to "Jesus" but you must take a hundred dollars."

"Why the hundred dollars?" Jackie asked curiously.

"Well, nobody in Chaiwan knows you, Miss Poon," David replied. "It's not as if it were the Walled City where you are protected. Chaiwan is a very dangerous area at night and you might get mugged. If you have a hundred dollars, they will take it and leave you alone, but if you have nothing they will be angry and beat you up."

"Don't be silly," Jackie reasoned. "I haven't got ten dollars, let alone a hundred. I'm not taking money – if I am on God's business then he will look after me. And anyway, if it would help you to understand how much God loves you then I wouldn't mind dying. I have nothing to lose."

David looked at Jackie incredulously for a moment then said, "You're crazy! You're mad!" But he glanced at his friend and went on: "We never met anyone who would die for us before."

Jackie arrived by minibus at 11:30 p.m. and spent a little time looking around Chaiwan. This enormous area at the end of Hong Kong Island consisted of resettlement blocks where tens of thousands of people were housed by the government. Each family had one room to live, eat and sleep in, with communal toilets and showers at the end of each floor.

Eventually Jackie arrived at the noodle shop where she was to meet the gang leader.

"What do you want?" the curly-haired Cantonese man asked.

"Take me to your leader," Jackie replied, clutching her huge Bible firmly.

"Who do you want to see?" the man grunted.

"I want to see 'Jesus'."

"Why do you want to see Jesus?" the man asked.

Jackie replied quickly, "I want to tell him about *my* Jesus."

The man looked amused then laughed to himself. "Are you sure you want to see Jesus?" He was trying to sound tough.

"Yes!" Jackie replied, becoming irritated. "I want to tell him about my Jesus," she repeated.

"Well, you're talking to him," the man replied.

Jesus the gang leader sat in the café and listened to Jackie talk. He understood what she was saying and before long he realised that even though he was a big gang leader he needed Jesus; he needed to ask Jesus to forgive the wrong things he had done; he needed Jesus in his life. And there, with coffee cups all around in the noodle shop, the gang leader called Jesus gave his life to Jesus. Just as Jackie was leaving, she remembered to tell the gang leader some important news: "Remember, you are supposed to tell other people about God." With that last comment Jackie walked away.

When Jackie saw him the next afternoon at a friend's house she hardly recognised the old "Jesus". He looked bright and keen, unlike the seedy villain of last night.

"Did you tell one person that you believed last night?" she asked eagerly.

"No, I didn't," he replied. "I told my whole gang. We stayed up until six in the morning looking at the verses you underlined in the Bible, and now they all want to believe, too."

The whole gang had given their lives to Jesus. Now people were becoming Christians all the time because people were telling them the good news of a God who loved them and a Jesus who died on a cross for them.

(To be continued…)

7 Thinking Big

	Programme	Item
Section 1	Welcome	
	Rules	
	Prayer	
	Praise	
	Game 1	Chinese Whispers
	Praise (x2)	
	Fun Item 1	
	Game 2	Chinese Writing
	Fun Item 2	
	Bible Text	Ephesians 5:16
	Announcements	
	Interview	
	Worship (x2)	
Section 2	Bible Lesson	Five Foolish Girls
Preaching	Illustration 1	Boy Scouts
Time	Illustration 2	Some Things We Have To Wait For
	Illustration 3	But Not Everything
	Story	Jackie Pullinger (7)
	Prayer	

 **Overview** The work Jackie had to do just escalated. God blessed her and gave her great favour with the government. They gave her houses, then villages, then even islands. But it all started when she was eight.

games

PreachingTime

Game 1

Chinese Whispers

PREPARATION	None.
PLAYERS	Five players per team.
SET-UP	Three players at A and two players at B per team.
OBJECT	The first player of each team is given the message: "Jackie Pullinger is a heroic woman!". This is whispered to the first player only once. The first player runs from A to B and whispers it to the next player, who then runs from B to A and whispers it to the next player, and so on.
WINNING	The first team to finish with something resembling the message wins.

Game 2

Chinese Writing

PREPARATION	A Chinese word with five characters on acetate. A piece of paper and pen per team.
PLAYERS	Five per team.
SET-UP	The Chinese word is displayed on an acetate. The pen and paper is placed at B.
OBJECT	The first player runs from A to B, copies the first Chinese character onto the paper as well as he or she can and returns. The next player does the same with the second character, and so on.
WINNING	The first team to complete the Chinese word wins.

BIBLE LESSON | **FIVE FOOLISH GIRLS (Matthew 25)**

"Make every minute count." *(Ephesians 5:16)*

Jesus told the following story:

The kingdom of heaven is like what happened one night when ten girls took their oil lamps and went to a wedding to meet the groom. Five of the girls were foolish and five were wise. The foolish ones took their lamps, but no extra oil. The ones who were wise took along extra oil for their lamps.

The groom was late arriving, and the girls became drowsy and fell asleep. Then in the middle of the night someone shouted, "Here's the groom! Come to meet him!"

When the girls got up and started getting their lamps ready, the foolish ones said to the others, "Let us have some of your oil! Our lamps are going out."

The girls who were wise answered, "There's not enough oil for all of us! Go and buy some for yourselves."

While the foolish girls were on their way to get some oil, the groom arrived. The girls who were ready went into the wedding, and the doors were closed. Later the other girls returned and shouted, "Sir, sir! Open the door for us!"

But the groom replied, "I don't even know you!"

So, my disciples, always be ready! You don't know the day or the time when all this will happen.

The story is there to remind us that we need to be ready at all times.

254 **The Jackie Pullinger Story**

Boy Scouts

Object needed: *Someone in a Boy Scout uniform, or a picture of a Boy Scout.*

Boy Scouts have a motto. Do you know what it is? *(Field some answers.)*

Their motto is "Be Prepared". If only our girls in today's parable had understood this, things might have been a whole lot happier for them.

God wants us to be prepared and he wants us to be ready for anything he wants us to do.

Some Things We Have To Wait For

Object needed: *A toy car or a picture of a car.*

Who would like to drive my car? *(Expect quite a few hands.)*

How many of you think you would be good at driving my car?

How many of you think that you would probably crash my car?

Now in this country there is a reason why you can't drive my car on the roads, apart from the fact that I will not let you and the fact that some of your legs are too short to reach the pedals. There is another reason. Why can't I let you? *(Field some answers. You're basically looking for the fact that they are too young.)*

And there are other things you can't do because you are too young. Can you thing of any? *(Get a full-time job, get married, etc.)*

So, there are some things you can't do because you are too young.

But Not Everything

Object needed: *A picture of John Wesley.*

There are things you *can* do now that some of you don't think you can. I'm thinking of all the things you can do for God right now. You may not be able to travel to faraway lands to live there and tell people about Jesus (although some of you may do just that with your mums and dads). But there *are* things you can do.

Some of the most famous preachers – people who tell large crowds about God – started preaching when they were eight, nine and ten years old.

This picture here is of a man called John Wesley. When he was alive he kept a journal – another name for a diary – of things which he saw. In his journal he talks about children as young as four and five praying for sick people and seeing them healed and made better. He talks of eight- and nine-year-olds telling adults about Jesus; the adults then became Christians. There really are some amazing stories in his diary.

But this is what we need to learn: Let's not wait until we're old – if we are ready and prepared, God can use us right now.

● STORY – Jackie Pullinger (7)

Jackie's work in Hong Kong went from strength to strength. Now many of the gang leaders were giving their lives to Jesus and many people in their gangs followed. The youth club was packed nearly all the time with people wanting to learn more about Jesus.

People who came with injuries were being prayed for and God was instantly healing them. People who came with drug problems were being prayed for and they instantly stopped taking drugs. Jackie was doing amazing things because she hadn't given up and God was blessing her.

It was clear that the youth centre was now much too small, so Jackie began to ask God to give her a bigger place. God told her he would. Shortly afterwards the Hong Kong government gave her a house. She called the house "The House of Happiness". Many drug takers became free of their drugs in that place.

Soon the house was too small. But Jackie

knew that God could give her all that she needed. She was prepared and she was ready. She was given another house. But still she knew God wanted more.

This time the Hong Kong government gave Jackie an entire village – a whole village to teach people about Jesus and see them set free from drugs. But Jackie continued to pray and God continued to bless her. Jackie married the man called Christopher that we heard about several sessions ago and still the work continued to grow.

Jackie was concerned that when Hong Kong was given back to the Chinese, she would have to leave and wouldn't be able to help the people any longer. She prayed and shortly afterwards she received a letter from the Chinese government.

They wanted Jackie to come and tell them how so many people were being set free from drugs. They wanted to hear about Jesus.

Shortly after that, the Chinese government gave Jackie an entire island where people could go to learn about God and see the amazing things he could do for them and through them.

Jackie did, and is still doing, amazing things for Jesus. But this is what I want you to know… IT ALL STARTED WHEN SHE WAS EIGHT YEARS OLD.

(I would pray for some of the children who want to be missionaries at this point, but you must do what you feel comfortable with and what you feel God is telling you to do.)

Special Events
Christmas, Easter And Harvest

Three One-off Lessons

CHRISTMAS SPECIAL
The Golden Box

	Programme	Item
Section 1	Welcome	
	Rules	
	Prayer	
	Praise	
	Game 1	Gold Coin Collection
	Praise (x2)	
	Fun Item 1	
	Game 2	Gold Coin Toss
	Fun Item 2	
	Bible Text	John 3:16
	Announcements	
	Interview	
	Worship (x2)	
Section 2	Bible Lesson	Nativity
Preaching	Illustration 1	The Sapphire Box
Time	Illustration 2	The Ruby Box
	Illustration 3	The Emerald Box
	Story	The Golden Box
	Prayer	

Overview Christmas means a lot of different things to different people – literally, lots of different things. But God didn't come to this world as a baby because of things; he came because of love.

games

Game 1

Gold Coin Collection

PREPARATION	A pile of chocolate money in a box at B and an empty box at A for each team.
PLAYERS	Four per team.
SET-UP	The players are lined up in relay formation at A. The box of chocolate coins is at B.
OBJECT	The players are to run in relay from A to B, collect a coin (only one) and place it in their team box at A. The team keeps going until the box at B is empty.
WINNING	The team that has the most coins wins.

Game 2

Gold Coin Toss

PREPARATION	A pile of chocolate money in each team box placed at A. An empty box per team positioned one metre past B.
PLAYERS	Four per team.
SET-UP	The players are lined up in relay formation at A.
OBJECT	The players run in relay from A to B and each tosses a coin into the empty box
WINNING	The team that has the most coins in their box wins.

Preaching Time

BIBLE LESSON NATIVITY

"God loved the people of this world so much that he gave his only Son, so that everyone who has faith in him will have eternal life and never really die." (John 3:16)

There are several ways to make this story interesting for the children:

1. Invite the children to act out the parts.
2. Use Jane Ray's illustrated nativity book The Story of Christmas, *showing the pictures as you tell the story.*
3. Use Joyce Dunbar's poem "This is the Star", and Gary Blyth's illustrations from the book of the same name.

In the days of Herod the King, in the town of Nazareth, there lived a young woman named Mary. She was going to marry a carpenter whose name was Joseph.

Now the angel Gabriel was sent from God to Nazareth, to the house where Mary lived. And the angel said,

"Hello, Mary! Blessed are you among women, for God has chosen you to be the mother of his Son. You shall give birth to a baby boy, and he shall be called Jesus."

And Mary said, "Let what you have said be done."

And the angel left.

Now, while Mary was waiting for her child to be born, an order went out for every person to return to the town of his birth, so that a count could be made of all the people in the land. And Joseph and Mary left Nazareth together to go to Bethlehem, where Joseph was born.

When they reached Bethlehem, Mary knew it was time for the baby to be born. But the town was filled with people and there was no room for them at the inn. So the innkeeper led them to his stable.

And there Mary gave birth to her son, and wrapped him in swaddling clothes. She laid him in a manger, with the ox and the ass standing by.

So what is Christmas all about? One of these boxes holds a clue about the most important part of Christmas. Let's look at them all:

Illustration **1**

The Sapphire Box

Object needed: *A sapphire-coloured box with a lid on it. Inside is a selection box.*

So what is Christmas about? Let's take a look at the first box and see what we find. *(Remove the lid and take out the selection box.)*

So maybe the most important part of Christmas is chocolate. God looked down on the world and decided that we needed chocolate. I'm not sure that's true. Chocolate is nice and I like to eat lots of it, but I don't really think it's the most important thing at Christmas time. If you took all the chocolate away, I think I would still survive – just about.

Illustration **2**

The Ruby Box

Object needed: *A ruby-coloured box with a lid on it. Inside it is some chocolate money.*

So what is Christmas about? Let's take a look at the second box and see what we find. *(Remove the lid and take out the chocolate money.)*

So maybe Christmas is about money. Loads and loads of money. Money to buy Christmas presents, and Christmas meals and Christmas trees and Christmas cards and... Well, there really is no end to the things you can buy... But the most important thing about Christmas can't be bought. Money is useful, but people who don't have much of it can still have a very good Christmas if they've got what's in the golden box.

So money is not the most important part of Christmas.

Illustration **3**

The Emerald Box

Object needed: *An emerald-coloured box with a lid on it. Inside is a television guide.*

So what is Christmas about? Let's take a look at the third box and see what we find. *(Remove the lid and take out the television guide.)*

Ah, now, this is the most important part of Christmas. Let me just have a quick look. Here it is. The Christmas Day movie. This has got to be the most important part of Christmas. Nothing beats sitting down and watching the television.

Let's see what else is on... *The Simpsons' Christmas Special.* That sounds interesting. And the *Barbie* movie – I know some boys who will like that one.

Television is interesting, but I don't even think that television is the most important part of Christmas. I think if it was a choice between television and the thing in the golden box, then it would have to be the golden box every time.

Let me put you out of your misery and tell you the story of the golden box.

● STORY – The Golden Box

Karen lived alone with her father. Her mummy had moved to another country many years before. Karen did miss her mum, but living with Dad was OK. Karen had spent the whole afternoon at the kitchen table with scissors; Dad could hear lots of cutting sounds as he sat in the living room watching television.

But when Dad eventually went to the kitchen to investigate, he was furious. "What a waste of money! Why have you used that good wrapping paper? You really are a silly girl."

Karen's dad told her off quite severely. They didn't have much money and the last thing Karen's father wanted was for her to waste their most expensive wrapping paper on her game. She had cut the wrapping paper up and now it was no good for anything. He grew even more upset when, after sending her to her room for cutting the paper up, he saw her pasting it onto an old box.

"What are you doing that for?" he asked.

"We could have used that paper for your granny's present."

A little later on, the same gold-wrapped present appeared under the Christmas tree. When Dad looked at the tag his anger soon subsided, and he felt almost a little embarrassed: he saw his own name on the tag.

That night was Christmas Eve and Karen went to bed early, as everyone does on Christmas Eve, hoping that the morning will come more quickly. Eventually, after a very sleepless night, Karen rushed into her dad's bedroom at 6 a.m. She shook him until he woke up. He was still very sleepy. He rubbed his eyes until the sleepiness had all gone. He stumbled into the bathroom to throw cold water over his face and then he made his way downstairs. He was feeling a bit grumpy about being up so early, but he smiled as Karen opened her presents: the Barbie doll and the lovely outfits, the new slippers, pyjamas with Harry Potter on, new school shoes… Eventually all her presents were opened and all that remained under the tree was the golden box.

Karen went over to collect it and handed it to her dad. He decided that he didn't mind being woken up at 6 a.m., for it must be a very lovely present to be wrapped in such a wonderful box. He took his time opening the lid and then he gazed inside.

He now became quite angry as he looked into the box. He looked at his little girl and spoke to her very strongly indeed: "Young lady, don't you know that when you give a present to someone, there's supposed to be a present inside?"

The little girl looked up with tears in her eyes and said: "Oh Daddy, it's not empty. I blew kisses into it until it was full. And then I put the lid on so none could escape. I've made you a box full of love."

The father was crushed. He fell on his knees and with tears in his eyes he hugged his little girl tightly.

We may all get presents this Christmas wrapped up in various ways, containing various wonderful things. But we all have a special box as well, an invisible box, a box full of love and joy and happiness from all the people around us. Sadly, there are boys and girls who have never known love, and there are some people who think that their boxes are empty, but that is where the true meaning of Christmas comes in. The Bible says this: "God loved you so much that he sent his only Son Jesus."

And Jesus came to make sure that we all have boxes full of love.

Many years later, when the girl had left home, her dad still had that golden box. He would often go to it and take out an imaginary kiss and remember the love of the little girl who had put it there.

God LOVED the world so much he sent Jesus. That was God's part. He LOVED. But the verse goes on: SO THAT EVERYONE WHO HAS FAITH IN HIM WILL HAVE ETERNAL LIFE. That's our bit…

(Possibly ask for a response.)

HAVE YOU GOT THAT FAITH IN YOUR INEART THIS CHRISTMA

EASTER SPECIAL
Substitutes

	Programme	Item
Section 1	**Welcome**	
	Rules	
	Prayer	
	Praise	
	Game 1	Egg And Spoon Race
	Praise (x2)	
	Fun Item 1	
	Game 2	Egg Catcher
	Fun Item 2	
	Bible Text	1 Corinthians 15:3
	Announcements	
	Interview	
	Worship (x2)	
Section 2	**Bible Lesson**	Mark's Crucifixion Account
Preaching	**Illustration 1**	The Brothers
Time	**Illustration 2**	Somebody Must Pay
	Story	The Lion, The Witch And The Wardrobe
	Prayer	

verview Atonement, substitution, propitiation… the Easter message is very complex. This curriculum series will look strictly at the substitution aspect: Jesus died in our place.

games

Game 1

Egg And Spoon Race

PREPARATION   An Easter egg per team.

PLAYERS   Five per team.

SET-UP   The traditional egg and spoon format, except the egg is replaced by an Easter egg.

OBJECT   The first player runs from A to B carrying the egg on the spoon. They then return to A; the next person then goes. This repeats until the whole team has gone. If the egg is dropped then the person must stop, replace the egg on the spoon and then continue.

WINNING   The first team back wins.

Game 2

Egg Catcher

PREPARATION   An Easter egg per team.

PLAYERS   Two per team.

SET-UP   The two people stand one metre apart.

OBJECT   The first person throws the egg to the second. If the second person catches it, he or she takes one step back and throws the egg back. This continues until the egg is dropped.

WINNING   The team that throws the egg the furthest wins.

Preaching Time

BIBLE LESSON   **MARK'S CRUCIFIXION ACCOUNT**

"Christ died for our sins according to the Scriptures." (1 Corinthians 15:3, New International Version)

The soldiers led Jesus away into the palace and called together all the soldiers. They put a purple robe on him and twisted together a crown of thorns and placed it on his head. They began to make fun of him, and they hit him again and again.

Then they led him away to be crucified. Jesus was so weak after his beating that when they tried to force him to carry his own cross he fell to the ground. They made a man called Simon from a place called Cyrene carry the cross for Jesus.

They brought Jesus to a place called Golgotha and there they crucified him. They literally nailed him to a cross. Nails pierced his ankles and his wrists and there he hung until he died.

Three days later, Jesus will prove that he is stronger even than death, and rise again from the grave, but let's not jump ahead. Let's think for a minute about the cross.

The man who had never done any wrong died for those who had done many things wrong. That's us – me and you. Jesus died for us.

Illustration 1

The Brothers

Objects needed: *A white shirt and a shirt stained with red.*

There were once two brothers who also happened to be identical twins. They grew up together, but they took two very different paths in life. One became a respectable businessman who worked hard at his job; the other became a thief and a criminal.

On one occasion the man who became the

criminal was robbing a house when the owners returned. In his panic he stabbed the owner and then escaped quickly. His shirt was covered in blood and he ran away fast, before the police could find him. He hadn't gone far when he heard the sound of the police catching up with him. He ran to his brother's house and began to knock on the door. His brother came quickly and let him in. The respectable brother realised what had happened, but was surprised at how soon the police came knocking on the door. He commanded his criminal brother: "Take off your shirt and go and hide out back. When they have gone, go to the hills and hide."

The criminal brother did as he was instructed. But as soon as he left the room his respectable brother put on the blood-stained shirt and opened the door to the police. The other brother knew nothing of this and escaped to the hills.

Several weeks later the criminal brother returned to find out if the police were still looking for him. He went to knock on his brother's door, but was astonished when he heard a man from across the street call out, "Sir! You will get no answer. They executed that man last week for murdering someone."

The brother began to cry. He realised that his respectable brother had given his life for him. He was heartbroken, but when he eventually recovered, he decided that he would live a respectable life from then on. After all, didn't he owe his brother that much?

Jesus was also innocent, but chose to die in our place. Surely we need to make some decisions about how we respond to that.

Somebody Must Pay

Objects needed: *Cans of pop.*

On a hot summer day I might be very thirsty. I might desperately want some Coke. I walk into the shop for my Coke and I see some in the fridge; my mouth waters just looking at it. I pick it up and begin to leave the shop, all the time looking at this amazing can of pop that I'm going to drink. Then just as I get to the door the shopkeeper shouts, "Stop! You haven't paid."

But I haven't got any money. I can't pay. I stand at the shop door, but until that Coke is paid for, I can't leave. Fortunately a kind old man sees how thirsty I am and pays the shopkeeper for me. I take my pop and go outside. It tastes lovely, but there was no way I could have enjoyed the Coke unless it was paid for. What is important is that *I* didn't have to pay for it. As long as someone paid, then the shopkeeper was happy.

You see, most things are not really free. Someone usually has to pay the price. We may have got our new trainers for our birthday, and to us they may be free, but someone paid.

Becoming a Christian is very similar. We can become a Christian for free. All it involves is asking Jesus to forgive the wrong things we've done and promising to live our lives for him. But although it may be free to us, someone had to pay. And that is what happened at the Crucifixion all those thousands of years ago. Jesus was taking the punishment for our sins – the wrong things we had done. Jesus took our punishment so that we didn't have to be punished. Jesus paid the ultimate price – his life – so that we didn't have to pay.

To become a Christian doesn't really cost us anything – it cost Jesus everything.

● STORY – The Lion, The Witch And The Wardrobe

Once there were four children called Peter, Susan, Edmund and Lucy. They were sent from London during the Second World War, to the house of a kind old professor who lived in the country. On the first morning, the children decided to explore the big house. It was full of interesting things and unexpected places. One room had a suit of armour; another had a harp in the corner. And one room was quite empty except for a big wardrobe with a looking-glass on the door.

"Nothing there," said Peter, and they trooped out again – all except Lucy. She thought that the wardrobe needed further examination. Opening the door, she found several long coats. She got into the cupboard and began to make her way through them. To her surprise the wardrobe seemed to go on for some distance. Her footsteps began to sound as if she was walking on crunching snow, rather than on wood. The coats no longer felt like coats but more like fir trees. Lucy kept walking until she came out the other side. The sight that greeted her amazed her greatly. For now she stood in a strange land surrounded by trees. Ahead of her was a lamp-

post and beneath her feet was freshly fallen snow. Lucy had entered the magical land of Narnia. She didn't understand how the wardrobe led to this strange land, but clearly it did.

It wasn't long before all the children had found their way to Narnia, and Peter, Susan, Edmund and Lucy found themselves in a magical place. It was a place of centaurs and unicorns, fauns and wood nymphs, talking animals and great birds. They learned of the emperor who had created Narnia and many other places; of Aslan who was an enormous lion who had been away from Narnia for some time; and of the queen of Narnia, who was really a witch and had cast an evil spell over the whole land, a spell which meant that it would be "always winter but never Christmas".

But it seemed that the wicked witch's spell was breaking. The snow, which had covered the land for some time, was beginning to melt and the news was that Aslan had returned.

Peter, Susan and Lucy were very excited about meeting this marvellous lion. But Edmund wasn't so keen. He had met secretly with the wicked witch; she had given him Turkish delight and promised him more if he brought his brother and sisters to her – she told Edmund that she wanted to meet them and make friends with them. But his brother and sisters refused to come with him. So, in the middle of the night Edmund crept away to meet with the witch.

While the others slept, Edmund crept into the castle of the wicked witch, expecting to get more Turkish delight. But when the witch saw that he was alone, far from giving Edmund more sweets, she was furious with him. Edmund had been tricked. The witch had tricked Edmund into becoming a traitor. She didn't want to meet Peter,

Susan and Lucy, she wanted to kill them. She knew about an ancient promise which said that when four brothers and sisters sat on a special throne at a castle called Cair Paravel, then the witch's spell would be broken and the wicked witch herself would die.

She commanded that Edmund be tied up. She knew that unless all four children sat on the thrones, she could not be destroyed. But just before the sun rose, Edmund escaped and went to look for his brother and sisters. Instead of chasing after him the queen smiled to herself. She knew that Narnia had a law. The law said that all traitors must die. The witch knew that she had the right to kill Edmund, but Edmund knew nothing of this.

He returned to his brother and sisters just as they arrived with the other creatures at a special place called the Stone Table. And there in the middle of all the creatures was Aslan himself, looking larger and more terrifying than anything that Edmund had ever seen before. His brother and sisters were bowing before him. Edmund approached cautiously. He didn't know how Aslan would treat him. After all, he had been tricked by the wicked witch and he was a traitor. But although Aslan was very fierce, Aslan was also eager to forgive – even traitors. The scene was set: Aslan was back, the four children could sit on the thrones at Cair Paravel and the wicked witch would be destroyed. But soon the witch arrived and she was demanding her rights.

"I have the right to kill the traitor!" she shouted.

The crowd went deathly silent. The witch stood with her army of strange monsters and weird creatures, and Aslan stood with the centaurs, unicorns and noble creatures of Narnia. Aslan knew that the witch's army was no match for his, but he also understood the law: Edmund should die. But Aslan knew of another law, an older law. And he stepped forward to talk to the witch. The witch looked puzzled at first, then she smiled and finally she laughed. The next thing the children knew, the wicked witch was moving away with her army behind her.

"Does that mean I don't have to die?" Edmund stuttered.

"Yes it does, Edmund."

Nobody understood what had happened and Aslan wouldn't say what he had said to the witch, but late that night Aslan could be seen walking off into the woods alone. Lucy and Susan followed him at a distance, but they would never have guessed what would happen next. Aslan walked to the stone table where the witch and her army were waiting. But instead of trying to fight them, Aslan walked into the very centre of them. Then the witch's army attacked Aslan and pushed him to the ground. They tied him with ropes and beat him. They pulled out all his fur and cut his mane. Then the queen ordered that Aslan be dragged onto the stone table. Holding a knife above her head, she killed Aslan. Lucy and Susan watched from a distance and cried bitterly, for now they realised what had happened: Aslan had agreed to give up his life so that Edmund could live.

Easter is about the same thing. It's about Jesus. It's about God's own Son dying, so that we can be forgiven for the wrong things we have done.

Lucy and Susan sat in the cold night until the morning sun began to rise and then they heard an almighty crash. They ran to the stone table to discover it broken in two. Through her tears Lucy sobbed: "What have they done to him now?" For Aslan's body was nowhere to be seen.

Then behind them there was a mighty roar. There stood Aslan, even more terrifying than before, his beautiful golden mane now restored and shining in the new-day sun. He was alive.

"The witch doesn't know everything," Aslan began, "for when someone who is innocent dies for someone who is guilty, even time works backwards and death cannot keep that person. But enough of that. Come quickly now, we have a battle to win."

And that's how Easter works as well. Because Jesus had never done anything wrong, death could not hold him and he rose from the dead three days later to live for evermore.

So Aslan and the girls sped off to fight the wicked witch and to see the children crowned in Cair Paravel, but to hear about all that you'll have to read the book for yourself. This is only the beginning.

(Adapted from C. S. Lewis's incredible work
The Lion, the Witch and the Wardrobe*)*

HARVEST SPECIAL
Sharing And Caring

	Programme	Item
Section 1	Welcome	
	Rules	
	Prayer	
	Praise	
	Game 1	Face Feeder (boys)
	Praise (x2)	
	Fun Item 1	
	Game 2	Face Feeder (girls)
	Fun Item 2	
	Bible Text	Proverbs 22:9
	Announcements	
	Interview	
	Worship (x2)	
Section 2 Preaching Time	Bible Lesson	James
	Illustration 1	Faces
	Illustration 2	A Big, Big World
	Illustration 3	Friends With Everyone
	Story	Starfish
	Prayer	

Overview At the time of year when many schools and churches are bringing food to share with others, this lesson is aimed at showing the importance of sharing and the need specifically to do something to help those in need.

games

PreachingTime

Game 1

Face Feeder (boys)

PREPARATION	A pile of mini chocolate bars at A. A huge face at B with a hole in the mouth. A line made with masking tape 1.5 metres away from the face.
PLAYERS	Five boys per team.
SET-UP	The team stands in relay formation at A.
OBJECT	The first player runs from A to the line 1.5 metres from B, throws the mini chocolate bar at the mouth, then returns to A. The team keeps revolving for two minutes.
WINNING	The team with the most chocolate bars through the mouth wins.

Game 2

Face Feeder (girls)

PREPARATION	A pile of mini chocolate bars at A. A huge face at B with a hole in the mouth. A line made with masking tape 1.5 metres away from the face.
PLAYERS	Five girls per team.
SET-UP	The team stands in relay formation at A.
OBJECT	The first player runs from A to the line 1.5 metres from B, throws the mini chocolate bar at the mouth, then returns to A. The team keeps revolving for two minutes.
WINNING	The team with the most chocolate bars through the mouth wins.

BIBLE LESSON JAMES

"The Lord blesses everyone who freely gives food to the poor." (Proverbs 22:9)

There is a book in the Bible called James. James has quite a few lessons in it, but one of the lessons that really does stand out is the part where James says that we mustn't tell people things such as: "I hope all goes well for you. I hope you will be warm and have plenty to eat" – and then do nothing at all to help them. James is quick to give us this warning: FAITH WITHOUT WORKS IS DEAD.

What does he mean? He means that it's not enough just to say nice things to people and wish them well when we don't do anything to help.

If we see people who are hungry, we should try and feed them. If they are lonely, maybe we could talk to them. If they are lost, maybe we could direct them.

God wants us to do things to help others.

Illustration 1

Faces

Object needed: *A three-dimensional pin sculpture (available from Argos and other novelty gift shops very cheaply).*

Invite a child to come to the front and ask them to close their eyes. Then, using the pin sculpture, very carefully take an imprint of their  face. Show it to the rest of the club – expect some laughter. Repeat this until you have ten people at the front.

A Big, Big World

Objects needed: *A figure "6" and nine zeros written on ten separate sheets of paper.*

How many people do you think there are in the world?

Hand the figure "6" to the first person and then give out a zero to each other person as you work through the illustration.

6... No, much more than that. There are more than six in this line.
60... No, there are more than that in this hall right now *(if there are!)*.
600... No, there are more than that in this village.
6,000... No, there are more than that in this town.
60,000... No
600,000... No
6,000,000... 6 million – No, still more.
60,000,000... No
600,000,000... No, still more.
6,000,000,000... Yes, nearly 6 thousand million people.

Friends With Everyone

Objects needed: *Two chocolate bars.*

The amazing thing is this: if we used this "pin sculpture" on all those people, they would all be unique, different and special.

Ask all but two of the volunteers to sit down.

But those 6 thousand million people are not all the same. Let's pretend that this person here is one half of the world and that person there is the other half. And let's pretend that this chocolate bar stands for everything that we need to survive.

Now let me show you what happens with the chocolate bar. I'm going to give it to this person here, because half the world has everything that they need to live. Now, should I give the other chocolate bar to the other person? Well, actually I can't. You see, this other half of the world doesn't have the things they need. They don't have enough to live properly. It actually gets a little worse. This first half here doesn't only have everything they need – they have more than they need.

Give the person with the chocolate bar the other chocolate bar.

Who has friends? How do you show your friend that you care for them? *(You'll get several answers. Keep going until you find the key word "share".)*

So because you care for your friends, you share? Well, what do you think our friend here with the two chocolate bars should do? Yes, he/she should share. And that really is how simple it is: if we did what God intended and shared what we have with those who don't, then we would all have enough.

(For more detailed information check out www.jubilee-kids.co.uk)

● STORY – Starfish

There's a certain beach in Australia where, a couple of times a year, something truly amazing happens: the tide comes in really high and washes hundreds of starfish onto the beach. Then the tide goes back out, leaving all these starfish stranded on the beach in the sun, dying.

On one of these occasions a young boy came onto the beach and started picking up the starfish one by one and throwing them back into the water.

After a while, an old man walked onto the beach and saw what the little boy was doing. He walked up behind the boy and smacked him from behind with his stick: "What are you doing? You silly boy," he croaked.

"I'm saving the starfish," the little boy replied.

"You really are a silly boy," the old man said with a little laugh. "You'll never get them all."

The little boy smiled, picked up a starfish and, holding it up to the man, said, "Mister, I may never be able to help all these starfish, but it certainly helps this one."

With that, the little boy took the starfish and threw it back into the sea.

We can't help all the refugees or help all the people who are starving, but if we all do what we can, if we all show that we care by remembering to share, then we really can change our world. We can show that we care by remembering to share.

APPENDIX 1
Handouts

Leaflet

FUSION PRESENTS:

FRANTIC
the children's event
for 5-11s

* Bouncy Castle * Multimedia * Face Painting
* Computer Games * Competitions * Dance
* Live Music * Fun Quizzes * Puppets
* Table Top Football * Wild Games * Stories
* Cafe Area
* Quizzes * Videos * Basketball
* Much more

MY CHURCH
My Street, My Town

Every Friday 6:15 – 8:15pm

Admission Only £1
My Church is a registered charity

Sample leaflet to advertise your children's club

Colouring Competitions

My Kids Club COLOURING COMPETITION

To be returned on Friday evening at the start of children's club

Name: _____

The best colouring will win a prize

Sample handout for home visits

APPENDIX 2
Visual Aids

Jesus' disciples gathered around him, and he taught them:

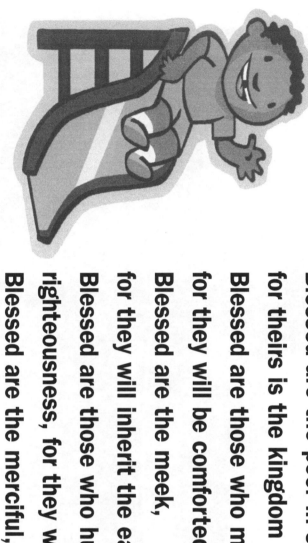

Blessed are the poor in spirit,
for theirs is the kingdom of heaven.
Blessed are those who mourn,
for they will be comforted.
Blessed are the meek,
for they will inherit the earth.
Blessed are those who hunger and thirst for
righteousness, for they will be filled.
Blessed are the merciful,
for they will be shown mercy.
Blessed are the pure in heart,
for they will see God.
Blessed are the peacemakers,
for they will be called sons of God.
Blessed are those who are persecuted because of righteousness,
for theirs is the kingdom of heaven.

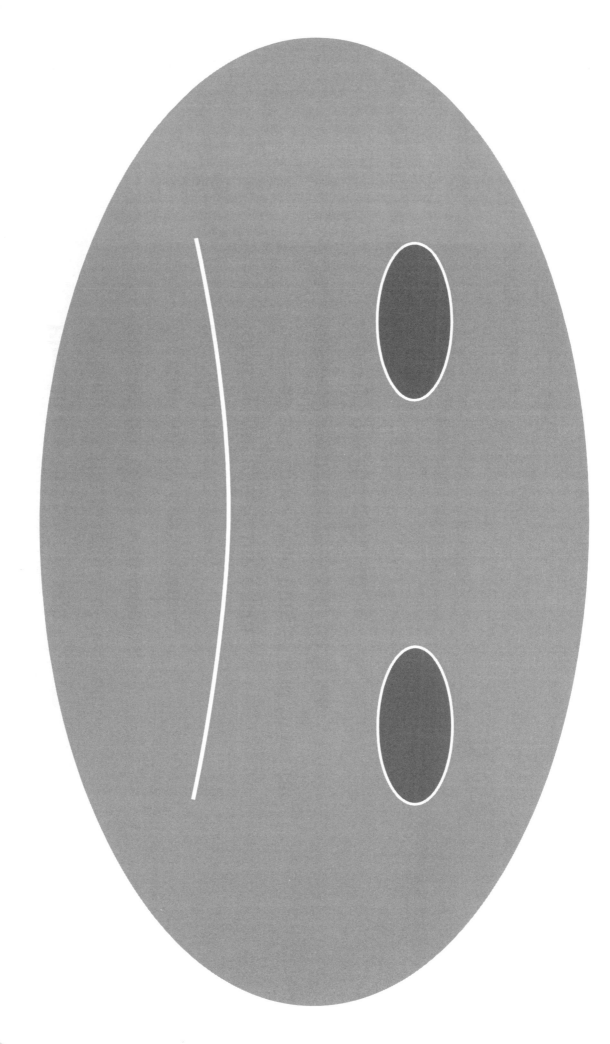

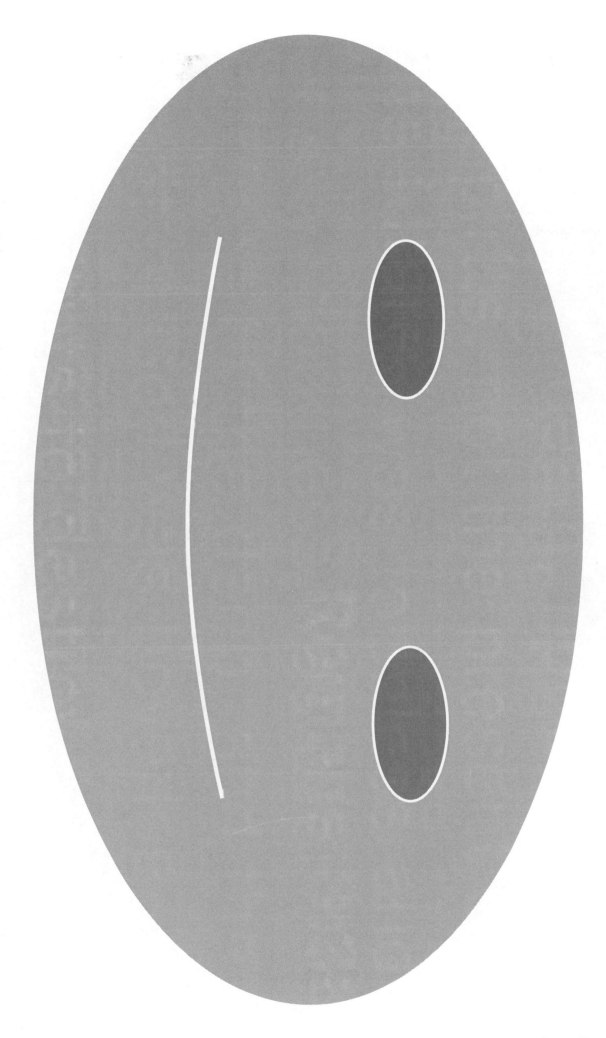

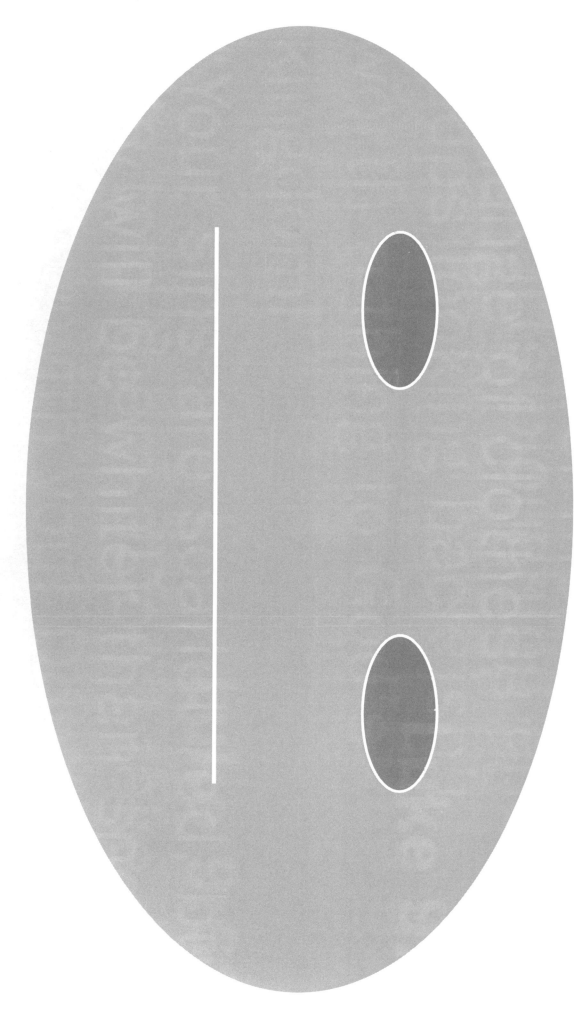

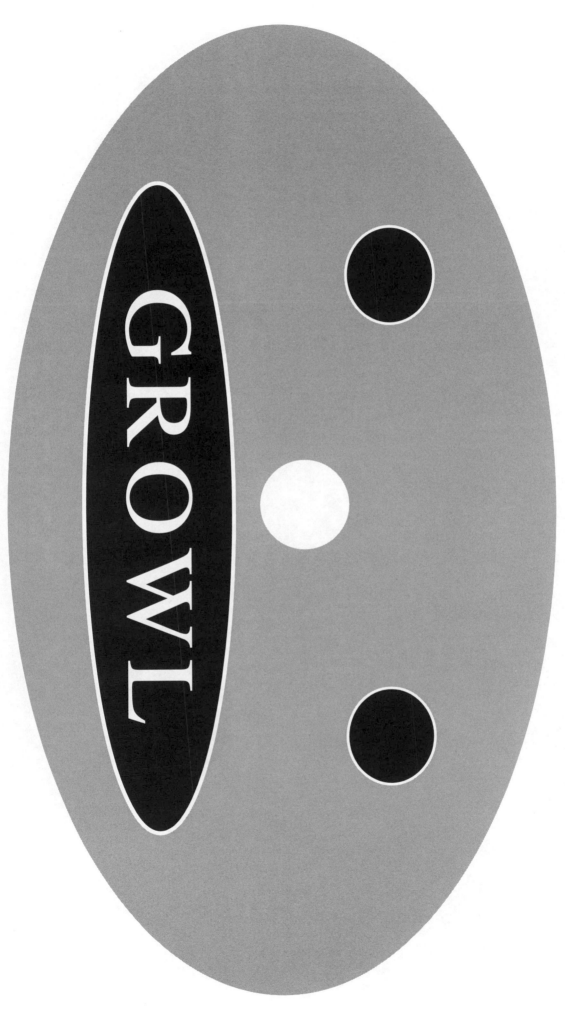

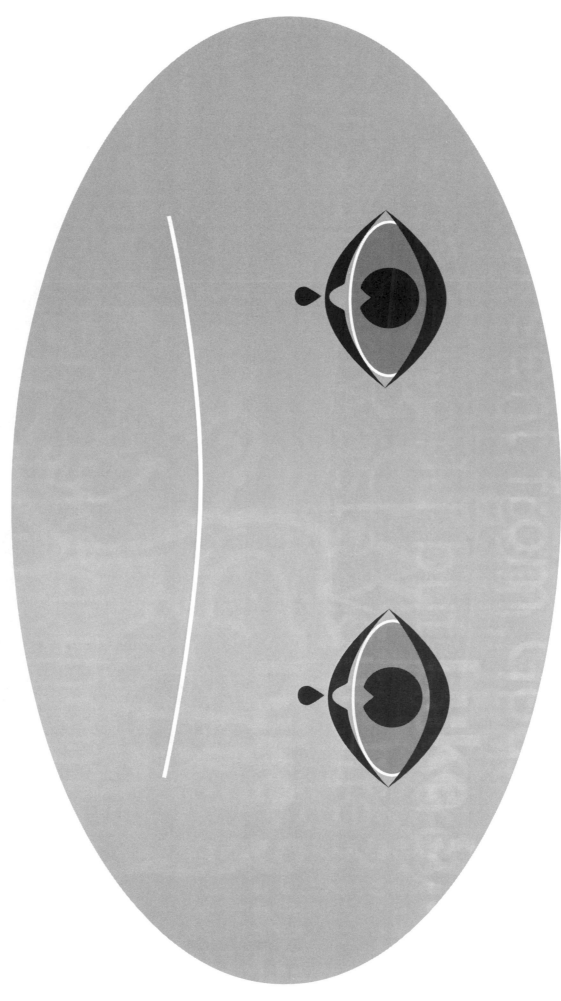

APPENDIX 3
Bible Texts

"Your sins are scarlet red, but they will be whiter than snow or wool."

Isaiah 1:18

"I am sure that nothing can separate us from God's love – not life or death, not angels or spirits, not the present or the future."

Romans 8:38

"Sin wants to destroy you, but don't let it!"

Genesis 4:7

"He told them, 'Don't take anything with you! Don't take a walking stick or a travelling bag or food or money or even a change of clothes.'"

Luke 9:3

"Jesus answered, 'You give them something to eat.'"

Luke 9:13

"Jesus then asked them, 'But who do you say I am?' Peter answered, 'You are the Messiah sent from God.'"

Luke 9:20

"What will you gain, if you own the whole world but destroy yourself or waste your life?"

Luke 9:25

"All at once they woke up and saw how glorious Jesus was. They also saw the two men who were with him."

Luke 9:32

"Jesus answered, 'Anyone who starts ploughing and keeps looking back isn't worth a thing to God's kingdom!'"

Luke 9:62

"The earth was formless and empty, darkness was over the surface of the deep, and the Spirit of God was hovering over the waters."

Genesis 1:2

"And God commanded the man, 'You must not eat from the tree of the knowledge of good and evil, for when you do so you will surely die.'"

Genesis 2:17

"Who shall separate us from the love of Christ?"

Romans 8:35

"The thief comes only to steal and kill and destroy; I have come that they may have life, and have it to the full."

John 10:10

"Ask, and you will receive. Search, and you will find. Knock, and the door will be opened for you."

Matthew 7:7

"Make a tree good and its fruit will be good, or make a tree bad and its fruit will be bad."

Matthew 12:33

"Blessed are the poor in spirit, for theirs is the kingdom of heaven."

Matthew 5:3

"Blessed are those who mourn, for they will be comforted."

Matthew 5:4

"Blessed are the meek, for they will inherit the earth."

Matthew 5:5

"Blessed are those who hunger and thirst for righteousness, for they will be filled."

Matthew 5:6

"Blessed are the merciful, for they will be shown mercy."

Matthew 5:7

"Blessed are the pure in heart, for they will see God."

Matthew 5:8

"Blessed are the peacemakers, for they will be called sons of God."

Matthew 5:9

"Blessed are those who are persecuted because of righteousness, for theirs is the kingdom of heaven."

Matthew 5:10

"O Jerusalem, Jerusalem, you who kill the prophets... how often I have longed to gather your children together, as a hen gathers her chicks."

Matthew 23:37

"Never will I leave you; never will I forsake you."

Hebrews 13:5

"Come, follow me!"

Matthew 4:19

"And surely I am with you always, to the very end of the age."

Matthew 28:20

"Love your neighbour as yourself."

Luke 10:27

"But God chose the foolish things of the world to shame the wise."

1 Corinthians 1:27

"Be imitators of God."

Ephesians 5:1

"The Lord will make you the head, not the tail."

Deuteronomy 28:13

"God did not give us a spirit of timidity."

2 Timothy 1:7

"God loved the people of this world so much that he gave his only Son, so that everyone who has faith in him will have eternal life and never really die."

John 3:16

"The thief comes only to steal and kill and destroy."

John 10:10

"I will bless you with a future filled with hope — a future of success."

Jeremiah 29:11

"If we cannot forgive those who sin against us, God will not forgive us."

Matthew 18:35

"God cares for you, so turn all your worries over to him."

1 Peter 5:7

"When you stood at the crossroads, I [God] told you, 'Follow the road your ancestors took, and you will find peace.'"

Jeremiah 6:16

"Jesus wept."

John 11:35

"And he will give you the desires of your heart."

Psalm 37:4

"Be bold and very courageous."

Joshua 1:6

"Anyone who believes me and is baptised will be saved. But anyone who refuses to believe me will be condemned."

Mark 16:16

"Jesus became wise, and he grew strong. God was pleased with him and so were the people."

Luke 2:52

"Simon Peter answered, 'Lord, there is no one else that we can go to! Your words give eternal life.'"

John 6:68

"He doesn't want any of these little ones to be lost."

Matthew 18:14

"Make every minute count."

Ephesians 5:16

"For to us a child is born, to us a son is given, and the government will be on his shoulders. And he will be called Wonderful Counsellor, Mighty God, Everlasting Father, Prince of Peace."

Isaiah 9:6

"Christ died for our sins according to the Scriptures."

1 Corinthians 15:3

"The Lord blesses everyone who freely gives food to the poor."

Proverbs 22:9

APPENDIX 4
Blank Lesson Plan

Lesson No

	Programme	Item
Section 1	Welcome	
	Rules	
	Prayer	
	Praise	
	Game 1	
	Praise (x2)	
	Fun Item 1	
	Game 2	
	Fun Item 2	
	Bible Text	
	Announcements	
	Interview	
	Worship (x2)	
Section 2 Preaching Time	Bible Lesson	
	Illustration 1	
	Illustration 2	
	Illustration 3	
	Story	
	Prayer	

Overview

games

Game 1

PREPARATION

PLAYERS

SET-UP

OBJECT

WINNING

Game 2

PREPARATION

PLAYERS

SET-UP

OBJECT

WINNING

Illustration 1

Object needed:

Illustration 3

Object needed:

Illustration 2

Object needed:

● STORY

APPENDIX 5
Resources

RESOURCES
TO REACH A NEW GENERATION

MUSIC

Children of the Cross, Jim Bailey (Kingsway)
God's Gang, Jim Bailey (Kingsway)
Ishmael's Collections, Ishmael (Kingsway)
King of Heaven, Doug Horley (Kingsway)
Lovely Jubbly, Doug Horley (Kingsway)
Shout to the Lord Kids 1 & 2, North Point Church (Integrity)
Soul Survivor Collections, Compilation (Survivor Records)
Whoopah! Wahey!, Doug Horley (Kingsway)

BOOKS

52 Ideas for Infant School Assemblies, Chris Chesterton & Elaine Buckley (Monarch)
52 Ideas for Junior Classroom Assemblies, Chris Chesterton & Pat Gutteridge (Monarch)
77 Talks for 21st Century Kids, Chris Chesterton (Monarch)
77 Talks for Cyberspace Kids, Chris Chesterton (Monarch)
Devil Take the Youngest, Winkie Pratney (Bethany House)
Don't Tell Cute Stories, Change Lives, Mark Griffiths (Monarch)
Fire on the Horizon, Winkie Pratney (Renew Books, Gospel Light)
Fusion, Mark Griffiths (Monarch)
Not Just Sundays, Margaret Withers (BRF)
The Prayer of Jabez for Kids, Bruce Wilkinson (Tommy Nelson Inc)
Reclaiming a Generation, Ishmael (Kingsway)
Streets of Pain, Bill Wilson (Word)
A Theology of Children's Ministry, Lawrence O. Richards (Zondervan)

VIDEOS

Miracle Maker (Bible Society)
The Testament Series (Bible Society)
The Veggie Tales Series, Big Ideas Production (distr. Word)

RECOMMENDED WEBSITES FOR RESOURCE MATERIAL

www.77talks.co.uk
www.armslength.com
www.duggiedugdug.co.uk
www.ishmael.org.uk
www.jubilee-kids.co.uk
www.kidzblitz.com
www.kingdomcreative.co.uk
www.tricksfortruth.com

PUPPETS AND GENERAL

For a spectacular range of puppets visit www.armslength.com or contact *TRICKS FOR TRUTH* on 01706 649921.

CAMPS AND EVENTS

www.activate.co.uk